The Indentured and Their Route

Praise for the book

'Bhaswati Mukherjee's compelling narrative of a hitherto untold story gives a voice without mediators to the descendants of the indentured.

As a memorial to its deeply troubled past, Mauritius possesses two UNESCO World Heritage Sites: Aapravasi Ghat, to recall the memories of indentured labourers, and Le Morne Cultural Landscape, which symbolizes resistance to slavery.

In 2007, Bhaswati, as India's Ambassador to UNESCO and India's representative to the World Heritage Committee, ensured, along with the Mauritian delegation led by the Minister of Culture, that Aapravasi Ghat was inscribed by acclamation on UNESCO's World Heritage List.

We, the descendants, remain attached to our original culture and civilization, which, in the melting pot of Mauritius, has become "Mauritian culture". Mauritius is our country and home while India is the ancient Mother land of legend. In the process, as Bhaswati points out, we have made a new identity for ourselves. As she says, identity is a raison d'être for human existence.

This book will have huge resonance for Mauritius and the 14 countries on the Indentured Labour Route.'

—**Mookhesswur Choonee**
Former Culture Minister, Mauritius; Mauritian Ambassador to India; Chairman, Gopio International; and Founder, The International Indenture Girmitiyas Foundation

'This is a gut-wrenching narrative about the journey of the indentured and their relentless quest for identity. I compliment the author for highlighting this forgotten history of India.

As Deputy Mayor of The Hague, I met the author, then India's Ambassador to the Netherlands, in 2010. Together we relived the journey of the *Lalla Rookh*, the first indentured vessel that came to Suriname.

The poems cited by the author from my collection of poems *Tamanna* or *Endless Longing* catalogue the suffering of the Girmitiyas, their fear of losing their identity and ultimately, culture as a memory and a saviour.

I compliment the author for recalling that Girmitiyas never forgot the language and culture of Mother India. As the author said, the children of the indentured now contribute to the greatness of Indian Diaspora. This book will resonate with the descendants of Girmitiyas wherever they are.'

—**Rabin S. Baldewsingh**
Government Commissioner in Kingdom of the Netherlands and Former Deputy Mayor of The Hague

'*The Indentured and Their Route* is a heartrending and utterly authentic vision of the trials that the early Indian migrants went through in distant lands. It is a story that for long needed to be told, and this must-read book does so compellingly.

Bhaswati Mukherjee utilizes her unique perspective as a diplomat-historian to put together a fascinating account. Her deeply researched book illuminates the dark corners of journeys forced on India's forgotten own. Ambassador Mukherjee's historical account compels reflection and deserves a wide readership.'

—**Rajiv Dogra**
Former Diplomat, Author and Television Commentator

The Indentured and Their Route

A Relentless Quest for Identity

Bhaswati Mukherjee

RUPA

Published by
Rupa Publications India Pvt. Ltd 2023
7/16, Ansari Road, Daryaganj
New Delhi 110002

Sales centres:
Bengaluru Chennai
Hyderabad Jaipur Kathmandu
Kolkata Mumbai Prayagraj

Copyright © Bhaswati Mukherjee 2023

The views and opinions expressed in this book are the author's own and the facts are as reported by her, which have been verified to the extent possible, and the publishers are not in any way liable for the same.

All rights reserved.
No part of this publication may be reproduced, transmitted or stored in a retrieval system, in any form or by any means, electronic, mechanical, photocopying, recording or otherwise, without the prior permission of the publisher.

P-ISBN: 978-93-5702-566-9
E-ISBN: 978-93-5702-568-3

First impression 2023

10 9 8 7 6 5 4 3 2 1

The moral right of the author has been asserted.

Printed in India

This book is sold subject to the condition that it shall not, by way of trade or otherwise, be lent, resold, hired out or otherwise circulated, without the publisher's prior consent, in any form of binding or cover other than that in which it is published.

Dedicated to India's lost children who never forgot their Mother land and who now form part of her great diaspora

CONTENTS

Foreword by Hardeep Singh Puri	*xi*
Preface	*xiii*
1. Slavery and Indenture: Dialectics or Inheritance?	1
2. From Famine to Bondage	12
3. Abolition of Slavery and Rise of Indenture	22
4. The Girmit	32
5. Beyond the Kalapani	43
6. Forgotten Memories: Cholera and Quarantine	63
7. Crossings	73
8. The Journey of the Indentured Woman: An Untold Story	113
9. India Rises against Indenture: Mahatma Gandhi and a New Dawn	145
10. Rise of India's Diaspora: Culture as Saviour and Redeemer	162
11. Old Sins Cast Long Shadows	178
Epilogue	191
Acknowledgements	199
Bibliography	202
Index	205

*India for thousands of years peacefully existed.
We, of all nations of the World,
have never been a conquering race,
And that blessing is on our head,
And therefore we live.*

—Swami Vivekananda

FOREWORD

Ambassador Bhaswati Mukherjee provides an illuminating narrative of the history of Indian indenture in her book *The Indentured and their Route: A Relentless Quest for Identity*. She builds a lucid and lyrical narrative of the external struggles and internal resilience of the 1.3 million Indian labourers who were inveigled into servitude across the 'Kalapani' as part of the so-called Great Experiment.

Revolving around the central concern of identity and how the indentured preserved links to their civilizational roots through language, poetry, music and religion, this book poignantly examines the lives of these 'lost Indians', their inheritances and their legacies. Mukherjee marries the flair and feeling of a writer with the accuracy and balance of a historian to animate real-life accounts and historical descriptions. In doing so, she has fascinatingly recreated the journey of these 'bound coolies' who worked in sugar colonies in Fiji, Mauritius, Suriname and other colonies in the Caribbean and later in Africa, most famously in Natal where Gandhiji successfully rebelled against the British.

This book describes the unimaginable scope of these migrations, which were circumscribed by stories of poverty, disease and fatal tragedy as much as they were by the shackles of the 'girmit'. The economic exploitation that India, on the cusp on industrialization in the mid-nineteenth century, suffered when it lost these human resources to British, French and Dutch colonies is remarkable. As with slavery, labour maximized the profits in the plantation colonies and enhanced the wealth of imperial Britain.

I was particularly struck by the author's analysis of the historiography of indenture, as she made a compelling case for why the unfreedoms of indenture should be studied in conjunction with the horrors of slavery. The abolition of slavery, in Britain in 1833 and in other European countries subsequently, was not the end of bondage but just the beginning of another inhumane process of capture over another people's liberty. As the author states in the preface, after slavery was abolished, it was virtually erased from our collective memory until the United Nations Educational, Scientific and Cultural Organization (UNESCO) and African states reminded the world of the 'Slave Route'.

The author attempts to do the same for the indentured by bringing to light the atrocities they had to face as well as their stirring fortitude in braving hardships to lay the foundations of new societies and economies, from Suriname to South Africa. Their quest for political empowerment is one of the most interesting examples of the evolution of democracy, pluralism and multi-ethnicity in modern history. It is also inextricably intertwined with the history of India. This book, ultimately, is not just an exposition of the lives of the Indian indentured but also a celebration of the Indian Diaspora that inherits from its ancestors a unique quality to persevere, assimilate and thrive.

Hardeep Singh Puri
Ministry of Petroleum and Natural Gas &
Ministry of Housing and Urban Affairs

PREFACE

Between the idea and the reality
Between the motion and the act
Falls the Shadow

—T.S. Eliot

Indenture and its painful origin fall in a grey area in our history. It has largely remained shrouded in the shadows. Romanian-born American writer, Nobel laureate and Holocaust survivor Elie Wiesel noted in *Night*: 'An executioner always kills twice; first, with his sword, then through forgetting.'[1] The same is true for indenture.

After slavery was abolished, it was virtually erased from our collective memories, until the UNESCO and the African states reminded the world of the Slave Route. Their intention was to ensure that the ashes of forgetfulness do not fall on it again.

The moment has come to do the same for indenture.

Collective amnesia about the indentured was accompanied by *déracinement*, involving the destruction of the memory of one's roots, culture, language and civilizational heritage. This loss of identity was particularly true for the indentured of Reunion Island, a French overseas territory in the Indian Ocean, close to Mauritius.

At what point did these unfortunates lose their identity? What is identity? It is the distinguishing character or personality that defines an individual. Identity, in this case, served as a saviour, a mechanism to hold on to the conflict-ridden and unsavoury

---

[1] Wiesel, Elie, *Night*, Hill and Wang, 2006.

present by constantly recalling the past with its language, poetry, music and religion. A sari, a dhoti, the Ramayana or the Quran become symbolic of a rapidly vanishing cultural heritage. These symbols, handed down over generations of the indentured underline that déracinement is only possible if one is willing to let go.

Former deputy mayor of The Hague, of Surinamese origin, Rabin S. Baldewsingh wrote of the fear of losing one's identity in his poem 'Trapped':

> Whilst wrestling
> With the fields
> I fled over the ocean.
> And here I am,
> trapped on the border between two cultures.
> Hearth and home are lost already;
> what will remain
> when identity slips away?
> The hat is larger than the head;
> how much longer can it cover the head?[2]

What defines indenture? How is it distinguished from slavery? The *Oxford English Dictionary* notes that indenture is a formal agreement binding an apprentice to a master or a contract by which a person agrees to work for a set period for a colonial landowner. For the colonizers who ingeniously devised this 'Great Experiment', its merit was being able to neatly sidestep the troublesome burden of slavery while denying to the newly enslaved and bonded, the principles of equality and natural justice. The *Merriam-Webster Dictionary* defines slavery as the state of a person held in forced servitude or a person who has been entrapped (through debt) and exploited. The *Cambridge*

---

[2] Baldewsingh, Rabin S., *Tamanna: Endless Longing*, Uitgeverij Surinen, Den Haag, 2013, p. 35.

Dictionary goes further and states that slavery is the condition of being legally owned by someone else and being forced to work for or obey them.

How, then, is slavery different from indenture? Many former slave masters argued that indenture was a form of migration to enable the indentured to lead better lives outside India. Was indenture a form of migration or a substitute for slavery? Migration results from the free choice of individuals to change their lives and destinies by moving to another land permanently or temporarily. However, the indentured neither benefitted from their enforced migration nor could they choose their destination; their colonial master had the lead and control. A book from the Oxford History of the British Empire Companion Series acknowledges, 'It is important to consider whether the Indian indentured labour had been inveigled into a new system of slavery.'[3]

The moot questions to be raised are: whether the distinction between slavery and indenture is cosmetic or were some rights enjoyed by the bonded that had been denied to the enslaved. The colonizers argued that the bonded had the security of their 'girmit' (contract). In reality, it was entered into by innocent, illiterate or credulous men. They had no way of knowing that their thumbprints would deprive them of their liberty for limited or unlimited durations. In some cases, they would pay with that most precious commodity of all, their life.

The slave, purchased like merchandize or a commodity, had no such contract but the end result appeared to be identical. A human was deprived of his fundamental human rights of liberty, freedom and life itself. It was, after all, the same slave ships that transported the indentured to far-flung colonies of the Empire. Again, it could be pointed out that there were no chains. True, but there was no escape either, except into the vast expanse of

---

[3]Harper, Marjory and Stephen Constantine, *Migration and Empire,* Oxford History of the British Empire Companion Series, Oxford University Press, 2010.

the open sea.

The journeys of the Girmitiyas have been documented through countless stories and poems that catalogue their narratives of the cruelty, torture and humiliation. These stories were written with their blood, sweat and tears. They watered the soil of countries and regions, such as Mauritius or the Caribbean, through their toil in the sugar plantations. Most were unfamiliar with sugar plantations. The 'jahaji bhais' (brothers through the crossing) obstinately clung to their precious oral traditions, language and culture.

Tragically, scholarship in this field of inquiry is marked by the frequent failure of historians, writers and intellectuals to transcend the geographical and conceptual parochialism that has now become a hallmark of contemporary 'plantation studies' in general and indentured labour studies in particular. The writers are invariably from the West and belong to the country of their former colonizers. They have dominated the narrative till date.

It is most unfortunate that the Indentured Labour Route, which brought the Diaspora to Suriname and Mauritius, with its many similarities to the Slave Route, did not, until recently, get the attention it deserved within the UN system, unlike the Slave Route. It is less well chronicled and sometimes conveniently forgotten.

It is frequently overlooked that their journey led to the formation of many modern democratic nation states. Their quest for political empowerment is one of the most interesting examples of the evolution of democracy, pluralism and multi-ethnicity in these regions. Their journey poignantly highlights not just the history of Suriname but of other countries, notably Mauritius and Guyana as well as Fiji and Reunion Island during this period. It is also inextricably intertwined with the history of India.

Equally unfortunate is the lack of interest internationally in the Indentured Labour Route despite its acknowledged role in shaping the contours of socio-economic, cultural and political life and contributing to the vibrant democratic politics of the post-colonial era. UNESCO contributed significantly to the international recognition of the infamous Slave Route, which encouraged the profound examination of its linkages with the 'Route des Engages' or the Indentured Labour Route. This helped debunk the popular myth of migration of the indentured from the 'miseries of their Mother land' to a glorious future outside India.

UNESCO's Executive Board recognized in November 2014 the establishment of an International Indentured Labour Route, to be developed by the 22 independent states concerned, including by Mauritius and Suriname. Its Secretariat is located at Aapravasi Ghat, Mauritius.[4] It marks the point where the indentured labour, drawn mainly from Bihar and United Provinces but also from the southern provinces of colonial India, passed through the gateway of Aapravasi Ghat, either to stay on in Mauritius to work as indentured labour in the sugar plantations or to sail on to further destinations, never to return to India.

The Executive Board noted that the Route 'is strongly associated with memories of almost half a million indentured labours moving from India to Mauritius to work on sugar canes plantations or to be transhipped to other parts of the World.'[5] For this reason, it has also been included in UNESCO's Memory of the World Register. This register represents the collective documented memory of the human civilization. It casts the long shadow of history and the legacy of the past on our present and the future.

The German philosopher Georg Wilhelm Friedrich Hegel noted: 'We learn from history that we learn nothing from history.' The reason for this, Hegel pointed out, is: 'The owl of Minerva

---

[4]'Aapravasi Ghat', *UNESCO World Heritage Convention*, https://tinyurl.com/492xrbct. Accessed on 27 July 2023.
[5]'Decisions Adopted by the Executive Board at Its 195th Session', *UNESCO*, https://tinyurl.com/3u8me822. Accessed on 11 August 2023.

spreads its wings only with the coming of the dusk.'[6] Hegel was reminding his readers that only at the end of human history, the end of time itself, can humanity understand its own history.

The quest for identity continues in one form or the other. When it is not denied, it flourishes into the great Indian Diaspora. When banished into the night, it results in conflict and war. It is a story waiting to be told. In its narration lies our salvation.

---

[6]Hegel, Georg Wilhelm Friedrich, *Philosophy of Right*, Dover Publications Inc., 2005.

1

SLAVERY AND INDENTURE: DIALECTICS OR INHERITANCE?

Whether enslaved or indentured, the victim will raise his head in defiance, knowing that freedom is never granted; it must be wrested from the master of the moment.

—Nouréini Tidjani-Serpos,
Former Deputy Director-General, UNESCO

Indenture as a quest for identity has its origin in one of the greatest migrations in India's history. The journey of indentured labourers from India to diverse destinations two centuries ago is an untold saga waiting for its chronicler. Slavery and indenture were two sides of the same coin. Like Hegelian dialectic, indenture's origin was rooted in the abolition of slavery. Popular outcry, revulsion and anger resulted in the progressive abolition of one of the horrors of human history, by the United Kingdom (UK) in 1834, by France in 1848 and by the Netherlands in 1863. Only after the United States of America (US), through the 13th amendment to its constitution on 31 January 1865, freed its vast enslaved population did the sugar plantations in far flung colonies finally fall silent.

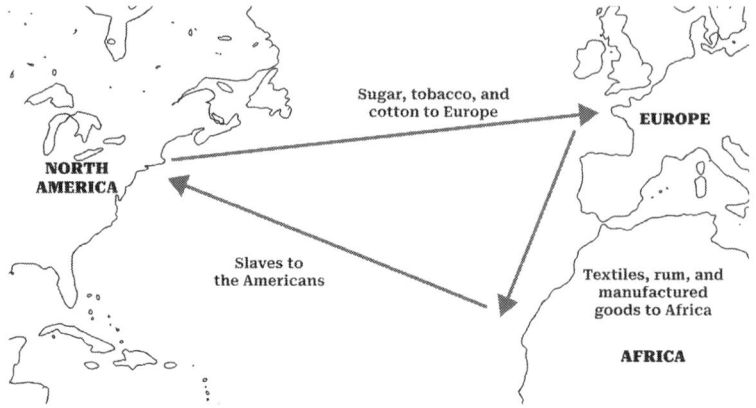

Figure 1: Old mercantile system based on slavery
Source: Map: Layerace/Freepik. This illustration has been designed using assets from Freepik.

The struggle to abolish slavery commenced from the early nineteenth century. Laws were adopted to reform the system. From 1 May 1807, British ships were not permitted to transport slaves. This was followed, on 1 March 1808, by the interdiction of the transportation of slaves by any ship to a British colony. The law was made more stringent in 1811, wherein offenders involved in slave trafficking could be punished under charges of transportation.

Efforts were made to persuade liberated slaves to continue working with their former slave masters. In fact, till 1834, former slaves were forced to work in the form of an apprenticeship, which implied that they actually remained in bondage. Emigration was difficult. Those liberated had nowhere to go. Gradually, many acquired economic freedom by farming their own plots in hitherto uncultivated territory.

The former slave masters were in a dilemma. The compulsions of sugar plantations demanded a form of labour synonymous with slavery. As Hugh Tinker, a reputed historian noted, 'There is a symbiosis which links sugar and servitude together.'[1] Plantation culture induced servility and loss of one's personality. The White servants were used as slave drivers. Author Dr Eric Williams concluded: 'White servitude was the historic base upon which Negro slavery was constructed. The felon-drivers in the plantations became without effort slave drivers.'[2]

Servility and human bondage were the hallmarks of the plantation economies of the time. The economics of sugar plantations was based on layers of intermediaries, similar to the Permanent Settlement established later in India. The big landowners were not content to remain away from the delights of the metropolis, whether London or Paris. The money from plantation labour was used to buy estates and titles back home while the landlord became a respected member of the House of Lords!

The agents who were left in charge were merciless exploiters assisted by overseers who could also be free men of colour. Extortion was the name of the game. It was not surprising that freed former slaves were reluctant to continue working on plantations if any other option was available. Once the British Parliament adopted the Slavery Abolition Act of 1833—followed by a seven-year apprenticeship for former slaves, later shortened to four years—the former slave masters understood that if they did not rapidly implement another system akin to slavery, economic ruin awaited them.

The Indian indentured were the dialectic on which the sugar plantations moved seamlessly from slavery to indenture. It is noteworthy that the plantation owners made no effort to protect the most important commodity of exploitation, regardless of whether it was the slaves or the indentured. This unfortunate approach also bound the slaves to their successors—the Indian indentured. Both

---

[1]Tinker, Hugh, *A New System of Slavery: The Export of Indian Labour Overseas 1830–1920*, Hansib, London, 1993, p. 3.
[2]Williams, Eric, *Capitalism and Slavery*, Penguin UK, London, 1944, pp. 16–19.

were desperate for their freedom and both were prepared to end their lives to regain their lost liberty.

The next stage came rapidly. The colonizers made their fatal choice in India's east, where her vast and impoverished masses were at the mercy of man-made famines and driven from their lands by the infamous 'Permanent Settlement'. Forced to cultivate opium, instead of food crops, to fuel the infamous Triangular Trade, the desperate and the marginalized believed that their salvation lay a short distance away, across the seas to a green paradise that awaited them.

Once again, in this tragedy-driven part of India, its suffering masses were deceived into undergoing the next stage of their servitude and destitution. The British Consul in Paramaribo, Suriname, quipped sardonically: 'The Suriname planter found in the meek Hindu a ready substitute for the Negro slave he had lost.'[3] He was mistaken! The so-called 'meek Hindu' actually was a born survivor. His 'meekness' masked an obstinate determination to cling to his culture, language and civilization despite all odds and to eventually return to his beloved Mother land.

For most, this yearning to return remained a dream. Of the 1.3 million Indian indentured labourers who left their Mother land from 1834 to 1917, when the Great Experiment ended, only about 21 per cent returned. The rest remained to seamlessly merge into the greater Indian Diaspora. That is another tale to be told!

As noted by Brij V. Lal, political thinker and well-known Girmitya historian from Fiji, 'In time, their [indentured] labour would lay the foundations of new societies and economies, from Suriname to South Africa. Their descendants form a distinct part

---

[3]Emmer, P.C., 'The Meek Hindu: The Recruitment of Indian Labourers for Service Overseas, 1870—1916', *Colonialism and Migration, Indentured Labour Before and After Slavery,* Comparative Studies in Overseas History 7, Ernst Van Den Boogaart and P.C. Emmer (eds), Martinus Nijhoff, 1986, pp. 187–208.

of the larger mosaic of a visibly growing community of the Indian Diaspora.'[4]

The debate between dialectics and inheritance was shaped by the silence of the two principal players: the slaves and the indentured. Their voices were never heard. The final conclusions of this debate can only be interpreted through the veil of their silence. The shipping off of more than a million of India's available labour force destroyed the nascent stirrings of industrialization, which had already been facing a severe setback with Bengal being lost to Robert Clive in 1757 in the Battle of Plassey. At that time, India was on the cusp of an industrial revolution. Now, decades later, the workforce disappeared, delivering a body blow to India's industrialists and to the burgeoning jute industry in Bengal and the tea plantations of Assam.

Case studies in Mauritius and Reunion Island leave the reader in no doubt of the dialectics between slavery and indenture and the latter's inheritance from the former. Nowhere is this more poignantly recorded than in Mauritius, which has successfully inscribed two sites on UNESCO's World Heritage List, to commemorate, recall and mourn the human tragedies played out against slaves and the indentured on Mauritian shores. Standing on Le Morne Cultural Landscape, which bore mute witness to the thousands of slaves who jumped over the cliffs into oblivion to escape slavery, one is awestruck by the brooding beauty of these steep cliffs overlooking the Indian Ocean. They are testament to the human soul's resistance to slavery.

The other, Aapravasi Ghat, marks the point where the indentured labourers, mainly from Bihar and United Provinces but also from the southern provinces of colonial India, passed through a gateway, never to return to India. Many of our ancestors forever left their footprints on the steps of this ghat. In the difficult

---

[4]Lal, Brij V., 'Indian Indenture: History and Historiography in a Nutshell', *Journal of Indentureship and Its Legacies*, Vol. 1, No. 1, 2021, pp. 1–15.

years ahead, the culture and memories that they refused to forget remained their only salvation.

In *Voices from the Aapravasi Ghat*, Khal Torabully simply stated:

> I keep in me the other culture
> The counter culture.
> The return to nature
> I deeply nurture.[5]

It can be reasonably asserted that those who survived the difficult experiences in the plantations of the far-flung British Empire were human beings of extraordinary courage and fortitude, similar to the African slaves brought in chains to work in the plantations of the deep south of the Americas.

Tinker has correctly depicted these inhumane conditions and has explicitly equated indenture with slavery.[6] He noted that the only acceptable distinction was that while slavery was lifelong bondage, indenture was temporary. Tinker's was the first definitive assertion of comparing indenture with slavery. Others, hesitant to revive the abolition debate, suggested that it was situated between slavery and free labour. This was the subject of much discussion among historians and political commentators.[7]

---

[5]Torabully, Khal, *Voices from the Aapravasi Ghat*, Aapravasi Ghat Trust Fund, 2013, p. 55.

[6]Tinker, Hugh, *A New System of Slavery: The Export of Indian Labour Overseas 1830-1920*, Hansib, London, 1993; Ali, Ahmed, *Girmit: Indian Indenture Experience in Fiji*, Ahmed Ali Fiji Museum Suva, Fiji, 2004; Saunders, Kay (ed.), *Indentured Labour in the British Empire, 1834-1920*, Croom Helm, London, 1984.

[7]Scholarship on indenture, much of which operates within the binary of slavery versus freedom includes Lai, Walton Look, *Indentured Labor, Caribbean Sugar: Chinese and Indian Migrants to the British West Indies, 1838-1918*, Johns Hopkins University Press, Baltimore, 1993; Mangru, Basdeo, *Benevolent Neutrality: Indian Government Policy and Labour Migration to British Guiana, 1854-1884*, Hansib, London, 1987; Northrup, David, *Indentured Labor in the Age of Imperialism*, Cambridge University Press, Cambridge, 1995; Saunders, Kay, (ed.), *Indentured*

Another subject of continuous debate was the origin and meaning of the words 'coolie' and 'Coolie Route'. European Orientalists of the time, including H.H. Wilson, were of the view that they had been derived from the Tamil word 'kuli' meaning 'wages'.[8] Early Portuguese colonizers defined the Indian dockers and load-bearers as 'culi'. Later, European ship-owners, including the British, referred to Indian labourers and dockhands as 'cules'.

Whatever its origin, there is no doubt that the word is pejorative. It was based on a racist perception of inferiority associated with the work being done by Indian labour. Later, it started being translated into a broader definition of racially inferior and illiterate Indian labour being used to replace the former slave. Over a period of time, it became difficult even for British historians, writers and politicians to deny that indenture, indeed, was an almost-perfect copy of slavery. It ensured that the status quo was maintained in the plantation economies and enabled the continued prosperity of the Empire, the Raj and the British monarchy.

It is now accepted that indenture was developed on the basis of racial segregation of labour, similar to slavery. In 1875, the Marquess of Salisbury, then Secretary of State for India, argued:

> We may also consider, from an Imperial point of view, the great advantage which must result from peopling the warmer British possessions which are rich in natural resources and only want population, by an intelligent and industrious race

---

Labour in the British Empire, 1834-1920, Taylor and Francis, London, 1984.

For a critique of the binary between slavery and freedom in the Indian context, see: Gyan Prakash, *Bonded Histories: Genealogies of Labour Servitude in Colonial India*, Cambridge University Press, Cambridge, 1990.

[8]Tinker, Hugh, *A New System of Slavery: The Export of Indian Labour Overseas 1830-1920*, Hansib, London, 1993, p. 42.

to whom the climate of these countries is well suited and to whom the culture of the staples suited to the soil, and the modes of labour and settlement are adapted.⁹

This form of racial classification of indentured labour also involved highly objectionable racist definitions of the likely utility of the subject races based on racial profiling. Predating apartheid, it reflected the imperial mindset, the so-called White Man's Burden and 'a global imperial vision in which multiple populations could be assessed side by side for their viability as a docile and effective labour force'.¹⁰

The Mercantilist Argument for Colonial Expansion

Figure 2: Age of unbridled capitalism based on indenture
Source: Dorf, Philip, *Our Early Heritage: Ancient and Medieval History*, Oxford University Press, 1940.

---

⁹Sanderson, Thomas Henry, *Report of the Committee on Emigration from India to the Crown Colonies and Protectorates*, HMSO, 1910, p. 7.
¹⁰Sturman, Rachel, 'Indian Indentured Labour and the History of International Rights Regimes', *The American Historical Review*, Vol. 119, No. 5, 2014, pp. 1439–65.

In 1871, a commission established to inquire into the treatment of immigrants in British Guiana, headed by William Frere, came to the following conclusions: Africans were driven to labour only by economic want and would 'get through their work with great speed, and if allowed, with great carelessness'. Indians, in contrast, were described as weaker as and less efficient than Africans, as prone to excessive subservience and mendacity, but as driven to labour by 'their love of saving and desire to return to their own country'. Chinese labourers 'possessed greater intelligence' than either of the other groups and were considered very careful and 'neat' in their work as well as 'much more independent than the Coolie', but 'the Chinese as a class were inveterate gamblers and opium smokers'.[11]

Indenturing of cheap labour from India to be used in the plantations and also as domestic labour illustrates the uneasy and often avoided comparisons to slave labour. As with the former, the rights of the subject populations were not governed by rule of law, human rights instruments or other legislation to regulate the superior, dominant and ruling White class. Their labour maximized the profits in the plantation colonies and enhanced the wealth of imperial Britain.

It was the age of unbridled and uncontrolled finance imperialism without any curbs. Apartheid was the natural corollary. This flow of labour was as much of a drain for India as the flow of wealth. India was being sucked dry of

---

[11]*Report of the Commissioners Appointed to Enquire into the Treatment of Immigrants in British Guiana*, William Clowes & Sons, 1871, pp. 90–1.

Another example of such comparative racial typologies of labour culture are contained in Bronkhurst, H.V.P., *The Colony of British Guiana and Its Labouring Population*, T. Woolmer, London, 1883, pp. 99, 140–9. Bronkhurst quotes a letter to the government by 'immigration agent-general' J.G. Daly on the cultural characteristics of emigrants from Madras (now Chennai) versus Calcutta (now Kolkata).

her human and material resources.[12]

It was also a story of uneven power relations, between labour in the colonies and capital in the ruling country under State patronage. Labour procured by indenturing from old colonies like India provided additional opportunities of extracting surpluses as those were deployed in the plantations where they had a near-slave status.[13]

It was the era of monopolistic capitalism. Ironically, it caused clashes of interest between two sets of colonizer capitalists, one in the so-called metropolises and the other in the plantation colonies. High sugar prices conflicted with the interests of the processing industry in Britain. Ultimately, sugar prices started falling, to the immediate detriment of the human rights of the indentured populations.

In a way, it represented another form of the Triangular Trade, similar to opium shipped from India to pay for Chinese tea, enslaving a generation of Chinese and with the profits going to Britain. In this instance, the Triangular Trade involved transporting Indian labourers to plantations for shipping raw materials, especially those used in manufacturing sugar, to Britain, with the profit from selling the finished product, in this case sugar, enriching the imperial coffers in London. It was a win-win situation for Britain. Capitalism and imperialism ensured that Britannia ruled the waves.

In the chain of events leading up to the First World War, the development of colonialism, finance imperialism and global capitalism was based on a profoundly racist division of the world's populations into subject and ruling races, inferior and superior, to

---

[12]Sen, Sunanda, *Colonies and the Empire: India 1870-1914*, Orient Longman, 1992, pp. 15–70.

[13]Sen, Sunanda, 'Indentured Labour from India in the Age of Empire', *Social Scientist*, Vol. 44, No. 1/2, 2016, pp. 35–74.

be coldly and calculatingly graded according to their contribution to labour and production. This thinking was reflected across the plantation indentured. How, then, can one distinguish between slavery and indenture, except in a dialectical context?

2

FROM FAMINE TO BONDAGE

There is shadow under this red rock,
And I will show you something different from either
Your shadow at morning striding behind you
Or your shadow at evening rising to meet you;
I will show you fear in a handful of dust.

—T.S. Eliot

It began at Plassey in 1757, the farcical battle where India lost her freedom. Colonization resulted in a series of famines ravaging India, not as a consequence of natural disasters but as a direct result of the callous colonial politics of the day. The Bengal Famine of 1770, which continued till 1773, killed approximately 10 million people, representing more than one-third of the population of Bengal at that time.[14] The Battle of Plassey was the turning point in the politics of hunger and famine in India.

From a historical perspective, the gradual impoverishment of India's East began as colonialism tightened its grip resulting in repeated famines in Bengal. Along with the merciless rise in taxation by the East India Company and the Permanent Settlement of 1793[15], a large number of small and middle level farmers were

---

[14]Mukherjee, Bhaswati, *Bengal and Its Partition: An Untold Story*, Rupa, 2021, p. 134.

[15]The Permanent Settlement of 1793, instituted by British Indian Governor General Charles Cornwallis, was an agreement to drastically raise land revenues.

deprived of their lands and marginalized.

Under Indian rulers, whether Hindu or Muslim, any natural disaster would be immediately addressed through a series of remedial measures so as to ensure that the drought-hit areas recovered and deaths by starvation were avoided. The tax to be paid by the peasant would be mitigated. Compensatory measures, including irrigation and distribution of food to those affected, would be immediately instituted. The tribute to be paid by the peasants to the rulers would be a reasonable figure of 10–15 per cent of their cash harvest. This ensured that during droughts, the agriculturalists had enough food supplies till the next monsoon. Death by starvation was, thus, avoided.

The fundamental rights of the peasants (called ryots) were protected during Mughal times through the agencies of *patwari*s and *kanungo*s, who were employed by the State for the purpose of maintaining the accounts of revenue collections. It was an inbuilt check in the system to prevent arbitrary exaction and exploitation.

After the Battle of Plassey in 1757, followed by the Treaty of Allahabad in 1765, the British took over the right of collecting the 'tribute', which they increased overnight from 10 to 50 per cent.[16] The tribute changed to a form of colonial taxation, although the nomenclature remained the same. The treaty also cemented the transfer of power to the East India Company. The diwani of the three provinces of Bengal, Bihar and Orissa was ensured in return for an annual payment of ₹26 lakh (£2.6 million). The fiscal rights secured by the British in this manner ensured revenue collection from the lucrative and rich eastern provinces of Bengal, Bihar and Orissa (present-day West Bengal, Jharkhand, Bihar, Odisha and Uttar Pradesh in India, as well as Bangladesh), turning the

---

It resulted in ruthless exploitation of the peasantry, since the revenue was not adjusted even during famines.
[16]Mukherjee, Bhaswati, *Bengal and its Partition: An Untold Story*, Rupa, 2021, p. 137.

tide of history for India and rendering her into a colony. The British agenda was one of ruthless economic exploitation, regardless of its social or human consequences. It was a policy devoid of any empathy or sympathy for Indians—the so-called natives. It was natural that such a policy would wreak havoc on Indian agriculture and economy, and lead to the impoverishment of its people. Famine was a natural corollary of such inhumane colonial policies. The wealth of the West started being accumulated through the graveyards and cremation grounds of the East.

The rapacious Warren Hastings, Governor General of Bengal, wished to take over all control of revenue collection.[17] Revenue collection was to be farmed out to the highest bidders under the supervision of European District Collectors. So high was the revenue burden on the hapless peasants that often it could not be collected at all. The entire agricultural system was destroyed. Hastings returned in disgrace in 1785. In 1786, Governor General Lord Cornwallis came to India with instructions to streamline the revenue administration and increase the wealth of the Company.

Twenty-three years after the first great famine of 1770, Cornwallis imposed the Permanent Settlement of 1793. It resulted in dispossession of about 20 million small farmers, who became destitute and landless. It also destroyed Bengal's growing industry, including its strong and productive textile industries, at a time when the benefit of the first Industrial Revolution was sweeping across Europe.

By 1813, finished Lancashire cotton goods started being imported into a region that had been famous from ancient times for its cotton and silk, woven by its traditional weavers. The results quickly became clear. Subsistence-level agriculture became the sole industry for survival. In the words of Governor General William Bentinck: 'The misery hardly finds parallel in

---

[17]Khan, Abdul Majed, *The Transition in Bengal, 1756-75: A Study of Saiyid Muhammad Reza Khan*, Cambridge University Press, 1969, pp. 294, 297–349.

the history of commerce. The bones of the cotton weavers are bleaching the plains of India.'[18] Despite efforts to whitewash it, history has judged that it was a sinister policy, dictated by naked mercantilism and profit.

The Company, ignoring starvation deaths that had started by 1771, enhanced the tribute to 60 per cent, so as to compensate for any decline in revenue. John Fiske, in his book *The Unseen World*, wrote that the Bengal famine of 1770 was far deadlier than the Black Death that terrorized Europe in the fourteenth century.[19] It is indeed ironic, as chronicled by historian Rakhi Chakraborty, 'the EIC [English East India Company] generated higher profits in 1771 than they did in 1768'.[20]

These sinister developments had commenced before Cornwallis. Some Company officials and European experts, including Alexander Dow, Philip Francis and Thomas Law, suggested a permanent assessment of land revenue, regardless of circumstances. It would also be fixed at the highest possible level. The standard assessment was fixed permanently at the assessment for the year 1789–90. It was fixed at ₹26.8 million (approximately £3 million). According to historian B.B. Chaudhuri's calculation, it 'nearly doubled' between 1765 and 1793.[21]

Cornwallis was from the landed gentry. His preference was for the zamindars, a comprador class of exploiters, with no sympathy for peasants. This also facilitated the task of revenue collection. Land in Bengal's fertile east became part of the zamindari estates. Earlier, zamindars had the right to collect revenue from land-owning peasants. The customary occupancy right of peasants

---

[18]Marqusee, Mike, 'Whitewashing the Past', *The Guardian*, 24 May 2002, https://tinyurl.com/5274s242. Accessed on 27 July 2023.
[19]Fiske, John, *The Unseen World, and Other Essays*, Houghton Mifflin, 1876.
[20]Chakraborty, Rakhi, "The Bengal Famine. How the British Engineered the Worst Genocide in Human History for Profit', *YourStory*, 2014, https://tinyurl.com/3p87eb57. Accessed on 27 July 2023.
[21]Mukherjee, Bhaswati, *Bengal and its Partition: An Untold Story*, Rupa, 2021.

was set aside. Now, they were reduced to the status of tenants and were at the mercy of the zamindars. There also was no written agreement about the amount of revenue, called *patta*, to be collected between the peasant and the zamindar, resulting in arbitrariness in revenue collection. Through subsequent regulations of 1799 and 1812, zamindars had the right to dispossess tenants of their land without court authorization.

Zamindars too were obliged to pay their revenue by a fixed date or sell their property. The colonial authority retained absolute control. As a result, between 1794 and 1807, about 41 per cent of the revenue collected from land, in cash and kind, in Bengal and Bihar was sold out in auction by impoverished zamindars.

Figure 3: Map of British Bengal Presidency in 1794

Source: Rennell, James, *A Map of the North Part of Hindostan or a Geographical Survey of the Provinces of Bengal, Bahar, Awd, Ellahabad, Agra and Delhi*, London, Laurie & Whittle, 1794.

The ruination of India was inevitable after the Treaty of Allahabad. Author William Dalrymple pointed out that through the treaty, '[the] collecting of taxes was henceforth subcontracted to a powerful multinational corporation, whose revenue collecting operations were protected by its own private army.' Dalrymple went on to sardonically term it as, 'an act of involuntary privatisation'. [22]

Lord Cornwallis pushed the policy without a proper evaluation of its effects in the medium and long run. He was aware that tenants and ryots had inviolable rights. As Governor General Lord Francis Edward Rawdon-Hastings later put it, these rights were based on a custom more ancient than all law. Lord Cornwallis chose to ignore them for reasons of expediency. In his minute of 3 February 1790, Lord Cornwallis noted:

> Every bigha [between 1/3 to 1 acre of land] of land possessed ryots, must have been cultivated under an express or implied agreement, that a certain sum should be paid for each bigha and no more. Every 'abwab' or tax imposed by the Zamindar over and above that sum is not only a breach of that agreement, but a direct violation of the established laws of the country. The cultivator, therefore, has in such case, an undoubted right to apply to Government for the protection of his property; and the Government is, at all times, bound to afford him redress.[23]

Lord Cornwallis erroneously thought he had introduced checks and balances into the new system. He noted:

> Whoever cultivates the land, the Zamindars can receive no more than the established rent, which in most places, is fully equal to what the cultivator can afford to pay. To permit him to dispossess one cultivator for the sole purpose of

---

[22]Dalrymple, William, *The Anarchy. The East India Company. Corporate Violence, and the Pillage of an Empire*, Bloomsbury Publishing, 2019, p. xxiv.

[23]Firminger, Walter Kelly, *The Fifth Report from the Select Committee of the House of Commons Vol. II*, R. Camray, Calcutta, 1812.

giving land to another, would be vesting him with a power to commit a wanton act of oppression, from which he would derive no benefit. [...] The Zamindar, however, may sell the land, and the cultivators must pay the rent to the purchaser.[24]

The Court of Directors, part of the colonial administrative system, thought otherwise, since they were aware of the rights of cultivators. While approving the proposal, they 'expressly reserved the right which clearly belonged' to government as sovereigns of interposing their 'authority in making, from time to time, all such Regulations as might be necessary to prevent the ryots being improperly disturbed in their possessions loaded with unwarrantable exactions'.[25]

In order to protect the rights of the cultivators, they noted:

Our interposition, when it was necessary, seemed also to be clearly consistent with the practices of the Mogul Government, under which it appeared to be a general maxim, that the immediate cultivator of the soil, duly paying his rent, should not be dispossessed of the land he occupied; that this necessarily supposed that there were some measures and limits by which the rent could be defined; and that it was not left to the arbitrary determination of the Zamindar, for that, otherwise, such a rule would be nugatory.[26]

Unfortunately, under relentless pressure from the zamindars, the infamous Haftam or Regulation VII of 1794 was enacted just one year after the Permanent Settlement. It gave zamindars unrestricted right of 'distraint', which was the seizure of property to clear outstanding dues of rent. This measure destroyed age-

---

[24]Ibid.
[25]Jha, Aditya Prasad, 'Tenants' Rights in Bengal and Bihar after Permanent Settlement (1793-1819)', *Proceedings of the Indian History Congress*, Vol. 23, 1960, pp. 78–90, https://tinyurl.com/57xf922f. Accessed 30 July 2023.
[26]Ibid.

old landholding rights and impoverished, marginalized and made landless ryots and cultivators who had tilled the soil for centuries.

The Haftam Regulation was criticized by Britain's judicial system. Justice Field noted:

> There is scarcely a country in the civilized world in which a landlord is allowed to evict his tenant with-out having recourse to the regular tribunals; but the Bengal Zamindar was deliberately told by the Legislature that he was at liberty to oust his tenants if the rents claimed by him were in arrear at the end of the year, leaving them to recover their rights, if infringed, by having recourse to those new and untried courts of justice, the failure in which might be punished with fine or imprisonment.[27]

As cynically noted by a contemporary English judge in 1802, 'But the fact is the ruin of one Zamindar being more conspicuous at the Suddar than that of 10,000 ryots, his interests naturally attract the attention of the legislature first.'[28]

President of the Board of Revenue Sir E. Colebrooke, in November 1814, noted that the absence of even a semblance of judicial enquiry before initiating the distraint of ryots' property for demanding rents was the root cause of the evil. As recorded by him, what was 'contained in the general Regulations for the Permanent designed for the protection of the Ryots or tenants, are rendered nugatory', and that the Courts of Justice, for want of definite regulations respecting their rights, were unable effectually to support ryots. He stated that he 'regretted the blunder that had been done by Cornwallis', of abolishing the office of the kanungos, through which rights of the ryots could have been ascertained

---

[27]Jha, Aditya Prasad, 'Tenants' Rights in Bengal and Bihar after Permanent Settlement (1793-1819)', *Proceedings of the Indian History Congress*, Vol. 23, 1960, pp. 78–90. https://tinyurl.com/57xf922f. Accessed 30 July 2023.
[28]Mill, James, *The History of British India*, Baldwin, Cradock and Joy, 1817.

and secured. He recommended the re-establishment of 'Kanungo Serishtah, or the institution of some similar office of registry and record' in Bengal and Bihar as had existed prior to 1793.[29]

Colebrooke was unaware or chose to ignore that the present system of kanungos could not effectively perform their duties, since the patwaris were hand in glove with the zamindars. R. Rocke, another member of the board, felt that '[the patwaris office] was in fact virtually abolished, in respect to its immediate objects, that is, as a check over the former Zamindars or farmers of the land revenue'.[30] As contemporary sources noted:

> The Patwarees were, in fact, the depositories of the local usages of the country, from whom it was always easy for the Revenue Officers of Government to collect correct information regarding the individual rights of the Ryots, in cases of disputes between them and the Zamindars or farmers. They were then considered the immediate servants of Government; but now, being dependent on the proprietors of the soil, the nature and intention of their original institution are materially altered, and instead of being the protectors and guardians of the rights and privileges of the cultivators of the soil, they are become the zealous and interested partisans of the new proprietors. Of course, little information can now be derived from that source, calculated to secure the Ryots from the grip of their new masters.[31]

As a result, even when the kanungo's office was re-established in Bihar by Regulation II of 1816 and in Bengal by Regulation I of

---
[29] *Selection of Papers from the Records at the East-India House, Relating to the Revenue Police, and Civil and Criminal Justice, under the Company's Governments in India Vol. I*, E. Cox, London, 1820, pp. 378–81.
[30] Jha, Aditya Prasad, 'Tenants' Rights in Bengal and Bihar after Permanent Settlement (1793-1819)', *Proceedings of the Indian History Congress*, Vol. 23, 1960, pp. 78–90, https://tinyurl.com/57xf922f. Accessed 30 July 2023.
[31] Ibid.

1819, it was ineffective and unsuccessful because the patwaris were totally biased in favour of the zamindars. Later, as the Company started embarking on expensive wars, they, too, lost interest in protecting the ryots. During the time of Governor General Lord Minto from 1807 to 1813, some efforts at mitigation were made, but they were not able to stem the rot. The collapse of the economy of East India followed along with the exodus of the desperate to the far-flung plantation colonies of the British Empire.

3

ABOLITION OF SLAVERY AND RISE OF INDENTURE

In my beginning is my end. [...]
Old stone to new building, old timber to new fires,
Old fires to ashes, and ashes to the earth
Which is already flesh, fur and faeces,
Bone of man and beast, cornstalk and leaf. [...]
We must be still and still moving
Into another intensity
For a further union, a deeper communion
Through the dark cold and the empty desolation [...]
The wave cry, the wind cry, the vast waters
Of the petrel and the porpoise.
In my end is my beginning.

—T.S. Eliot, 'Four Quartets' (Part II: East Coker)

Between slavery and indenture lay a devious colonial plot. The imperial mind was highly innovative when plotting the destiny of the poor natives they had colonized.

Between the abolition of slavery in 1833 and the rise of indenture, the pioneers of British imperialism introduced the system of apprenticeship for a six-year period. It was an attempt to entice the newly freed slaves into a new form of slave labour. After all, American President George Washington and British Prime Minister William Gladstone were both slave owners! The experiment failed, since the newly liberated slave rightly believed that no commodity was more precious than liberty.

The leaders of the anti-slavery movement had initially preferred the principle of 'poor law reform' so that the local White population could have the opportunity to work on the plantations. They would be supported by former slaves working for regular salaries. The Poor Law Amendment Act along with the Emancipation Act were intended to facilitate this social transition in the plantation colonies, which had been totally dependent on slave labour until then.[32]

The failure to recruit former slaves after Emancipation led to renewed efforts to recruit sections of the marginalized in Western societies. Unchecked capitalism had resulted in huge imbalances in wealth distribution and created large sections of population who were unemployed and desperate. These so-called White immigrants were offered contracts of three to five years to work on the sugar plantations.

Between 1834 and 1837, around 3,000 English, 1,000 Scots and about the same number of Germans and some Irish were sent to the Caribbean. It is significant to note that such immigration, except for convicts transported to distant colonies, was a matter of choice freely entered upon and usually decided on the basis of material advantage to the individual. No such freedom of choice was available to the non-White indentured. Initially, it was the floating and destitute living a precarious existence in Madras, Bombay (now Mumbai) and Calcutta who were persuaded to move out of India. The Western perception of the early indentured was highly negative.

---

[32]For a brief exposition of these views, see: Roberts, David, *Paternalism in Early Victorian England*, New Brunswick, 1979, pp. 2–9.

All four draft plans for the Emancipation Bill generated within the Colonial Office in 1833 were intended to create circumstances in the plantation colonies, which would be conducive to the growth of regular habits of industry among emancipated slaves. The apprenticeship period following Emancipation was viewed as a time for establishing such regular industrial routines.

The experiment to recruit White Europeans totally failed as far as the lower levels of the plantation economy were concerned. Europeans were unused to hard labour in alien climatic conditions. Tinker correctly noted that the experiment was doomed to fail because of 'the unsuitability of raw, un-acclimatised Europeans for field work in the tropical sun, with the added temptation of unlimited drink'.[33] There were many such examples of failed White immigration. The White émigrés were undisciplined, not amenable to the plantation routine and often fell sick under tropical skies.

Their approach and attitude were problematic. Europeans wished to be the 'managers', in a situation similar to the earlier slave owners. They demanded higher wages with no manual labour. Their preference was for temperate rather than tropical colonies. The perception of a dual-labour market based on race, where they would be working alongside people of colour, was rejected. Their approach, based on White supremacy, was fundamentally racist, since many of the early European settlers were semi-literate, had behavioural problems and hailed from marginalized sections of Western capitalist societies at a time when welfare states had not been established.

The preference for Indian indentured was equally based on racist presumptions typical of the early Victorian Age, as authors Marjory Harper and Stephen Constantine noted, 'Indian indentured labourers were recruited and managed by white Europeans whose own terms and rewards of employment were distinctly higher and privileged. In fact, the two streams of empire migration did not just conveniently coincide but were deliberately so engineered and structurally related.'[34]

---

[33]Tinker, Hugh, *A New System of Slavery: The Export of Indian Labour Overseas 1830–1920,* Hansib, London, 1993, p. 56.
[34]Harper, Marjory and Stephen Constantine, *Migration and Empire,* Oxford History of the British Empire Companion Series, Oxford University Press, 2010, p. 5.

Figure 4: Of human bondage: Plantation economy with slaves and the indentured

Source: 'File:Slaves working on a plantation—Ten Views in the Island of Antigua (1823), plate III—BL.jpg', *Wikimedia Commons*, https://tinyurl.com/mr2u6wem. Accessed on 17 August 2023.

Indenture, after slavery, was hailed by the imperialists as a new and great experiment! According to available records, 1,474,740 indentured were recruited by the British between 1834 and 1920, with Indian indentured dominating the migration. The Indian indentured numbered at 1,258,861, which was around 85 per cent of the total. Over one-third of the Indian indentured were sent to Mauritius, another one-third to the Caribbean. The remaining reached South Africa, East Africa, Malaysia and Fiji.[35]

Indian migrants sometimes went to other plantation colonies. Very few returned to India. As a result, in Mauritius, as an example, Indians made up 72 per cent of the population by 1910. In Fiji, Indian migrants equalled the indigenous population.

---

[35] Burn, W.L., *Emancipation and Apprenticeship in the British West Indies*, Jonathan Cape, London, 1937, p 291.

There was great demand for Indian migrants in the West Indies. In view of the failure to attract former slaves, and with White immigration not being a successful alternative, there was a serious labour vacuum in the Caribbean, which Colonial Secretary Lord Stanley thought of addressing through Indian indentured from India or through transportation from Mauritius. In 1842, around 34,525 Indians arrived in Port Louis, Mauritius.[36] On approval of Lord Stanley's proposal by the British Indian Government, in mid-1844, the shipment of Indian indentured to the Caribbean, notably Jamaica, Trinidad and British Guiana, commenced.

Figure 5: Faces of *sorrow*: Indian indentured in Caribbean plantations
Source: "'Labourer at Worship", Jamaica, c1905. Artist: Adolphe Duperly & Son', *Getty Images*, https://tinyurl.com/yf93348n. Accessed on 21 August 2023.

---

[36]Tinker, Hugh, *A New System of Slavery: The Export of Indian Labour Overseas 1830–1920*, Hansib, London, 1993, p. 81.

With the abolition of the Corn Laws in 1846, followed by the abolition of sugar duties, sugar prices fell, leading to a crisis in plantation economies.[37] While Jamaica refused any more Indian indentured, leading to a precipitous decline in output from their plantations, British Guiana and Trinidad continued with the experiment. This helped stabilize the economies of both colonies. By 1860, the sugar exportation of the British West Indies was back to pre-Emancipation levels.[38]

Not all the Indians who left India were indentured. Some went as so-called free labour, although the line dividing indenture and free labour was thin and frequently blurred. Free labour migrated to Mauritius, South Africa, the Caribbean, Burma (now Myanmar) and Ceylon (now Sri Lanka). Other free labour included the former indentured whose contracts had expired. They settled in the plantation colonies and became small landowners. This was particularly true of freed Indians in Mauritius, Fiji and the Caribbean.

Whether indentured or free, the subservience and acceptance by the Indians of a low social status led to the popular inference that they were similar to their predecessors who were now emancipated slaves. Over time, they came to deeply resent the parochial attitudes of the Whites and to realize that their labour was essential to maintain the momentum of sugar plantation economies. Emancipation had coincided with the abolition of preferential imperial tariffs, establishment of free trade and subsequently, a catastrophic fall in sugar prices. The route to prosperity lay in the recruitment of Indian indentured. As a result, Mauritius became the largest sugar producer and exporter.

The migrants were regarded as pawns to be moved around the British Empire to ensure profit maximization from a hybrid

---

[37]Rice, Duncan C., "'Humanity Sold for Sugar!' The British Abolitionist Response to Free Trade in Slave-Grown Sugar", *The Historical Journal*, Vol. 13, No. 3, 1970, pp. 402–18.
[38]Deerr, Noël, *The History of Sugar*, Chapman and Hall, London, 1950, p. 377.

combination of capital, labour and land, which defined the plantation economies of the time. These huge streams of global migrations had the unintended consequence of transporting the social and cultural values of the indentured to their final destinations. This resulted in the establishment of rainbow nations—multiracial and multi-ethnic states—in these distant colonies.

Clearly, 'in evaluating the effects of empire migration, the economic consequences are self-evidently monumental'.[39] Settlement was accompanied by environmental degradation and destruction, elimination of the indigenous and native populations and the development of racist ideologies based on the concept of racial superiority and the White Man's Burden. As correctly noted, 'Empty spaces or virgin lands were cultural terms and rarely objective descriptions.'[40]

It was unfortunate that European settlers and builders of empires looked at these acquired assets, the plantation economies, through coloured glasses that influenced their approach to the indentured who arrived there to create these plantations for the profit of the colonizers. It also influenced their perception of ownership and identity.

The abolition of slavery coincided with the predominance of free trade and capitalism. Ideally, the nation at the forefront of emancipation of slaves should have vigorously debated the social, economic and human rights conditions of the indentured in the plantations. That was not to be, and that era passed. The UK was no longer interested in its role as the redeemer. Profit was the new religion. Morality and moral values were no longer at the heart of the debate.

Early Victorian England was profoundly racist. The British were convinced that former slaves and indentured Indians, from

---

[39] Harper, Marjory and Stephen Constantine, *Migration and Empire,* Oxford History of the British Empire Companion Series, Oxford University Press, 2010, p. 150.
[40] Ibid. 9.

pagan religions and questionable cultural and social customs, were unfit to run plantations. They were suitable for the lowest rungs of labour. Their redemption, according to the missionaries, lay in their conversion and acceptance of their inferior status and of the so-called superior values of the European civilization. Historian William Green noted:

> Europeans at the summit of that hierarchy were of questionable character. Their presumed responsibility involved inculcating in the lower orders 'proper' civic attitudes, Christian values, and a respect for 'ennobling labour'. If, in retrospect, this social attitude appears both arrogant and futile, it was, in the 1840s, entirely in keeping with provincial English practice and in essential harmony with the concept of cultural uplift maintained by missionary bodies.[41]

In the decades that followed, the British colonial government's approach to immigration of free labour or the transportation of the indentured as a way of controlling the increasingly impoverished sections of Indian society was challenged by the rise of Indian nationalism. The early Indian nationalists condemned indenture as an example of inequality, exploitation and marginalization of Indians in British colonies.

Gopal Krishna Gokhale, a political leader, social reformer and Mahatma Gandhi's mentor, highlighted in 1912 that indenture was 'a monstrous system, iniquitous in itself, based on fraud and maintained by force'.[42] Gokhale's comments were echoed 70 years later by Tinker.[43]

The position taken by Gokhale and others posed a dilemma

---

[41]Green, William A., 'Emancipation to Indenture: A Question of Imperial Morality', *Journal of British Studies*, Vol. 22, No. 2, 1983, pp. 98–121.
[42]Cumpston, I.M., 'A Survey of Indian Immigration to British Colonies to 1910', *Population Studies*, Vol. 10, No. 2, 1956, p. 7.
[43]Tinker, Hugh, *A New System of Slavery: The Export of Indian Labour Overseas 1830–1920*, Hansib, London, 1993.

for Whitehall, symbolized by Joseph Chamberlain's speech to the Imperial Conference in 1897. On one hand, he said that the right of self-governing colonies to control an influx of Indians who are 'alien in civilization, alien in religion, alien in customs' was confirmed. Paradoxically, he also highlighted the importance of bearing in mind 'the traditions of the Empire, which makes no distinction in favour of, or against, race or colour'.[44]

The Western imperialist powers, having been strongly criticized by Indian nationalists and the small liberal English lobby, had to reluctantly acknowledge that indenture was antithetical to freedom and could find no place in the modern Western nation state. The brutal exploitation of the poor and marginalized by forcing them into exile was, as William Green pointed out, 'a further testimonial to European racism and to the arrogance of great power'.[45]

Who would inherit these vacant spaces being cultivated at the whim of the colonizer? After all, European settlers were as alien to these lands as the Indian indentured. At some point in the clash of conflicting ideologies and diverse social and racial origins, a new nationalism arose, through which the indentured captured political power. This was also driven by hostility to entrenched racial prejudices against Indians across the Empire. It also helped shape a distinctive identity for the Indian indentured.

The Europeans, instead of offering accommodation, insisted on absorption and assimilation. While they succeeded to a certain extent in Reunion Island, they were rejected elsewhere. Similarly, systematic efforts at conversion also failed. Not only did the migrants cling to their respective religions and their social and

---

[44]*Proceedings of a Conference between the Secretary of State for the Colonies and the Premiers of the Self-Governing Colonies at the Colonial Office, London, June and July 1897*, HMSO, London, 1897, pp. 13–14, https://tinyurl.com/ymtzj6te. Accessed on 30 July 2023.

[45]Green, William A., 'Emancipation to Indenture: A Question of Imperial Morality', *Journal of British Studies*, Vol. 22, No. 2, 1983, pp. 98–121.

cultural identities, but their customs and practices also thrived in these alien lands. An Indian storekeeper, Mr Telucksing, from Durban, South Africa, stated to the Wragg Commission: 'I have not suffered in my caste in any way by coming across the ocean to Natal, because I have observed all my religious ceremonies and I have done nothing to debar me from enjoying my caste privileges.'[46]

The consequences of these ill-considered policies cast a long shadow over events in the twentieth century and beyond. It remade geographies in Africa and Asia, often with huge bloodshed and human suffering. It led to the partition of India and borders being created on imperial whim across Asia, Africa and the Arab world.

Some argue that the creation of the UK itself was a product of English imperialism based on the principle of the 'core' and 'periphery'. This could unravel at some point post-Brexit. Imperialism and corporate rapacity have a lot to answer for and belong to the wrong side of history. As Dalrymple noted, this story must be narrated not just because imperialism persists till today but also because, 'it is not obviously apparent how a nation state can adequately protect itself and its citizens from corporate excess.'[47]

∼

---

[46]Harper, Marjory and Stephen Constantine, *Migration and Empire*, Oxford History of the British Empire Companion Series, Oxford University Press, 2010, p. 179.

[47]Jasanoff, Maya, 'The Anarchy by William Dalrymple Review—The East India Company and Corporate Excess', *The Guardian*, 11 September 2019, https://tinyurl.com/yzuunbmy. Accessed on 27 July 2023.

4

THE GIRMIT

> *May the stream of my life flow into*
> *the river of righteousness.*
> *Loose the bonds of sin that bind me.*
> *Let not the thread of my song be cut while I sing;*
> *And let not my work end before its fulfilment.*
>
> Rig Veda 11.28. 1–9[48]

The girmit or so-called contract lay at the core of the Indian indenture process, which, over time, became a global phenomenon, spread over Africa, Asia and the Pacific as well as the Caribbean. It commenced in 1838 when the earliest indentured left for Mauritius and British Guiana and ended by decree in 1917, when the First World War was still raging globally.

With a thumbprint substituting for a signature to convey the signatory's agreement to conditions written in an alien language and no translation, this deceptive document triggered one of the biggest transplantations of people in human history. Around two million Indian indentured left their homes and settled in the plantation colonies of the British Empire. They would understand only later that by affixing their thumbprints on this document, they lost their freedom, perhaps forever in some cases.

---

[48]Brodbeck, Simon, 'Introduction', *The Bhagavad Gita*, Juan Mascaró (trans), Penguin Classics, 2003.

The Girmit

What was the girmit? Technically, it symbolized a legal contract between supposedly equal partners to regulate a work agreement on the basis of pecuniary considerations. In reality, after the failure of the 'apprenticeship' experiment, recruiters took no chances in ensuring a foolproof contract for innocent and credulous Indians who thought they were being given a chance to have a new and bright future. Since the arrangement was state regulated, the responsibility and liability also lay with the British Indian Government.

Why was a written agreement defined as the girmit? Since there was no equivalent word for a contract or agreement in an Indian language, the legal undertaking loosely translated was termed as the girmit. It was supposed to be freely accepted by both sides. Since it was written in English, the potential recruits, who had no formal schooling, affixed their thumbprints on the document. It regulated the terms and condition of employment which, by 1870, were uniform in content and application. Since the work revolved around manufacturing sugarcane, the girmit laid down the conditions of employment, including remuneration and the possibility of medical and housing facilities. For the Girmitiyas, as they came to be known, the most important written undertaking was the offer of a return passage to India, usually after 10 years of residence.

At the macro level, British rule was an intolerable burden for India, which had the most deleterious effect on her poorest and most deprived. At the micro level, in the villages and agricultural sector, the impact was so severe that there was no other option but to look for remunerative employment. The outward-bound flow increased dramatically after recurrent famines in Bengal, Bihar and the United Provinces.

Dadabhai Naoroji, in the 1860s, underlined that the British continuously drained India of her wealth as 'the price of her rule in

India'.[49] Neither did India receive any compensation, then or now, nor was there any regret on Britain's part, then or now. Naoroji calculated in 1870 that the drain could be valued at approximately £12 million. From 1870 to 1872, the drain averaged £27.4 million annually. By the end of the nineteenth century, the drain was valued at about £20 million annually.[50] Dr Irfan Habib calculated that the drain was about 9 per cent of national income from 1783 to 1782 and 4.41 per cent in 1880. He further calculated that Britain gained over £2 million from 1789 to 1790 and the amount increased to £4.7 million by 1801.[51]

The outward flow of India's wealth deprived her of the benefits of Industrial Revolution and destroyed her agriculture and industry. Combined with the Permanent Settlement and man-made famines, where no succour was available, the girmit appeared to be the only option available to millions to escape starvation. It was no coincidence that most of the indentured came from Bengal, Bihar and Orissa, which had been most affected by the Permanent Settlement. Peasants became tenants and later were driven out of their holdings.

The adverse impact of imperialism is also clear from the demography and caste origin of this exodus. According to the 'Indentured Immigration Records', many of those who opted to be recruited were from the agricultural sector.[52] The actual process of recruitment was based on the core premises of deception and subterfuge. The vast Indo-Gangetic plains with the teeming millions, who were driven from their lands though the imperialism and loot of the Company, provided easy succour to the recruiters.

---

[49]Naoroji, Dadabhai, *Poverty and Un-British Rule in India*, Government of India, Publications Division, Delhi, 1996, p. iv.
[50]Ibid.
[51]Habib, Irfan, *Essays in Indian History: Towards a Marxist Perception*, Anthem Press, London, 2002, p. 304.
[52]'Indian Immigration Archives', Mahatma Gandhi Institute, https://tinyurl.com/5eeas2zk. Accessed on 14 August 2023.

Who were the potential victims? It is of particular interest that although Calcutta was the main port of embarkation, very few Bengalis boarded those ships.[53] Initially, the tribal areas of Bihar and its hinterland provided a fertile ground for the sirdars (recruiting agents). Passenger lists for the ships *Hesperus* and *Whitby,* which left for British Guiana in 1838, indicate 405 Girmitiyas aboard the two vessels, of whom 72 came from Hazaribagh, 49 from Bankura, 36 from Ramgarh, 27 from Midnapur and 20 from Nagpur. A caste and religious breakup of the Girmitiyas revealed that 34 per cent were Dhangars or the herding tribals, 8 per cent were Muslims, 5 per cent each were Rajputs and Kurmis, 4 per cent each were Bauris and Bhuiyas, and the remainder were Kshatriyas, Gowalas and Bagdis.

From the 1870s, the focus of recruitment shifted to the United Provinces of Agra and Oudh. Within the United Provinces, the Eastern (Poorbea) districts that furnished the bulk of the emigrants—districts such as Basti, Gonda, Faizabad, Sultanpur, Azamgarh, Gorakhpur, Allahabad (now Prayagraj) and Ghazipur.[54]

The testimony of some who were subject to deception during recruitment confirms the flawed process. One indentured, Munshi Rahman Khan, stated:

> While I was standing on the bridge of the canal and looking at the water, two Muslims, who later proved to be money minded devils, came to me. [...] 'We would like you to have a job?' They said it was a government job. [...] They happily told me. 'Then you could become a sardara [headman] and receive a salary of 12 annas per day. The work has to do

---

[53]Lal, Brij V., *Girmitiyas: The Origins of the Fiji Indians,* Journal of Pacific History, Canberra, 1983.

[54]Vertovec, Steven, '"Official" and "Popular" Hinduism in the Caribbean: Historical and Contemporary Trends in Suriname, Trinidad and Guyana', *Across the Dark Waters: Ethnicity and Indian Identity in the Caribbean,* David Dabydeen and Brinsley Samaroo (eds), Macmillan Caribbean, 1996, pp. 108–30, 112–13.

with sugar...' Hearing such tempting words I became very happy. [...] To get such a high salary at that time [in India] was very difficult.[55]

There are only a few such first-hand sources available of the process of recruitment. One riveting account is contained in Brij V. Lal's *Chalo Jahaji*. The recruitment process is described as follows:

> This is the coolie-recruiters' harvest-time. Will not the generous Sirkar [government] pay him in silver rupees for every son of the soil won by his persuasive tongue for service in the far-off countries? Well Ramjani knows his 'happy hunting-grounds'. He seldom attempts his arguments in the remote jungle villages; he values his skin too highly for that, for new ideas do not find favour in these communities. Yet Ramjani knows well that it is just these men that, once secured, are the best working article.[56]

The anonymous writer explained to the reader about the journey to Calcutta and the embarkation:

> In company with other parties of coolies, under charge of 'forwarding agents', he starts for Calcutta.[57]

There is proven documentary evidence that some Girmitiyas were the victims of deception or forced recruitment through

---

[55]Munshi Rahman Khan was born in Hamirpur, United Provinces, in 1874. He arrived in Suriname in 1898, at the age of 24, and was employed on the plantation named Skerpi.
For more information, see: Khan, Munshi Rahman, *Autobiography of an Indian Indentured Labourer Munshi Rahman Khan (1874-1872): Jeevan Prakash*, Kathinka Sinha-Kerkhoff, Ellen Bal and Alok Deo Singh (trans), Shipra Publications, Delhi, 2005, p. xiii.
[56]Lal, Brij V., *Chalo Jahaji: On a Journey through Indenture in Fiji*, Australian National University Press, 2012.
[57]Ibid.

kidnapping by recruiters. For instance, Pudai, a male juvenile was kidnapped in 1876 in Allahabad and illegally detained at the depot in Kydganj.[58] In another instance, a married woman, Partabia, was tricked and taken to the depot in Calcutta. She was put in illegal detention and not released even when her father and father-in-law came to the depot to look for her.[59] In the case of Partabia, the concerned *arkatia*s (sub-recruiters) were tried in a court of law charged with kidnapping and found guilty. The punishment, however, did not reflect the severity of the crime they committed. Two were given six months of rigorous imprisonment and the third simple imprisonment for three months.[60] In some cases of proven malpractices, the licenses of the arkatias were cancelled. Here again, through manipulation and deception, many arkatias were able to have their licenses restored.

Who were the recruiters? According to the Immigration Ordinance of October 1881, a recruiter was licensed under the Act to recruit emigrants on behalf of an emigration agent.[61] Sub-recruiters, called arkatias, were sent to district towns and villages with instructions to recruit agricultural labour, usually men. There were some woman arkatias, usually related to the recruiter, whose primary responsibility was to hire women. Once an agreement was procured, they were taken to the district officer in charge of registration. They stayed at a sub-depot before being taken as a group by train to Calcutta.

---

[58]Deen, Shamshu, *Solving East Indian Roots in Trinidad*, HEM Enterprises, 1994, p. 288.
[59]Ibid.
[60]Mahase, Radica, *Why Should We Be Called 'Coolies'?: The End of Indian Indentured Labour*, Routledge, 2020.
[61]*Proceedings of the Lieutenant-Governor of Bengal*, General Department, Emigration, Calcutta, 1900, p. 502.

Figure 6: Indentured waiting patiently at a plantation in Suriname

Source: 'File:Tropenmuseum Royal Tropical Institute Objectnumber 60008926 Suriname, Tadja Feest Op Een Plantage.jpg', *Wikimedia Commons*, https://tinyurl.com/39duwuf3. Accessed on 30 July 2023.

Recruitment was a lucrative business. The arkatias were paid per head per Girmitiya.[62] Major D.G. Pitcher noted: '[The] sub-agents received for the most part a monthly salary, in addition to certain commissions on each recruit payable on embarkation.'[63] The stakes were high, since the recruiters were paid ₹35 for female Girmitiyas and ₹25 for male Girmitiyas.[64] After 1868, when the colonial government fixed a quota of 40 women per 100 men for every ship carrying the indentured, the additional pressure on the arkatias to recruit women resulted in greater malpractices and forced migrations. As a result, the entire recruitment process was

---

[62]Ibid.
[63]'Results of Major Pitcher's Inquiries into the System of Recruiting Labour', *Proceedings of the Lieutenant-Governor of Bengal*, General Department, Emigration, Calcutta, 1883.
[64]*Report of the Committee on Emigration from India to the Crown Colonies and Protectorates*, HMSO, London, 1910, p. 21.
   This report has been referred to as Sanderson Report across the text.

subject to coercion, deception and, in some cases, especially for women Girmitiyas, kidnapping and abduction.

The arkatias never gave a clear picture either of life in the plantation colony or of the nature of the work and conditions of employment to their potential recruits. Most were informed that a far better life and destiny awaited them with unlimited wealth and prosperity. This also caused unrest on the plantations, since they had a rude awakening when they reached their final destination.

As a result, the Protector of Emigrants in Trinidad suggested to the British Indian colonial government that it was imperative for the Girmitiyas to be made aware in advance of the terms and conditions of work.[65] Accordingly, the British Indian Government, in 1898, decreed that the Protector of Emigrants and depot agents in Calcutta should instruct recruiters and registering officers that the potential recruits be fully briefed regarding their terms of engagement as well as their future life in the plantation colony.[66] A Hindi translation of the Bill to Consolidate and Amend the Law Relation Emigration was published in the Bihar Gazette on 19 December 1899.[67] It was further translated into other important local languages, notably Bengali and Urdu.

However, since the majority were either totally illiterate or literate in other local languages, the above measures did not provide much relief. The Girmitiyas continued to put their thumbprints on the girmit without any knowledge of the terms and conditions of the contract.

Even for those who understood the language of the contract, the document titled 'Terms of Engagement of Intending

---

[65]*Proceedings of the Lieutenant-Governor of Bengal*, General Department, Emigration, Calcutta, 1898.
[66]Ibid.
[67]'Letter to the Secretary of the Government of Bengal, General Department from Babu Kalli Coomar Mitter, Hindi Translator to the Government, Calcutta, 20th December 1899', *Proceedings of the Lieutenant-Governor of Bengal*, General Department, Emigration, Calcutta, 1900, p. 60.

Emigrants' was modified at will, either by the colonial planters, the local authorities or the imperial government depending on circumstances. For example, the document stipulated that the Girmitiya was entitled to a return passage to India free of charge on completion of their contract and stipulated stay in the colony. This was frequently modified to deny the indentured their legal right to a free passage. Many were forced to contribute one quarter of the total cost or to pay for the entire passage.

Similarly, the provisions for medical care were totally ignored by many plantation owners as well as the stipulated minimum wages for each worker. The legal provision was 12 annas (local currency) for an able-bodied man for one day's work, while a minor (between 10 and 12 years of age) would receive 8 annas per day with wages being paid on a fortnightly basis. Workers were never fully paid on time. The contractual obligation regarding free time was never respected. The indentured were required to possess passes to allow them to leave the plantation. Compradors from among them were appointed to control them. The similarity to slavery was now too glaring to hide.

The conditions of employment continued to be violated, leading to unrest and dissent. The indentured were at the mercy of the White supervisor or the comprador sirdar. Horrifying stories started coming back to India, resulting in a strong public reaction across the country. Reports of abuse and ill-treatment persisted. The imperial government found itself under pressure. Some action had to be taken to assuage public opinion. In 1875, Lord Salisbury, the Secretary of State for the colonies, wrote to the British Indian Government enquiring if the private contractual system should not be better regulated under direct supervision of the colonial government in India.

> While, then, from an Indian point of view, emigration, properly regulated, and accompanied by sufficient assurance of profitable employment and fair treatment, seems a thing

to be encouraged on grounds of humanity, with a view to promote the well-being of the poorer classes; in this view also, it seems proper to encourage emigration from India to the colonies well fitted for an Indian population.[68]

The British Indian Government's response was negative. It was couched in diplomatic language as follows: 'Our policy may be described as one of seeing fair play between the parties to a commercial transaction, while the Government altogether abstains from mixing itself in the bargain.'[69]

The real reason was the problem of legal liability and lawsuits by the anti-slavery lobby in the UK. Pressure from Indian nationalists, horrified by the continuing reports of gross abuses, ultimately forced the hand of the British Indian Government. Indenture was formally abolished in 1917.

In retrospect, the colonial policy of 'divide and rule' was successfully used to keep the Indian indentured away from the free slave population in the colonies. Isolating them within the plantations and permitting some limited practice of their social and cultural customs were deliberate policies of the colonial authorities. The Indians were never allowed to integrate with other ethnic groups. It was a system resembling apartheid, with artificial separation of ethnic groups and complete control over both groups. It has been noted:

> A labour force can be more easily subjugated and controlled when it is seen as inferior [...] in all the territories, the difference between immigrants and planters extended beyond ethnicity. [...] Indians were never encouraged to

---

[68]Gillion, K.L., *Fiji's Indian Migrants: A History to the End of Indenture in 1920*, Oxford University Press, Melbourne, 1962, p. 22.
[69]Lal, Brij V., *Leaves of the Banyan Tree: Origins and Background of Fiji's North Indian Migrants, 1879 -1916: Vol. 1*, 1981, The Australian National University, PhD dissertation.

develop a sense of identity and they were generally treated as an inferior people.[70]

Unfortunately, the fractures and divisions from this separation haunt us till today. The ultimate abolition of indenture reflected the complexities of imperial governance of the times. Ships could no longer safely transport the indentured in the middle of the First World War. The historical context of abolition is a sobering reminder of the cynicism of the colonial policies of the day.

Gandhi agreed to support the Allies in the First World War in return for the promise of autonomy for India. That promise too was broken immediately after the war concluded with a decisive victory for the UK. Betrayal followed despite the decisive role and contribution to victory by Indian soldiers in the trenches, braving German mustard gas. The Spanish Flu in 1918, which reportedly killed around 14 million Indians, was followed by Jallianwala Bagh massacre on 13 April 1919, just two years after the abolition of indenture. India continued to remain a colony of the British Empire.

∽

---

[70]Mahase, Radica, *Why Should We Be Called 'Coolies'?: The End of Indian Indentured Labour*, Routledge, 2020, p. 7.

5

BEYOND THE KALAPANI

> *The die is cast,*
> *the Rubicon's been crossed;*
> *no lamenting now*
> *the opportunities lost,*
> *no counting the cost;*
> *the time for choosing's past,*
> *and we are caught, alas,*
> *in an everlasting mist.*
>
> —Adolf Wood, 'The Game of Chance'

Where and how did it begin? The process of recruiting the indentured was complex. Many are not aware of how the notion of crossing the oceans was deeply intertwined with India's religious, cultural and social norms of the day. From ancient times, the crossing of the metaphorical 'Kalapani'[71] has been derived from a notion that the separation from the river Ganges, called Ma Ganga, would break the cycle of reincarnation and would imply an immediate loss of one's caste. A ban on sea travel is mentioned in the fifth century BC sutra of Baudhayana. These deeply ingrained social prejudices continued into the nineteenth century. Enlightened leaders who tried to defy them were faced with social ostracism. As an example, Dwarkanath Tagore, the

---

[71] 'Kalapani' or 'Kala Pani', which means 'black water' in Hindi or Bhojpuri, represents the proscription of crossing the seas as sanctified in certain religious texts.

grandfather of Rabindranath Tagore, 'faced excommunication by the inner circle of his family' following his return from his first trip to Europe in 1842.[72]

As a result, recruiters never mentioned the journey across the vast Indian Ocean and beyond, the crossing of the Kalapani, which would come as an unpleasant surprise to the indentured once the journey commenced. Innocent and credulous, these men were lured from their homes and families under false promises of wealth and prosperity to promised lands close to India. The colonizers took full advantage of the desperation of the poor seeking what they were told would be a rosy future.

India was in the throes of recurring famines, not as a consequence of natural disasters but as a direct result of the ruthless colonial policies of the day. The situation was aggravated by the Permanent Settlement, which drove millions of peasants from their lands into poverty and destitution.

These prejudices and superstitions were enhanced by persistent reports of high mortality rates which combined with the distrust of the then Indian elite towards the entire process of recruitment impacted the numbers willing to be shipped out. There were disturbing reports of high mortality rates and racist treatment, which stirred nascent nationalist sentiments led by the Indian elite. Judge Pitcher noted that 'educated native gentlemen' were very sceptical about the motives of the British in authorizing emigration in the interests of populating distant 'desert lands'.[73]

The journey originating from the port of Calcutta was made ironically in the same ships used earlier to transport slaves

---

[72] Mortuza, S., 'Beyond "Kalapani" and Tagore's Search for a Shared Regional Identity', *Journal of the Indian Ocean Region*, Vol. 13, No. 3, 2017, p. 284, https://tinyurl.com/2ddsav37. Accessed on 31 July 2023; Mandal, Somdatta (ed. and trans), *Wanderlust: Travels of the Tagore Family*, Visva-Bharati, Kolkata, 2014.
[73] Bates, Crispin, and Marina Carter, 'Kala Pani Revisited: Indian Labour Migrants and the Sea Crossing', *Journal of Indentureship and Its Legacies*, Vol. 1, No. 1, 2021, pp. 36–62, https://tinyurl.com/2p8pzx97. Accessed 14 August 2023.

from Africa to North America and Europe. The challenges on the journey to unknown destinations, with the scourge of malnutrition, skin infections and cholera lurking at every corner of the unsanitary holds of these ships, resulted in an unacceptably high mortality rate. This fact was reluctantly acknowledged even by the colonial authorities.

The journey itself marked the beginning of an odyssey across the Kalapani, a tragic journey into exile across the tempest tossed Indian Ocean. Those who were lucky enough to survive cholera on-board spent their days doing hard labour and nights dreaming of their Mother land. In between, they tended to the orphans, whose parents had been mercilessly thrown overboard, having fallen victim to disease.

In 1894, the Protector of Emigrants tried to justify the excessive death rate at Calcutta depot, noting:

> Although the scarcity in the North-Western Provinces and Oudh had not reached the more acute stage of famine, it was still sufficiently severe to urge crowds of half-starved adults and emaciated children to the different recruiting centres, with the result that the Calcutta depots eventually became asylums for a large number of people in a more or less anaemic and unhealthy condition.[74]

Tables 1 and 2 list the percentage of dropouts before the journey from Calcutta as well as in Mauritius, where the indentured had a long wait in difficult conditions before travelling to their final destination in the Caribbean. It was only after the stirring of nationalism and the rise of the Indian national movement, along with public awareness and indignation at their miserable plight that the numbers of potential Girmitiyas started falling sharply.[75]

---

[74] *Yearly Reports on Emigration*, 1894.
[75] Emmer, P.C., 'The Meek Hindu: The Recruitment of Indian Labourers for Service Overseas, 1870–1916', *Colonialism and Migration, Indentured Labour*

Table 1
Number of indentured emigrants ordered and dispatched (in statute adults) via Calcutta

	All Colonies		Suriname	
	Demand	Supply	Demand	Supply
1884	18,639	13,867	1,350	1,535
1885	6,430	5,331		
1886	7,010	5,975	320	329
1887	4,625	4,565		
1888	7,180	6,541	1,000	470
1889	9,945	10,041	1,200	1,134
1890	13,826	12,154	1,256	1,162
1891	13,867	14,401	698	653
1892	10,558	10,416	1,370	1,340
1893	10,510	10,068	700	750
1894	14,638	14,865	1,219	1,152
1895	9,487	9,976	1,340	1,341
1896	8,776	9,611	1,166	1,128
1897	7,024	7,379	1,300	1,287
1898	6,358	6,035	600	590
1899	9,733		918	918
1900	11,171	11,225		
1901	11,290	11,460	1,250	643
1902	10,455	10,494	625	1,254
1903	9,893	8,794		
1904	7,501	6,901	239	238
1905	8,157	8,933	165	165
1906	13,276	13,362	1,200	1,188
1907	8,414	6,889	1,800	1,002
1908	9,276	10,160	1,800	1,801
1909	9,347	8,420	1,833	1,833
1910	12,153	8,340		
1911	9,706	8,861		
1912	10,447	8,227	1,600	1,154
1913	5,167	6,175	1,638	1,675

Before and After Slavery, Comparative Studies in Overseas History 7, Ernst Van Den Boogaart and P.C. Emmer (eds), Martinus Nijhoff, 1986, pp. 187-208.

1914	5,132	2,588	800	705
1915	5,846	2,314		
1916	9,071	3,666	1,050	280
Total	314,911.5	287,058.5 = 91 per cent	28,439	25,844 = 91 per cent

Source: de Klerk, C.J.M., *De immigratie der Hindostanen in Suriname*, Urbi et Orbi, Amsterdam, 1953, p. 70.

Table 2
Causes of non-embarkation of intending emigrants

a) Between first registration and entry into Calcutta Depot (expressed in percentages of the total number of first registrations)		
	All Colonies	Suriname
Deaths	0.03	0.03
Desertions	1.14	1.04
Rejections	7.19	5.65
Unwilling	0.46	0.85
Claimed by relatives	0.29	0.11
Detained	0.77	0.45
Unaccounted for	5.62	3.80
Total	15.50	11.93
b) Between entry in Calcutta Depot and embarkation (expressed in percentages of the total number 0f first registrations)		
Deaths	0.49	0.62
Desertions*	2.48	3.13
Rejections	13.5	16.60
Unwilling	1	1.3
Claimed by relatives	0.4	0.6
Total	17.87	22.25
Days in depot	27	43

Source: de Klerk, C.J.M., *De immigratie der Hindostanen in Suriname*, Urbi et Orbi, Amsterdam, 1953.

Note: *1880-1890: 4.2 per cent; 1880-1890: 4.9 per cent; 1906-1916: 0.9 per cent; 1906-1916: 1.4 per cent

The difficulties for the hapless passengers began as soon as the ships had embarked on the long voyage. Crossing the seven seas or Kalapani was a challenge. Social segregation enforced by the rigidly hierarchical caste system left the indentured trapped inside a converted slave ship, with no options to practise their religion, food habits or familiar social customs. The sanitary conditions onboard were primitive because the passengers were packed inside with little regard for hygiene and health.

The overseers and the 'masters' of the ship were soon confronted by rising mortality due to cholera and other diseases that were rampant or severe depression leading to suicides on-board. Those dying of cholera were just thrown overboard, leaving behind orphans who were often taken care of by complete strangers.

A descendant of the bonded from Suriname, Rabin S. Baldewsingh, wrote poignantly of that painful journey of his ancestors in the first ship, the *Lalla Rookh*[76], that set sail with the indentured from Calcutta to Suriname:

> This trek is so lonely;
> Under the spell of fate.
> I am not the only one
> in this narrowness of imprisonment
> where men
> play men
> where men
> surpass animals.
> This is surely no dream
> this weeping, this grief.
> No, this trek will not lead to liberation;
> it is the isolated destination in hell.

---

[76]The *Lalla Rookh* was the first ship to carry Indian indentured labourers to the plantation colony of Suriname from Calcutta. It reached its destination on 5 June 1873.

The only compensation lay in the Bhojpuri[77] folk songs and poems and short stories narrated or sung or jealously guarded in the memories that never faded and were passed down the generations. It is, after all, in the same manner that Indian oral traditions have survived through millennia. The journey is now documented through countless stories and poems in Bhojpuri and other languages. A popular folk song composed on the theme of *bidesia* (foreigner) by Bhikhari Thakur carries a powerful message.[78]

> In the regime of British, I was compelled to leave country [...]
> How would I cross the black-water O migrant.
> In the dark room the night was not passing,
> How do I express my pain O migrant?[79]

Reports of conditions on-board began to reach India. Popular folk songs and poems warned of the dire situation, akin to slavery, in sugar plantations. Anti-indenture lobbies came up in the affected areas. Although early nationalists had failed to comprehend the abuses, later nationalist leaders started a country-wide agitation. Recruitment numbers started falling.

---

[77]Bhojpuri is a dialect of Hindi spoken primarily in the Indian states of Bihar, Jharkhand and Uttar Pradesh, along with parts of Nepal.

[78]Pandit Beniram, a contemporary of Bhartendu Harishchandra, was a great composer of *kajari*, a kind of Bhojpuri song. Beniram composed a 'Kajari Bidesiya' around 1860s. See: Singh, Sri Durga Prasad, *Bhojpuri ke Kavi aur Kabya* (The Poets and Poetry of Bhojpuri), Bihar Rashtra Bhasha Parishad, Patna, 1958.

During the second decade of the twentieth century, Bhikhari Thakur composed a play titled *Bidesiya* that became very popular in northern India. The theme of the play centred on migration and the separation of family/the newly married wife. See: Singh, Nagendra Prasad (ed.), *Bhikhari Thakur Rachanawali* (The Compositions of Bhikhari Thakur), Bihar Rashtra Bhasha Parishad, Patna, 2005.

[79]Upadhyay, Vishwamitra, *Lokgiton me Krantikari Chetna* (The Revolutionary Zeal of Folk Songs), Publication Wing, Ministry of Information and Broadcasting, Government of India, 1997, pp. 42–3.

In an iconic poem titled 'Kisan', Maithili Sharan Gupt lyrically expressed the campaign of deception by arkatias to lure the innocent, marginalized and desperate onto these ships.

> A person just asked me on the bank of the Triveni
> Oh! I moved to pity to see you.
> You seem sad, what troubles do you have?
> It is hard to live on, as this country is ruined!
> But there is no need to be worried now,
> you have the blessings of God now.
> Today, and just from today your troubles are over,
> your bad days are over.
> Clothes-food and a monthly salary of fifteen rupees,
> Work that gives you name and fame and also leisure.
> You will be sailing the seas and wonderful sights you will see. [...]
> You will remember me; someone there was who was concerned about me!
> I was surprised, is he human or divine;
> But later I came to know about that arkatia
> Beware! Countrymen, yes in your country
> Many devils roam in the guise of humans.[80]

Initially, the colonial masters who were forced to review the conditions were of the view that the problem could be resolved by changing the diet and introducing Indian or 'native' food. The officers of the Indian Civil Service were condescending about the food on-board. A typical example was the pronouncement by George A. Grierson, a linguist and administrator in the Indian Civil Service of Irish origin, who quipped: 'A man can eat anything on-board ship, a vessel being like the temple of Jagannath, without caste restrictions.'[81]

---

[80]Gupt, Maithili Sharan, *Kisan* (Farmer), Sahitya Sadan, Chirgaon, Jhansi, 1916.
[81]Grierson, G.A., *Report on the Result of His Enquiry into the System of Recruiting*

The colonizers were forced to acknowledge that food habits, if abruptly changed, in total disregard of religious or social and cultural taboos or preferences, can have serious consequences and could threaten the continuation of indenture itself. They needed to understand: 'The indentured ship holds a mirror back onto Indian society to demonstrate the limits of colonial regimes concerning food, health, and taste.'[82]

Criticism came from other quarters, including from the well-organized anti-slavery and humanitarian movements. Their most damning criticism was that Prime Minister Gladstone, a former slave trader, had devised indenture for free labour to run his sugar plantations, which had fallen silent. One complaint was that recruitment was based on the kidnapping of Indian labourers who were then forcibly drafted on-board ships. Gladstone's first term as Prime Minister of Britain was from 1868 to 1874. There is no doubt that Gladstone had descended from a family of notorious slave traders. He initially spoke out strongly for the rights of slave owners.[83]

A Board of Enquiry set up by the British Indian Government in 1838 demonstrated a lamentable lack of interest and knowledge of Indian dietary habits. This was evident in the India Emigration Act V of 1837, the first law to regulate indenture emigration. It provided the following guidance for rations on-board:

Labourers for the Colonies, Government of India, Department of Revenue and Agriculture, 1883, pp. 19.

[82]Kumar, Ashutosh, 'Feeding the Girmitiya: Food and Drink on Indentured Ships to the Sugar Colonies', *Gastronomica*, Vol. 16, No. 1, Spring, 2016, pp. 41–52.

[83]Scoble, John, *British Guiana: Facts! Facts! Facts!,* Johnson and Barrett, London, 1840; Barrett, William Garland, *Immigration to the British West Indies: Is It the Slave-Trade Revived or Not?,* Gray and Warren, London, 1859; Jenkin, Edward, *The Coolie: His Rights and Wrongs,* George Routledge and Sons, New York, 1871; Kale, Madhavi, *Fragments of Empire: Capital, Slavery and Indian Indentured Labor in the British Caribbean,* University of Pennsylvania Press, Philadelphia, 1998.

Table 3
Guidance for rations for indentured on-board:
India Emigration Act V, 1837

Ingredient	Quantity (in chatak[84])
Rice	14
Turmeric	½
Dal	2
Onions	½
Ghee or oil	½
Tobacco	1
Salt	¼

Source: *East India (Coolie Emigration): Copy of Mr. Geoghegan's Report on Coolie Emigration from India*, HMSO, 1874, p. 4.

These directions, which ignored the traditional and seasonal diets of the indentured, resulted in severe malnutrition and indigestion on-board. The Act was amended in 1843 and the daily dietary requirements of those on-board were regulated as follows:

Table 4
Amended daily dietary requirements of
indentured on-board: Act XXI, 1843

Ingredient	Quantity (in ounces[85])
Rice	20
Turmeric	1
Dal	4
Onions	1
Oil	1½
Tobacco	1

---

[84] 1 chatak = 58.32 grams
[85] 1 ounce = 28.35 grams

Salt	1½
Ghee	1
Tamarind	2
Chillies	1½

Source: *East India (Coolie Emigration): Copy of Mr. Geoghegan's Report on Coolie Emigration from India*, HMSO, 1874, p. 13.

This too was totally inadequate. The colonial government reluctantly added parched rice and gram as well as sugar for emigrants during bad weather. Deputy Commissioner of Emigration Steamers A.C. Campbell wrote: 'Parched rice (*chura*), gram (*sattu*), and other similar articles of food which natives are used to, should be utilised for at least one meal each day, and that rice and other cooked food should be distributed but once a day.'[86]

Sattu was the staple diet for peasants from eastern India.[87] Sattu also features in popular songs while chura was eaten by migrant peasants searching for work in the fertile Gangetic Plain.[88] A popular folk song depicts a husband requesting his wife to pack chura quickly so that he can use it for his journey:

---

[86] Kumar, Ashutosh, 'Feeding the Girmitiya: Food and Drink on Indentured Ships to the Sugar Colonies', *Gastronomica*, Vol. 16, No. 1, Spring 2016, pp. 41–52.

[87] Dr Shahid Amin provides the following details on sattu: 'Parched gram ground into flour is more an ingredient than a preparation of food. It is the most common portable food of the country-side. A peasant while travelling would tie a pound or so of sattu in his gamcha and make a "dish" by mixing it with the right amount of water and kneading it into dough. This is then eaten garnished with green chillies and/or some onions. A few pounds of sattu would be enough for a peasant to survive for a couple of days.' See: Crooke, William and Shahid Amin (eds), *Glossary of North Indian Peasant Life*, Oxford University Press, 1989, p. 151.

[88] Upadhyay, Krishna Dev, *Bhojpuri Lokgit, Bhag-1* (Bhojpuri Folk Songs, Part 1), Hindi Sahitya Sammelan, 1990, p. 323.

O pretty woman do husk chura,
O pretty woman I shall go to the country of Magh.
The pretty tearful woman husks chura and shows a smiling face.
[Her husband] boosts her morale with a smile.[89]

Despite these interim measures, mortality rates on the ships, in particular on the Calcutta route, caused a public outcry. The colonial government of Bengal was pressured to hold an inquiry. Dr Frederic John Mouat, a professor of medicine and jail superintendent in Bengal, was appointed to head it.[90] His findings were alarming. High mortality rates were due to appalling sanitary conditions on-board, the transportation of germ-laden water from the Hooghly River, a sudden and radical change in diet of the indentured labour, and inexperienced and uncaring medical officers.

As expected, Western medical historians, Laurence Brown and Radica Mahase, in a cover up, tried to suggest that the indentured passengers were resistant or refused Western medicine.[91] This is absurd and cannot explain why—after remedial measures, including a change in diet were introduced—mortality rates declined significantly, from 1860s until the end of the system.

Dr Mouat, in concluding the inquiry, suggested fresh provisions specifically for emigrants:

---

[89]Ibid. 286. Translation by Ashutosh Kumar.
[90]Lawrenson, Ross, 'Frederic John Mouat (1816-97) MD FRCS LLD of the Indian Medical Service', *Journal of Medical Biography*, Vol. 15, 2007.
[91]Brown, Laurence and Radica Mahase, 'Medical Encounter on Kala Pani: Regulation and Resistance in the Passage of Indentured Indian Migrants, 1834-1900', *Health and Medicine at Sea, 1700-1900*, David Boyed Haycock and Sally Archer (eds), Boydell Press, Woodbridge, Suffolk, 2009.

Table 5
Amended dietary changes by
Dr Mouat to reduce on-board mortality

Ingredient	Quantity[96]
Rice	20 oz
Chillies	½ oz
Salt	1 oz
Firewood	2 lbs
Tobacco	1 oz
Mustard seeds	½ drm
Salt fish	2 oz
Ghee	1 oz
Black pepper	1¼ drm
Onions	2 oz
Coriander seeds	2 drm
Tamarind	2 oz
Dal	4 oz
Ginger oil	½ oz
Turmeric	½ oz
Garlic	½ drm

Source: *East India (Coolie Emigration): Copy of Mr. Geoghegan's Report on Coolie Emigration from India*, HMSO, 1874, p. 25.

Dr Mouat also prescribed mutton on a weekly basis. To that end, six sheep or goats for every 100 men were taken aboard for the voyage. During bad weather, when cooking was very difficult, the following provisions were allowed:

---

[92] oz = ounce; lb = pound 1 seer = 933.10 grams; 1 ounce = 28.35 grams; 1 drm = 180 grams; tls = tablespoon

Table 6
Amended dietary provisions prescribed by Dr Mouat for bad weather

Ingredient	Quantity
Chura or aval	1 seer or 2 lbs
Bhut, gram or cuddeley	½ seer or ½ lbs
Biscuits	½ seer or 1 lb
Sugar	1 chatak or 2 oz

Source: *East India (Coolie Emigration): Copy of Mr. Geoghegan's Report on Coolie Emigration from India*, HMSO, 1874, p. 25.

The colonial government was initially unaware of the extent to which caste and religious practices were intertwined in the food habits of the indentured. This became evident once meat was introduced in their diet. Initially, tinned meat was introduced. This was opposed even by the Muslim indentured, since the ritual 'halal' slaughter was intrinsic to their meat consumption. Moreover, both Hindus and Muslims needed to be reassured that beef and pork were not being served in the guise of preserved meat. They insisted that preserved mutton should be attached to the bone to ensure that beef and pork were not on offer. Bigger bones would be proof that the animal was a cow and not a goat.[93]

Historians specializing in this period of colonialism such as Warwick Anderson and Richard Wilk note that the concern of colonialism for dietary preferences and cultural and social order, emanating initially from the need to reduce mortality rates and continue the indenture system, was ultimately rooted in the notion of perpetuating colonialism and controlling subject populations.[94]

---

[93] Kumar, Ashutosh, 'Feeding the Girmitiya: Food and Drink on Indentured Ships to the Sugar Colonies', *Gastronomica*, Vol. 16, No. 1, Spring 2016, pp. 41–52.

[94] Anderson, W., 'Excremental Colonialism: Public Health and the Poetics of Pollution', *Critical Enquiry*, Vol. 21, No. 3, 1995, pp. 640–69; Anderson, W., *The Cultivation of Whiteness: Science, Health, and Racial Destiny in Australia*, Basic

Beyond the Kalapani 57

The available source material provides valuable inputs into the evolution of the system. For instance, in his biography *Jiwan Prakash*, Munshi Rahman Khan, an indentured labourer from Suriname, wrote:

> Till we reach [Calcutta], we were allowed to cook our own meals as we pleased as we were given raw food materials. Every one followed his own rituals and system. They wore their *janeu* [sacred thread], *tikka* [forehead mark], *kanthi mala* [sacred necklace] etc. according to their caste and religion and followed the system of caste and creed. [...] They had managed to preserve their religious sanctity.[95]

This changed on the journey. Many Brahmins and other high caste people, due to poverty and out of desperation, hid their upper caste status and joined as indentured labourers.[96] According to Girmitya historian Brij V. Lal, this transformation was the beginning of a new and powerful ship-based bond known as jahaji bhai.[97]

Khan's autobiography describes how the high- and low-caste people ate together.

Books, New York, 2003; Warwick, A., *Colonial Pathologies: American Tropical Medicine, Race, and Hygiene in the Philippines*, Duke University Press, Durham, 2006; Wilk, Richard A., 'Taste of Home: The Cultural and Economic Significance of European Food Exports to the Colonies', *Food and Globalisation: Consumption, Markets and Politics in the Modern World*, Alexander Nutzenadel and Frank Trentmann (eds), Berg, New York, 2008.

[95]Khan, Munshi Rahman, *Autobiography of an Indian Indentured Labourer Munshi Rahman Khan (1874-1972): Jeevan Prakash*, Kathinka Sinha-Kerkhoff, Ellen Bal and Alok Deo Singh (trans), Shipra Publications, Delhi, 2005.

[96]The best examples are Totaram Sandhaya and Baba Ramchandra, who declared their caste as Kshatriya during emigration. Totaram's emigration pass shows him as a Kshatriya. Baba Ramchandra wrote that he entered into contract after changing his caste.

[97]Lal, Brij V., *On the Other Side of Midnight: A Fijian Journey*, National Book Trust, Delhi, 2005, p. 2.

In order to get food, we had to line up in two separate queues, one for men and the other for women. There was no separation based on caste, religion or class. At this point in time no Brahmin or Kshatriya protested that they would not sit along and eat with Muslims or Chamars [lower castes]. This is because they all had become Sudras. [...]
Rice and rotis were served thrice a week while on Sundays we were given chura or biscuits. Every fifteenth day, fresh sheep meat and rotis was given to us. Daal, vegetable, tamarind chutney, tinned meat and lime juice was also provided daily. [...] On board, there were no distinctions between high castes and low castes, Hindus or Muslims, or other racial distinctions.[98]

Colonial surgeons' contemptuous approach to the customary dietary beliefs and traditions of the indentured was both arrogant and racist.[99] Dr Bakewell, health officer of shipping in Trinidad, quoted Dr Pearse's description of the Indian labourer as:

> A deeply scorbutic, low fed coolly [sic] with a fatty degeneration of cornea, proneness to low diarrhoea, puffy gums, flesh and rapid sinking of vital power at times. [...] He [coolie] inherited it, he was born with it and his ancestors for thousands of years have been in the same condition.

---

[98]Khan, Munshi Rahman, *Autobiography of an Indian Indentured Labourer Munshi Rahman Khan (1874-1872): Jeevan Prakash*, Kathinka Sinha-Kerkhoff, Ellen Bal and Alok Deo Singh (trans), Shipra Publications, Delhi, 2005, p. 79.
[99]See: Lieffers, Caroline, '"The Present Time Is Eminently Scientific": The Science of Cookery in Nineteenth-Century Britain', *Journal of Social History*, Vol. 45, No. 4, 2012, pp. 936–59; Mitra, Rajarshi, 'The Famine in British India: Quantification Rhetoric and Colonial Disaster Management', *Journal of Creative Communications*, Vol. 7, Nos. 1–2, 2012, pp. 153–74; Dixon, Jane, 'From the Imperial to the Empty Calorie: How Nutrition Relations Underpin Food Regime Transitions', *Agriculture and Human Values*, Vol. 26, No. 4, 2009, pp. 321–33.

They have been for the most part vegetable feeders using a small portion of animal food.[100]

The colonial medical officials compared this diet to that of so-called English emigrants (transported convicts) to Australia. Once again, demonstrating their colonial mindset and ignorance about the beneficial effects of an Indian vegetarian diet, they noted that the latter 'belonged to a class which for centuries has been living on a much better diet than the Hindoo; that he habitually eats wheaten bread and drinks beer, and that even [though] he cannot afford meat, he is able to eat cheese, which is the most concentrated form of nutriment that can be taken.'[101]

The contemptuous attitude towards the indentured influenced the behaviour of the crew in case of any grave danger to the ship, such as an impending shipwreck. A horrific incident was the wreck of the vessel *Syria* on 11 May 1884, off the coast of Fiji, on the Nasilai Reef. Of the passengers, 56 indentured died and three of the Indian crew lost their lives despite the efforts of Dr William MacGregor, the then chief medical officer and acting colonial secretary of Fiji. *Syria* had been on its maiden voyage to Fiji. She had been carrying a disproportionately high number of passengers from Bihar (52 per cent of the total passengers aboard) along with women and children.

Dr MacGregor disliked all Indians whom he regarded, in his own words, as 'necessary evils'.[102] In his detailed account to Governor Sir Arthur Gordon, he painted a complete picture of the horror of the wreck and the abandonment of the Indian passengers. He wrote:

---

[100]Kumar, Ashutosh, 'Feeding the Girmitiya: Food and Drink on Indentured Ships to the Sugar Colonies', *Gastronomica*, Vol. 16, No. 1, Spring 2016, pp. 41–52.
[101]Ibid.
[102]Joyce, R.B., *Sir William MacGregor*, Oxford University Press, Melbourne, New York, 1971, p. 73.

The scene was simply indescribable, and pictures of it haunt me still like a horrid dream. [...] People falling, fainting, drowning all around one; the cries for instant help, uttered in an unknown tongue, but emphasized by looks of agony and the horror of impending death, depicted on dark faces rendered ashy grey by terror; then again, the thundering, irresistible wave breaking on the riven ship, still containing human beings, some crushed to death in the debris, and others wounded and imprisoned therein; and all to be saved then or never [...] Some sacrificed their lives to save others; some, such as the strong lascar crew thought only of themselves, and rushed into the boats surrounded by dying women and children. [...] In spite of everything that could be done the loss of life was fearful.[103]

Shipwrecks were not the only cause of mortality on these long journeys. More frequent were severe bouts of cholera, fever, typhoid and dysentery caused by unsanitary conditions, poor diet and contaminated drinking water. The mortality figures were striking. In 1859, on-board the *Thomas Hamlin*, en route from Calcutta to Guyana (then called Demarara), 82 of the indentured contracted and died of cholera. On the Mauritius route, the most tragic journey was of the *Shah Allam*, which caught fire in 1859. Only one indentured passenger survived out of 400. The tragedy lingers in the collective memories of the former Girmitiyas globally.[104]

Ultimately, it was the Kalapani discourse that symbolized the indentured route. It included the falsehoods used to induce innocents to agree to the journey, the horrors of the journey itself and the sudden and enforced loss of one's culture. These became powerful instruments for Indian nationalists to call for the abolition of indenture.

---

[103]Ibid. 72–73.
[104]Lubbock, Basil, *Coolie Ships and Oil Sailers*, Brown, Son & Ferguson Ltd., 1987, pp. 30–32, 58–60, 68.

Folk culture, music and poetry highlighted these evils. Some regretted the use of deception in recruitment.[105] Others explained why the crossing was called Kalapani. The well-known poet from Lucknow, Shikohabadi (1819–1881), lamented: 'The prisoners' evil fate made the water black [Kalapani]. [...] In the darkness of the evening of exile, they were granted the kohl of Solomon.'[106]

Figure 7: The sailing ship *Mersey* launched for the Nourse Line, which was used for transporting the indentured to British colonies.

Source: 'Mersey', State Library Victoria, https://tinyurl.com/5hf5k5a6. Accessed on 21 August 2023.

Madan Mohan Malaviya, too, in a powerful speech, elaborated on the evils of the crossing: 'He [the indentured] was never informed that the moment he would set foot on-board the steamer all

---

[105]Kumar, A., 'Songs of Abolition: Anti-Indentured Campaign in Early 20th Century India', *Indian Diaspora Socio-Cultural and Religious Worlds*, P. Kumar (ed.), Brill, Leiden, 2015, p. 47.

[106]Anderson, C., 'A Global History of Exile in Asia c. 1700–1900', *Exile in Colonial Asia: Kings, Convicts, Commemoration*, R. Ricci (ed.), University of Hawaii Press, Honolulu, 2016.

his cherished ideas and beliefs about caste and religion would have to be abandoned under sheer compulsion[…] in conditions under which he would never have consented to dine if he was a free man.'[107]

By that time, even rural areas had become aware of the horrors of the crossing. Sital Persad, a former indentured labourer and later the chief interpreter of the Department of Immigration in Suriname, was sent to his native village in India in 1914 to facilitate the recruitment process. He reported that he was repeatedly questioned whether indentured were 'treated as animals overseas and what happened to single women'.[108]

It was Tagore who summed up the intellectual dilemma of articulating the metaphorical and symbolic language of the crossing. The challenges posed to Brahmanical orthodoxy through caste-imposed sanctions to voyagers of the Kalapani were analysed by him from the perspective of the *bhadralok*. Once again, it was Gandhi who understood and appreciated the indignity of the crossing in its total perspective better than all before or after him.

---

[107]IOR, EP, 10001, (1916), p. 333.
[108]Emmer, P.C., 'The Meek Hindu: The Recruitment of Indian Labourers for Service Overseas, 1870–1916', *Colonialism and Migration, Indentured Labour Before and After Slavery,* Comparative Studies in Overseas History 7, Ernst Van Den Boogaart and P. C. Emmer (eds), Martinus Nijhoff, 1986, pp. 187–208.

6

FORGOTTEN MEMORIES: CHOLERA AND QUARANTINE

*Any man's death diminishes me,
because I am involved in mankind,
And therefore never send to know
for whom the bells toll;
it tolls for thee.*

—John Donne

Had John Donne (1572–1631) penned this verse not for the millions of victims of the Black Death, which devastated London in 1348, but for the cholera-infested ships transporting the indentured to their destinations, the British masters would not have cared, since their priorities were different then and their hearts beat to the tune of profit.

The pain of cholera, quarantine, high mortality rates and the arrogant and racist treatment of the sick remained definitive collective memories of the crossing and its aftermath. It haunted jahaji bhais till the end. Quarantine and its administration differed from one plantation colony to another. It was particularly harsh on Reunion Island. In Mauritius, the conditions for isolation in Aapravasi Ghat were more humane. In both Reunion Island and Fiji, the sick were quarantined on small, isolated islands away from the mainland.

The most riveting first-hand account of this came from the voyage to Fiji of the ill-fated *Leonidas*, a 1,600-tonne vessel that transported over 60,000 Indian indentured migrants to Fiji between 1879 and 1916. On that fatal journey, on 28 January 1879, the *Leonidas*, carrying over 500 indentured to Fiji, ran out of luck. A European sailor was struck down with cholera three days after departure from Hooghly. It soon spread among the indentured due to the unhygienic and unhealthy conditions on-board. It was regrettable that for reasons of economy, the invariable practice of the shipping owners, in this case James Nourse, one of the two shipping contractors to the Fiji government, was to replenish the water tanks of the ship with the cholera-contaminated waters of the Hooghly River.

"LEONIDAS... sailed for some time up and down outside the port... but the next morning, the ship "was found to be in a pest-stricken condition."...

Figure 8: The *Leonidas* on cholera-enforced quarantine, patrolled by police ships at the Fijian port of Levuka

Source: Neogi, Tathagata, 'This Day in History: Leonidas Arrives in Fiji', *Medium*, 14 May 2018, https://tinyurl.com/3dr9w63h. Accessed on 31 July 2023.

Despite all the precautions taken by Surgeon Superintendent Dr J. Welsh, including quarantining in the ship's hospital all the cholera-infected migrants, the outbreak could not be controlled. Dr Welsh's testimony provided the details: 'The diet for all on-board was lowered, and children were dosed with castor oil, laudanum and rum, and fed on arrowroot and sago for four or five days.'[109] These measures, though well-intentioned, were most inadequate and 19 lives were lost. The mortality rate of 3.8 per cent was well above the average of 1 per cent for the entire period of indentured migration to Fiji.

For the migrants, on a long journey to an unknown destination, with the breakdown of centuries-old social values on-board, the bonds between strangers were of immense psychological value. The continuous working routine also helped diminish the sense of alienation. It also provided moral support in near-death situations.

Some accounts are of particular interest. According to Brij V. Lal:

> A typical day began at 6.00 a.m., the voyage fostered a sense of community among the migrants, irrespective of their social positions in India: they were 'coolies' all. The sense of comradeship formed during the crossing endured. Years after their girmit had expired, the indentured labourers would hobble long distances on foot to meet their jahaji bhais (ship mates) and reminisce over the shared ordeals of the voyage.[110]

On arrival, just off the port of Levuka on the island of Ovalau on 14 May 1879, the *Leonidas* was unable to dock at the harbour because of complete darkness.[111] This, in retrospect, proved to be

---

[109]Welsh, J., Letter to Dr William MacGregor, 16 May 1879, *House of Commons Papers*, XLIV, HMSO, 1880, p. 60.
[110]Lal, Brij V., *Chalo Jahaji: On a Journey through Indenture in Fiji*, Australian National University Press, 2012.
[111]Ibid. 143–51.

a blessing. The colonial authorities, initially, had no information about the dreaded and fatal cholera infection that had spread among the passengers.

When J.B. Thurston, the colonial secretary, went in an open boat to facilitate the docking of the vessel, Surgeon Superintendent Dr Welsh warned him of the many cases of cholera and small pox aboard the ship. Thurston immediately informed Acting Governor George William Des Voeux. It was decided to send Chief Medical Officer Dr MacGregor to get further information. The latter confirmed that although the cholera cases had diminished, there were also cases of small pox. The Governor was of the mind that the ship should be sent back to the high seas without off-loading the indentured. Governor Des Voeux wrote to Sir Michael Hicks of the Colonial Office in London:

> Had it been possible to ensure that the vessel, if prevented from entering the harbour, would leave the group altogether without touching anywhere or receiving any visits from natives or others, it might have become a question of whether she should not be sent away, even at the imminent risk to 500 lives, rather than that 100,000 lives should be subject to danger scarcely less grave. But having no man-of-war at hand or other means of prevention, it would be almost certain that the ship, if sent away, would put at one of the many islands lying in any course which could be taken' for leaving the Colony, and in that case, while the 500 would perhaps have been sacrificed, the 100,000 would have been in still greater jeopardy.[112]

In retrospect, this was a crucial decision. Had the *Leonidas* been sent back to the high seas, Fiji would have not had witnessed repeated cholera epidemics thereafter. It was this fatal journey that brought cholera to Fiji. The Governor decided that the ship

---

[112]Ibid.

should be steered clear of the Barrier Reef and anchored in the harbour to the leeward of the town. Unfortunately, during this operation, the *Leonidas* ran aground in low tide. Providentially, the ship was able to float again on high tide the next day and was safely anchored in Levuka harbour. To quarantine it fully, a military ship was placed between the *Leonidas* and the harbour. Three other military boats patrolled the waters so as to ensure that no cholera patient would reach the harbour. Armed guards were ordered to shoot any unlikely quarantine breakers at sight. The crew was kept under continuous supervision to ensure that the quarantine was respected.

As had become the common practice in other plantation colonies, a tiny island, named Yanuca Lailai, of about 100 acres, was selected as a quarantine bay. Native Fijians were ordered to construct some makeshift huts made of wood and grass called Fijian *bures*. As narrated by Brij V. Lal: 'The Fijians worked with "extraordinary activity" and within three days the task was completed, together with a hospital, storehouse, and quarters for the depot keeper. Later thirty more houses were added for married couples and others with families.'[113]

The journey of the ship, carrying so many infected cholera patients to this tiny island, was both challenging and dangerous. The island was over 10 miles away. Contact between the infected passengers and those on the mainland had to be avoided at all costs. Fijian Chief Roko TuiTailevu (Ratu Abel, the eldest son of Chief Cakobau) was approached for assistance to transport infected passengers to the island, and he provided 50 armed men. Twelve days after the *Leonidas* arrived in Levuka, the passengers were transported in rowing boats to the island. The process was completed in three days. The *Leonidas* finally left for the Americas.

The deboarded passengers were quarantined for three months, till 15 August 1879. During their quarantine, 15 more

---

[113] Ibid. 146.

died, from the after effects of cholera, dysentery, diarrhoea and typhoid.[114] Dr MacGregor was considered to have played a key role in containing a possible epidemic. Governor Des Voeux paid tribute in dispatches to Dr Macgregor's 'remarkable presence of mind combined with fertility and readiness of resource. [...] his untiring energy and sustained exertion.'[115]

The local Fijians, particularly Chief Cakobau, enquired about the two diseases aboard the *Leonidas*. Unfortunately, some Europeans, in order to turn public opinion against the Indian indentured, tried to insinuate that the diseases had been brought to Fiji by the Indians. This was noted in the dispatches to London about the circulation of misinformation at the behest of 'certain whites passing there [who] had not failed to seize the opportunity for mischief in representing the presence of the smallpox as the natural result of the Government action in introducing coolies.'[116] This was denied by the Governor who clarified that it was a European who had first contracted cholera aboard the *Leonidas*.

There were different narratives about cholera and quarantine in the different plantation colonies. Cholera had a chequered history on Reunion Island. It resulted in one of the harshest quarantine regimes of the time. The nineteenth century witnessed an influx of Indian indentured after the abolition of slavery by England in 1833. Public health and sanitation for the workers was virtually absent. There was initially no established quarantine centre (lazaret). This resulted in draconian measures to control contamination and spread of the dreaded disease. Decontamination centres were set up in the capital Saint-Denis under medical supervision. In the case of ships reaching Reunion

---

[114]The data was obtained from the Department of Revenue and Agriculture (Emigration), April 1882, Pros. 90-93, The National Archives of India (NAI).
[115]Lal, Brij V., *Chalo Jahaji: On a Journey through Indenture in Fiji*, Australian National University Press, 2012.
[116]Ibid.

Island with cholera patients on-board, they were not allowed to dock and the infected workers had to remain on-board.

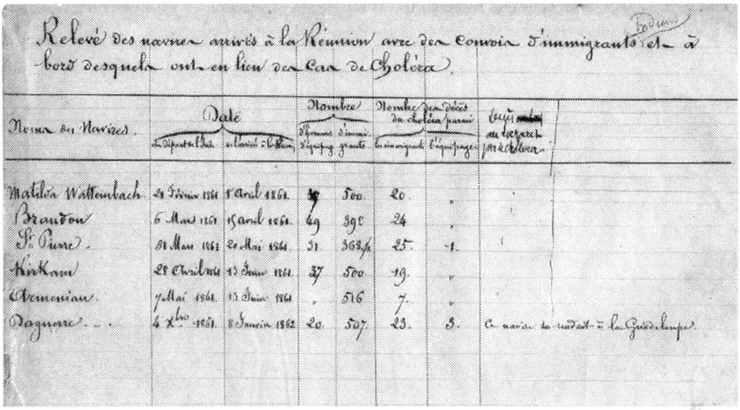

Figure 9: A survey of the ships that arrived on Reunion Island with convoys of Indian immigrants and on-board which occurred cases of cholera, 1830–1987

Source: Departmental Archives of Reunion – 12 M 63, *Société de plantation, histoire et mémoires de l'esclavage à La Réunion*, https://tinyurl.com/mhzu5d65. Accessed on 22 August 2023.

It was only in 1850 that a lazaret (an isolation hospital) named 'La Grande Chaloupe' was opened on Reunion Island. However, due to sustained pressure from the sugar plantation industry and the captains of ships who wished to dock, cases of small pox were often suppressed. Sometimes infected indentured were allowed to bypass the lazaret and enter Reunion Island directly. This affected public health and led to repeated cholera epidemics in Reunion Island.

The first recorded outbreak was in January 1820. Cholera came to Reunion Island from Mauritius through infected passengers aboard the steamer *Pivert*. A year earlier, there had been a cholera epidemic in Mauritius in November 1819, carried there by the English frigate *La Topaze*, which had sailed from Calcutta, India. Due to strict quarantine measures, Reunion Island was able to escape two subsequent cholera epidemics in Mauritius in 1854 and 1856.

The next cholera epidemic was recorded on 6 March 1859. This time, the infected passengers, all indentured, had come from East Africa by the steamer *Mascareignes*. It was particularly unfortunate that the captain Mr d'Agnel confirmed that there were no cholera cases on-board. In fact, the navy surgeon Alfred Vaillant had recorded that cholera cases had been present aboard the ship since it had left the East African coast. This information was not given to the doctor aboard the ship.

As a result of this false testimony, cholera spread rapidly in Reunion Island. The mortality rate was highest among the poorest and most marginalized, notably freed slaves. A confession was obtained from the ship's crew about the denial of cholera cases on-board through an enquiry conducted by Dr Petit, the chief navy physician and director of the health department of Reunion Island. A trial for endangerment to public health was held on 24 January 1860. The captain and the crew were exonerated on the testimony of physicians in Reunion Island that cholera was not an infectious disease.[117]

In Suriname, like on Reunion Island, cholera was introduced by vessels carrying the indentured from India. The earliest recorded case is of an English ship *Sheila*, which left Calcutta on 9 October 1882 with 451 Indian indentured labourers. During the journey, as recorded by Dr Schelkly, the medical officer in charge of the quarantine quarters, a virulent form of cholera broke out on 16 October 1882 and continued for 12 days. As a result, by the time the ill-fated *Sheila* reached its destination on 12 January 1883, there had been 37 deaths due to cholera. The ship was quarantined by the colonial administration of Suriname for three weeks.

---

[117]Gaüzère, B.A. and P. Aubry, 'Cholera Epidemics on Reunion Island during the 19th Century', *Medecine et santé tropicales*, Vol. 22, No. 2, 2012, pp. 131–36, https://tinyurl.com/2smhj6ve. Accessed on 16 August 2023.

An enquiry conducted by Dr Schelky pinpointed the reasons for the outbreak to be contaminated drinking water stored in unsanitary conditions, insufficient ventilation, inadequate toilet and sanitation facilities and the possible presence of the disease in one of the passengers prior to departure for Suriname, which indicated that the colonial authorities in Calcutta had not conducted a rigorous examination of the passengers before embarkation.

Written testimony and reports by the ship's surgeon and Dr Schelky provide detailed information about the facilities on-board, the diet of the indentured and the provision of drinking water. This can be seen from the dietary chart in Table 6.

There were similar reports of cholera epidemics on ships carrying Indian indentured workers to different parts of the West Indies. One such account was given regarding the journeys of the ship *Clarence* from 1858 to 1873. According to the account, the living area for the indentured was similar to the space available on slave ships.

Some ship surgeons tried to claim that there was more living space available for the indentured. It was claimed that on slave ships, the space allocated to each slave was approximately 3–5 superficial feet[118]. The improvement on ships carrying indentured labourers was only superficial. The reality was that on most ships, each indentured was allocated about 15 superficial feet to survive. As a result, the conditions were ideal for the rapid spread of cholera.[119]

It is significant to note that there was a separate section titled 'Cholera on Emigrant Ships' in the *Proceedings of the Sanitary Commissioner of the British Government of India*. Extracts from available records, including discussions between the captain and the physician on-board underline the presence of cholera on most

---

[118]1 superficial foot = 1 ft x 1 ft x 1 in
[119]"Physical Conditions on the Ship", *Sailing the British Empire: The Voyages of The Clarence, 1858-73*, https://tinyurl.com/82uj4ks6. Accessed on 16 August 2023.

ships carrying the indentured from India. This adversely impacted both the flow of indentured from India and their acceptance in the different plantation colonies.

There can be no doubt, as testified by Tinker, that the indentured were abused and exploited on these ships carrying them to their distant destinations.[120] One can conclude that conditions on-board were conducive to the spread of dreaded diseases, especially cholera. The treatment of the afflicted was usually without compassion or mercy. The disease itself attracted social solecism and racial commentaries. It symbolized the imperial attitude underlying colonial conquest. Jules Harmand, the ideologue of French colonialism, said in 1910: 'The basic legitimization of conquest over native peoples is the conviction of our superiority, not merely our mechanical, economic and military superiority, but our moral superiority. Our dignity rests on that quality...'[121]

The treatment of cholera victims, indentured from India and transported under inhuman conditions in former slave ships to different plantation colonies, must be understood in the context of Harmand's definition of racial superiority. This was the defining ideology of the colonizers. The memories of cholera and quarantine will haunt the survivors and their descendants for all time to come. Yet it risks being forgotten, since written records are scarce and the oral testimonies passed on by descendants through generations are contemptuously rejected by Western historians. Alas, it remains yet another forgotten memory.

---

[120]Northrup, David, *Indentured Labor in the Age of Imperialism, 1834-1922*, Studies in Comparative World History, Cambridge University Press, New York, 1995.
[121]Curtin, Philip D. (ed.), *Imperialism*, Walker, New York, 1971.

7

CROSSINGS

Mauritius: Aapravasi Ghat, Solitude, Slavery and Unrest

> *Four great gates has the city of Damascus...*
> *Postern of Fate, the Desert Gate,*
> *Disaster's Cavern, Fort of Fear...*
> *Pass not beneath, O Caravan, or pass not singing.*
> *Have you heard*
> *That silence where the birds are dead yet*
> *something pipeth like a bird?*
>
> — James Elroy Flecker, 'The Gates of Damascus'

'Mirich Dwip' (Mauritius) was the origin of the British Great Experiment. It was the first organized attempt to substitute slavery with indenture after the abolition of the former.

Recorded history chronicles the arrival of five Dutch ships on Mauritian shores on 17 September 1598, under the command of Vice Admiral Wybrandt van Warwijck. The Dutch named the unpopulated island 'Mauritius' after Dutch Stadholder Maurits van Nassau. In 1715, Mauritius was claimed by France, and in 1721, they named the island Ile de France. In 1767, the French government bought Ile de France from the French East India Company. By the end of the eighteenth century, slaves constituted over 80 per cent of the island's population.

In 1787, Port Louis was made into a free port, open to ships of all nations. During the American War of Independence, Ile de France was used as a major naval and military base for French campaigns against the British in India. Due to its strategic position, Britain had its eyes set on Ile de France. On 3 December 1810, the French finally capitulated. Under British rule, the island was once more named Mauritius.

Aapravasi Ghat,[122] situated in Port Louis, Mauritius, was a pivotal point in the journey of the indentured from India across the Kalapani. From 1834 onwards, ships would break journey here. The *Atlas* was the first ship to reach Mauritius on 2 November 1834 and to dock at the ghat. The sick, especially the cholera patients, from the ships would be quarantined separately. The rest would pass through the gates, either to work as indentured labour in the sugar plantations on Mirich Dwip or elsewhere, wherever their destiny led them.

Many of the indentured, after a short stay at Aapravasi Ghat were transported in other ships to the Caribbean and to Reunion Island. Many names are now legendary. The *Lalla Rookh* made her first historic journey on 5 June 1873 to Suriname from Calcutta via Mauritius. The numbers of the indentured swelled rapidly. By 1870, Mauritius had 352,401 Indians. By 1907, Guyana's total population of Indians had swelled to 127,000, Trinidad to 103,000 and Natal to 115,000.

For the indentured, Aapravasi Ghat was the gate of no return because their liberty and freedom were lost forever. For the Girmitya route, Aapravasi Ghat replicated the Door of No Return on Gorée Island in Senegal, which marked the rapid descent into

---

[122]Built in 1849 to receive indentured labourers from India and owned by the Mauritian Ministry of Arts and Culture, its buildings stand as a historic testament to indenture in the nineteenth century. Among its key structural components are the remains of sheds for housing, kitchens, lavatories, a building used as a hospital block and highly symbolic flight of 14 steps upon which all immigrants had to lay foot before entering the immigration depot.

hell for the newly enslaved. Many of the newly indentured would work alongside the now liberated slaves in the plantations, hoping to regain their freedom. Little did they know that liberation was a long way off. In fact, the arrival of the first indentured in Mauritius on 2 November 1834 is now celebrated as a national holiday, with 2 November 2022 marking the 188th anniversary of the first arrival of the indentured from India.

Inscribed on UNESCO's World Heritage List in 2006, the wording selected by UNESCO is poignant. Aapravasi Ghat—as the first site chosen by the British government in 1834 for the Great Experiment of using indentured, rather than slave labour—is strongly associated with memories of almost half-a-million indentured labours moving from India to Mauritius to work on sugarcane plantations or to be transhipped to other parts of the world.

Figure 10: Commemorative plaque at Aapravasi Ghat marking the arrival of Girmitiyas on 2 November 1834

Source: '180th Anniversary of Arrival of Indian Indentured Labour in Mauritius', *Ministry of External Affairs, Government of India*, https://tinyurl.com/mvensu3e. Accessed on 21 August 2023.

The history of Mauritius is unique. An uninhabited island, settled by different waves of colonizers, its sugar plantations provided huge revenues to the colonizers through the unpaid labour of slaves and indentured. As a memorial to its deeply troubled past, Mauritius is home to two UNESCO World Heritage Sites—Aapravasi Ghat, to recall the memories of indentured labour, and Le Morne Cultural Landscape, which symbolizes resistance to slavery.

Le Morne, built at the foot of the Le Morne Brabant Mountain, with its steep drop to the Indian Ocean, has a haunting atmosphere, as if it the tormented souls of the dead still linger on. On my several visits there to pay homage to the departed, I felt the towering cliffs standing testament to the agonizing drop into oblivion, into the waiting ocean, of the thousands of slaves who preferred suicide to a life without liberty.

Figure 11: Le Morne, a UNESCO world heritage site in Mauritius
Source: '180th Anniversary of Arrival of Indian Indentured Labour in Mauritius', *Ministry of External Affairs, Government of India*, https://tinyurl.com/mvensu3e. Accessed on 21 August 2023.

Member States of UNESCO, especially those whose citizens had been enslaved in that dark period, have built a memorial park with statues symbolizing the resilience of the human spirit under different forms of slavery. Known as the International Slave Route Monument at Le Morne, it was completed on 1 February 2009. Situated in a garden, the site was deliberately selected because of its linear connection between the sea and the Valley of Bones, a macabre reminder of the mass suicides of the enslaved, some reaching the beach and others the ocean, all in a free fall. Standing there, one can see the clear eastward view to the edge of the mountain, the caves on the cliff faces, which gave shelter to the runaway slaves for a while, and the sheer drop to the ocean.

The two statues there, donated by UNESCO Member States, depict graphically, as seen in Figure 12, a slave in free fall to the ocean and, in Figure 13, an enslaved man without hope but clinging to his culture and social origin. In Figure 12, Mauritian sculptor Jean Michel Hotentote, through his creation, shows a slave

Figure 12: In free fall to eternal liberty
Source: Le Morne Cultural Landscape, Le Morne Heritage Trust Fund

Figure 13: Despair, enslavement and salvation
Source: Le Morne Cultural Landscape, Le Morne Heritage Trust Fund

emerging from a cave in the rocks before throwing himself into the Ocean, towards the direction of his country, Madagascar. The second, as seen in Figure 13, by a famous artist from Madagascar, J. Rabemananjara, is a sombre statue of a slave in traditional clothing from Madagascar called *lamba* representing resistance to slavery. The sitting position and his enchained hands and feet represent resistance to enslavement while preserving his culture.

The misfortunes of those who endured slavery and coolitude have been expressed poignantly by the famous poet and thinker, Khal Torabully:

> So four feet
> Would be arrival of Columbus
> Then three feet when coolies came
> Leaning on their motris [luggage]
> Or their contract for five years of bliss.[123]

The soil of Mauritius became the 'epitome of the struggle between free labour and slavery'.[124] One of the first planters to employ indenture confided in 1835 to an associate that 'their cost is not half that of a slave'.[125] The inference to be drawn is that indenture was a cheaper form of slavery. Ultimately, about half a million indentured came to Mauritius, making it the largest recipient of indentured labour in the British Empire.[126] The dark steps to the

---

[123]Torabully, Khal, *Voices from Aapravasi Ghat: Indentured Imageries*, Aapravasi Ghat Trust Fund and Khal Torabully, 2013.
[124]Colonial Office Series (CO) 167/210, Nicolay to Grey, 21 May 1839, Minute of Labouchère; CO 167/252, Gomm to Stanley, 1 March 1844, Enc. Merchants Committee to Col. Secy, 20 February 1844; Parliamentary Papers (1842 xxx [26]), Stanley to Smith, 22 January1842; Cumpston, I.M., *Indians Overseas In British Territories, 1834-1854*, London, 1969, pp. 35–6, 85.
[125]Colonial Office Series (CO) 167/182, Bergstein to Gaillardon, 23 January 1834; pp. 1845 xxxi (641), *Report of Labour Committee*; Quenette, Rivaltz L., *La fin d'une légende: En marge de l'abolition de l'esclavage*, Port Louis, 1970, p. 57.
[126]Tinker, Hugh, *A New System of Slavery: The Export of Indian Labour Overseas 1830-1920*, Hansib, 1993.

brooding entrance of Aapravasi Ghat marked the point where half-a-million indentured Indians stepped on the soil of Mauritius, never to return.

In 1810, when Mauritius became a British settlement, it had a very small population and limited arable land. It was densely forested. Its population numbered approximately 7,000 White people, 8,000 free people of colour and 63,000 slaves.[127] The new settlers from Britain were of the view that sugarcane cultivation was the solution to the island's economic difficulties. They granted Mauritians sugar tariff equality with Caribbean produce. As a result, until the slump in the 1860s, Mauritius overtook all other British colonies on sugar production. This feat was achieved due to the labour of the Indian indentured.

Figure 14: The gate of no return—Aapravasi Ghat

Source: 'File: First footprints at Aapravasi ghat museum, Port Louis, Mauritius.jpg', *Wikimedia Commons*, https://tinyurl.com/y95364uj. Accessed on 21 August 2023.

The plantation owners believed that the so-called meek Indian, employed at half the cost and with longer working hours, was the

---

[127]Howell, B.M., *Mauritius, 1832-1849: A Study of a Sugar Colony*, 1951, University of London, PhD dissertation, p. 8; Kuczynski, R.R., *Demographic Survey of the British Colonial Empire*, Vol. II, Oxford University Press, London, 1949, p. 738.

best option for profit maximization. The indentured had no option to switch employers while under contract. Yet, this preference was politically sensitive. An open preference for the exploitation of indentured Indians over the employment of newly freed slaves would have caused social unrest. The uncomfortable truth was that the plantation owners had complete control over all labour. As noted by contemporary historian W. Rodney: 'This alone justified the continuation of indenture-ship, irrespective of the cost to the individual proprietor and to the general tax-payer.'[128]

The colonial government also cleverly played off the indentured against the newly emancipated slaves, now called 'apprentices'. For example, Charles Grant (first Baron Glenelg) believed, 'The importation of free labourers was likely at this critical period to have a most useful influence on the conduct of the apprenticed population.'[129]

It was claimed that [a] peaceful transition from slavery to post-slavery conditions [was] more successfully achieved in Mauritius than in perhaps any other part of the British Empire in the nineteenth century.'[130] Such accounts deliberately ignore the high costs of this policy to the social harmony of the region. The newly freed slaves were forced off the plantations to make way for the cheap Indian indentured workers. This poisoned race relations in Mauritius till its independence.

Journey to Mirich Dwip: Braving the Unknown

How were the Indians inveigled into braving this journey to Mirich Dwip? The recruitment initially targeted innocent tribal people of India. An authenticated report stated:

---

[128] Rodney, W., 'Guyana: The Making of the Labour Force', *Race & Class*, Vol. 22, 1981, p. 337.
[129] Glenelg, Letter to Nicolay (39), 31 January 1838, pp. 1837–8 lii (180).
[130] Beachey, R.W., *The Slave Trade of Eastern Africa*, Cambridge University Press, London, 1976, p. 31.

On 9th September 1834, 36 lost-looking Dhangars [tribal people from the Chota Nagpur region] met some recruiters in Calcutta and were asked if they would be willing to go to Mauritius as indentured labourers. The absence would be of short duration and remuneration attractive. Mirich Dwip [Mauritius] was said to be just off the coast of Bengal, and they would be back home before their absence was noticed in the village. The Dhangars agreed. [...] Thereupon, they were taken to the chief magistrate at the Calcutta Police Court, who read out and 'explained' the terms and conditions of the contract to be signed. The men affixed their thumbprints on the document, affirming their understanding of what was on offer and that they were emigrating voluntarily. The Vice-President in Council of the Government of Bengal approved the transaction and authorised the departure of the indentured labourers.[131]

Thus was the deed of deception sealed. The conditions on the ships were appalling. Consequently, tribals had a high mortality rate. Recruitment was diversified to enmesh more of the marginalized and desperate. Between 1 August 1834 and 31 December 1835, 14 ships transported emigrants from Calcutta to Mauritius. By 1839, over 25,000 Indians had been introduced into the colony.

The geographical origin of the indentured is an interesting case study of the socio-economic conditions of India under colonial rule. According to one case study, of 2,187 males who reached Mauritius from 1842 to 1844 were 107 different and identifiable castes or communities.[132] They included tribal groups like the Mundas and Bhuiyas, Scheduled Castes like Chamars and

---

[131]Lal, Brij V., *Levelling Wind, Remembering Fiji*, ANU Press, 2019, pp. 21–44.
[132]Brennan, Lance, John McDonald and Ralph Shlomowitz, 'The Geographic and Social Origins of Indian Indentured Labourers in Mauritius, Natal, Fiji, Guyana and Jamaica', *South Asia: Journal of South Asian Studies*, Vol. 21, No. 1, 1998, pp. 39–71, 2007, https://tinyurl.com/287c7p5v. Accessed on 16 August 2023.

Mochis, pastoral and cultivating castes like Gowalas, cultivators like Kurmis, and Muslims[133]. There were 24 Brahmins (1.1 per cent) and 44 Rajputs (2 per cent) in the sample. A much smaller number of females (from 57 castes) migrated on the same vessels.

Table 7 demonstrates the pattern of gender recruitment in districts of North India under colonial rule.

Table 7
Caste identifications of a sample of North Indian female emigrants to Mauritius 1859–1871

Group	1859–1864		1865–1871	
	No.	Percentage of total population	No.	Percentage of total population
Muslim	275	19.2	250	20.9
Chamar	162	11.3	167	13.9
Dusadh	114	7.9	101	8.4
Gowala	82	5.7	25	2.0
Rajput	54	3.8	41	3.4
Koeri	42	2.9	46	3.8
Kurmi	44	3.1	40	3.3
Kahar	46	3.2	32	2.7
Brahmin	15	1.0	44	3.7
Ahir	0	0.0	44	3.7
Other	601	41.9	409	34.11
Total	1,435	100	1,199	100

Source: Brennan, Lance, John McDonald, and Ralph Shlomowitz, 'The Geographic and Social Origins of Indian Indentured Labourers', *South Asia: Journal of South Asian Studies*, Vol. 21, 2007, pp. 39–71, https://tinyurl.com/287c7p5v. Accessed on 16 August 2023.

---

[133]The Muslim group did not include those who identified themselves as Mughals (1), Pathans (3), Sheikhs (1) and Julahas (6).

The methods of recruitment were varied. Before government regulations were implemented to stop abusive methods of recruitment in 1842, local recruiters—called duffadars, arkatias and maistries, who were paid on a per head basis—lured the potential indentured to the agency houses in the main port towns, notably Calcutta.[134] Their coercive methods led to a public outcry and a temporary suspension of indentured emigration in 1839.

This was succeeded by state regulated agencies in the 1840s. However, the abuses continued, since the objective was to get indentured at the lowest terms of employment while preventing others from offering better terms. The abuses have been recorded in detail.[135]

The strategy of using returned indentured on the plantations to recruit from the people in their districts was introduced as an ingenious method to circumvent criticism from abolitionists outside the country and from within India. Defined as 'returnee recruiting', it was a favoured method 'because it was cost-effective, and avoided many of the problems associated with directly coercive methods of labour recruiting'.[136]

In reality, the recruiters, called sirdars, were another level of sub-exploiters inserted by the colonialists to lure and deceive the innocent. They ensured a steady flow of indentured and were rewarded with sirdarships and responsibility for the management of the indentured on the plantations.

---

[134]In 1842, the India Act XV was passed, which regulated emigration of Indians who fell under the authority of East India Company to Mauritius.
[135]Tinker, Hugh, *A New System of Slavery: The Export of Indian Labour Overseas 1830-1920*, Hansib, 1993, pp. 63-80; Carter, Marina, *Indian Labour Migration and the Indenture Experience in Mauritius,* 1987, Oxford University, D.Phil. thesis, pp. 50-118.
[136]Carter, Marina, 'Strategies of Labour Mobilisation in Colonial India: The Recruitment of Indentured Workers for Mauritius', *The Journal of Peasant Studies*, Vol. 19, Nos. 3-4, 1992, pp. 229-45.

This new system of recruitment received the official stamp of approval after an envoy of the colonial government in Mauritius visited India in 1843. He strongly recommended that returnee recruits be used, since they had already created, '*un puissant stimulant pour une emigration croissante* (a powerful encouragement for greater emigration in larger numbers)'.[137]

There are fascinating first-hand accounts of such returnee recruiters. One Dhibby Deen, from Gorakhpur in eastern Uttar Pradesh, carried a letter authorizing the payment of his return passage and that of 'any able bodied men who may wish to accompany him, not exceeding 50 in number'.[138]

Of more significance than the inducements offered to join rival agencies, however, was the potential for independent recruiting. One returnee, Rama, wrote to his brother Lutchmun in Mauritius: 'If you and Hittoo bring money we shall be able to recruit 1,000 people in one month.'[139]

Of even greater interest was the determination of the returnees to collect their spouses and family members and return to Mauritius. This would determine the future history of Mauritius and set it apart from other British settlements. The approach of the colonial government in Mauritius was also different. 'Family migration to Mauritius was not designed to secure cheap female labour as such; it acted rather to ensure the reproduction of the work force in a colony which had come to rely totally

---

[137] Anderson, Letter to Dick, 11 November 1843, Parliamentary Papers 1844 xxxv (356).

[138] Chapman, Barclay, Letter to Colville, Gilmore & Co, Calcutta, 23 November 1840.

Returnee recruiters were also active in Madras as seen in the case of Ramaswamy from Madurai. Emigration Agent Madras, Letter to Secy. Govt. Madras, 24 February 1843, Mauritius Archives PL Series (PL) 57.

[139] Protector of Emigrants, Letter to the Colonial Secretary, 18 March 1852, Mauritius Archives PB Series 5.

The letter was translated from the Nagari script.

on immigrants for the production of its principal crop.'[140] This positively impacted the settlement of the returnees in Mauritius. Several measures were taken by the British colonial government in Mauritius to encourage such family reunions. Colonial records reveal that by 1852, returnees who were reunited couples were given a bonus of £1 for each spouse. By 1852, local recruiters in Calcutta were being paid only for bringing families.[141] Returnees could claim their female relatives upon arrival after paying for the cost of the voyage. They were also permitted to send their families to and from Mauritius as passengers.

The supply of the indentured ultimately exceeded the demand for such labour. Along with falling sugar prices due to over production, the system came under pressure and underwent further modification. Sub-exploiters moved up the hierarchy and became employers of the indentured. The returnees and sirdars became landowners, since large plantations were increasingly being cut into small plots and sold. The wheel had turned full circle! Returnees or the new landowners established settlements that came to be termed as Indian settlements or villages. Indian cultural traditions and practices re-emerged and a new Indian elite emerged from the indentured.

Marina Carter, historian and commentator, noted: 'The rapidity and scale of the demographic revolution wrought by Indian immigration in Mauritius was without parallel amongst British colonies in the post-emancipation period.'[142] The importance of the role of family migration in enabling the emergence of a new

---

[140] Carter, Marina, 'The Family under Indenture: A Mauritian Case Study', *Journal of Mauritian Studies*, Vol. 4, No. 1, 1991.
[141] Emigration Agent Calcutta, Letter to Col. Secy., 17 February 1852; EA Madras, Letter to Col. Secy., 10 April 1852; EA Calcutta, Letter to Col. Secy., 28 March 1853, RA 1176; EA Calcutta, Letter to Col. Secy, 20 October 1855, RA 1314.
142 Carter, Marina, 'Strategies of Labour Mobilisation in Colonial India: The Recruitment of Indentured Workers for Mauritius', *The Journal of Peasant Studies*, Vol. 19, Nos. 3–4, 1992, pp. 229–45.

settler class in Mauritius cannot be overemphasized. The role of a pre-existing Indian mercantile and landowning class who loaned money and rented land to former indentured workers facilitated the emergence of this new elite.

However, several impediments remained. The new settlers did not enjoy equality vis-à-vis their former White employers. On the contrary, Indians were denied equal access to resources on equal terms with White colonists. They also did not earn equal wages, equal systems of justice or social equality. These came later, through a long struggle, aided partly by Gandhi.

The role of Gandhi in sensitizing the indentured Indians about their rights and liberty has been fully documented only recently. Gandhi was in regular contact with Barrister Manilal Doctor, who went to Mauritius, as advised by Gandhi during a meeting in London in 1906.

In one of his letters in 1911 from Tolstoy Farm in Transvaal, close to Johannesburg, South Africa, Gandhi informed his mentor, Gopal Krishna Gokhale: 'Mr Manilal Doctor has, as you are aware, done very good public work in Mauritius and gained the affection of the poor Indians there to whom he became a friend in need.'[143]

Manilal Doctor reached Mauritius from London in 1907 and began the long and arduous process of political and social emancipation, which culminated in the freedom of the nation on 12 March 1968. Until his return to India in 1911, he took up the cases of human rights violations of the Indian indentured, leading to a national movement for social and political change.

Gandhi's own stopover in Mauritius, while travelling from Durban to Bombay in 1901, triggered the process of change that led to a political struggle for equal rights among Mauritians of Indian origin. Gandhi's stay in Mauritius coincided with the outbreak of bubonic plague on the island. As a result, he stayed

---

[143]'How M.K. Gandhi's Mauritian Visit of 1901 Fell into Oblivion', *Le Mauricien*, 1 October 2021, https://tinyurl.com/3d3yvcww. Accessed on 16 August 2023.

for only two weeks. In a significant speech on 13 November 1901, Gandhi highlighted the contribution of Mauritians of Indian origin to the development of Mauritius. He called upon them to actively participate in future in the politics of Mauritius.[144]

Gandhi was instrumental in campaigning against indenture resulting in British India's Imperial Legislative Council officially banning indenture in 1917. At that time, he enlisted the support of Manilal Doctor who, at Gandhi's instance, attended an important meeting of the Indian National Congress (INC) to campaign against indenture.

On his final return to India on 9 January, 1915, at the request of Gopal Krishna Gokhale, Gandhi often spoke of the plight of indentured Indian labourers in Mauritius. He played an important role, as the President of the INC in 1924, in sensitizing the public about the plight, living conditions and great suffering of the indentured. He often spoke movingly of their inhuman exploitation.

Gandhi disapproved of returnee recruitment, which had just commenced, with indentured workers returning from Mauritius to inveigle more of their countrymen and countrywomen into this trade. Between the 1910s and 1940s, Gandhi encouraged prominent Mauritians, including R.K. Boodhun, P. Lutchmaya, J.N. Roy and B. Bissoondoyal, to work for the rights and liberty of the indentured.

Hazareesingh, a prominent Mauritian historian and writer, wrote to Gandhi about the purpose of his visit to Mauritius. To this, Gandhi replied:

My dear Hazareesingh,

I was on my way to Nandi Durg when your letter reached me. I stayed in Mauritius for about ten days while my boat was lying at anchor. There was no other purpose in my visit

---

[144]Prasad, D., *Public Life of Manilal Doctor*, Rite-Print-Pak, Mumbai, 1992, p. 15.

to your Island, and this is why only a few people may have been aware of my presence there. I stayed in the house of some mussulman friends. I also met the Governor at a social function. Please convey my greetings to all my fellow countrymen.

Yours Sincerely
M.K. Gandhi,
Wardha.
26.5.36[145]

The letter was diplomatically worded! It did not reveal that Gandhi, during his visit, had admonished Indians and recommended that they start a political movement for their rights. Freedom did not come without major social upheavals. Industrial strife and protests culminated in major events in August 1937, September 1938 and the infamous incident on 27 September 1943, which can never be forgotten.

On that day, four Indo-Mauritians, including Anjalay Coopen, were shot in cold blood at Belle Vue Harel Sugar Estate in the Riviere du Rempart district. Anjalay had been pregnant and in her martyrdom lay the birth of the Mauritian Labour Party and the inexorable movement towards freedom. Today, her life-sized statue stands next to the Mauritian Supreme Court in Port Louis. It inspires every Mauritian of the need to resist tyranny and to struggle for freedom. Anjalay was a true follower of Gandhi.

As the iconic chairman of the Aapravasi Ghat Trust Fund (AGTF), the late Mahen Utchanah, wrote on 2 November 2014:

> Their struggle led to the famous general elections of August, 1948, when gradually political power passed from the hands of the Franco-Mauritian oligarchy and British officials into the hands of the descendants of indentured workers and

[145]Ibid.

their leaders, as they fulfilled their tryst with destiny and history.[146]

During my many visits to Mauritius from May 2014 to October 2017, I was deeply moved by the articulation of the memories of so many of my ancestors, who left their Mother land behind and came to a new home in Mauritius, climbing the steps of the Aapravasi Ghat for the first time. These new Mauritians remained attached to their original culture and civilization, which, in the melting pot of Mauritius, has now become 'Mauritian culture'. Mauritius is their country and home while India is their ancient Mother land of legend.

There are many legends of the oral and intangible heritage they brought with them, including the Bhojpuri songs that are still sung in Mauritius, Guyana, Suriname and all over the Caribbean. These are songs that recall that while the days are full of work, the nights bring back memories of their Mother land, India.

The history of Mauritius underlines the importance of looking for indentured thought and experience as seen, felt and witnessed by the immigrants and their descendants, rather than through the tinted cultural lenses of others. We need to reflect on the importance of giving indentured labour and their descendants a voice without mediators. The indentured and their descendants need to have the opportunity to present their versions of their experiences.

A victim of slavery and indenture, Mauritius symbolizes the need to commence a much-delayed dialogue on the global post-colonial heritage of both and the manner in which they have contributed to the universal dialogue on the humanism of diversity. Such a dialogue can promote a better understanding of the common cultural and civilizational links between peoples and

---

[146]Peerthum, Satteeanund, and Satyendra Peerthum, *The Struggle of the Descendants of Indentured Labourers in Early Modern Mauritius (1921-1945)*, Cathay Printing Ltd., Pointe aux Sables, 2014, p. vii.

lead to the strengthening of cultural diversity and the enrichment of humanity.

Reunion Island: Destruction of Identity, the Déracinement of a People

> *Words, after speech, reach into silence.*
>
> —T.S. Eliot

A mountainous and uninhabited island, only 200 kilometres from Mauritius, Reunion Island was occupied and settled by the French in 1664. From the sixteenth century, encouraged by the French East India Company, slaves and *engages* (French for Girmitya) were part of the unpaid workforce of the French aristocracy and colonial administrators of Reunion Island. Human exploitation reached new and complex levels on this island.

Named Bourbon Island after the Bourbon dynasty, Reunion Island's experiments with slavery and indenture are a microcosm of the history of France. France abolished slavery after the French Revolution of 1789 and subsequently, once again, during the Reign of Terror on 4 February 1794. It was restored in 1802, shortly before the coronation of Napoleon as emperor.

As a signatory to the Additional Act on slavery adopted at the Congress of Vienna in 1815, France and Reunion Island remained in defiance of international law by continuing to import slaves till 1848. As the only French colony in the Indian Ocean, this was more marked for Reunion Island, since England had proclaimed its abolition in her colonies in 1833. Slavery was finally abolished on 27 April 1848 due to the vigorous abolition campaign during the Second Republic by the famous writer, politician and abolitionist Victor Schoelcher.[147] Commissioner of the Republic

---

[147]Schmidt, Nelly, *Victor Schoelcher*, Fayard, Paris, 1994.

Sarda Garriga declared the abolition of slavery on 20 December 1848, despite strong local opposition to this proclamation. Reunion Island was unique in that, unlike Mauritius, slavery and indenture existed in parallel universes, but with very different social and economic consequences. Before 1848, Indian engages worked alongside African slaves. Their living conditions were akin to slavery.

Indenture had a chequered history in Reunion Island. The forcible transfer of Mauritius from France to England in 1810 deprived the French of their supply of sugar. It put pressure on Reunion Island to develop its own sugar plantations. These nascent plantations were developed by slaves till 1848. After its abolition, efforts were made to keep the freed slaves in a 'forced employee' system that was not enforceable by 1851 because of strong opposition. It was succeeded by 'compulsory labour' under rigorous control and supervision. Slowly, slavery gave way to indenture.

Former slave masters were encouraged by the arrival of the well-connected and aristocratic Eugène Panon Desbassayns de Richemont, who came to Pondicherry (now Puducherry) on 12 March 1826, as commissioner of the navy and administrator of the French trading posts in India. He served as the Governor of Pondicherry from 18 June 1826 to 2 August 1828.

Richemont discovered the loopholes in French law, which permitted 'Indian servants' to be brought to Reunion Island, provided they had an employer known as 'Le Mastere'.[148] Richemont manipulated the stipulation in the existing laws, which provided that domestic help could be brought from India, provided they had a mastere of a householder to look after them. On arrival, they

---

[148] Under local decree of 18 January 1826, the indentured had to be employed by an official resident of the island who would undertake to pay any costs if their workers were sent back home. In reality, these were indentured labour contracts in disguise.

were treated akin to slaves. On 27 April 1827, with the adoption of the Second Abolitionist law, the provision was extended to indentured labour. So severe were the conditions and the adverse media coverage and public outcry that on 6 March 1839, the French colonial authority was pressured to issue the Pondicherry Decree prohibiting the export of *engages*. Nevertheless, the illicit trafficking to Reunion Island continued for some time.[149]

The decree of 29 July 1848 reversed the 1839 decree and permitted the export of *engages* from India, especially from ports along the Coromandel Coast. There was, initially, a slow and small flow of indentured mainly from Tamil Nadu and recruited from former French colonies likes Pondicherry, Karikal and Yanaon. The earliest record dates back to April 1828 when the ship *La Turquoise* brought 15 Telinga workers from Yanaon, a French settlement in India.[150] In 1830, more than 3,000 Indian indentured workers arrived on 21 boats.[151] They were duly registered.

Between 1842 and 1916, around 49,890 emigrants left for French colonies. On 20 December 1848, the *Mahé de Labourdonnais* brought the first 500 men to Reunion Island from Pondicherry and Karikal. The numbers were small. Before 1870, only 4,700 reached Reunion Island.

There were conditions attached to their recruitment. By the decree of the Pondicherry commissioner on 23 June 1849, the *engages* had to be at least 21 years of age. In theory, an emigration commission would need to testify that the *engages* were leaving

---

[149] At least seven shipments arrived from India between 1839 and 1848. Regarding the question of the links between slavery in India and indentured labour in the Mascarene Islands, see: 'Le coolie-trade vers La réunion au XIXe: une traite déguisée?', V. Chaillou-Atrous and P.E. Penot (eds), *Mélanges offerts à Jacques Weber*, Les Indes Savantes, 2019, pp. 135–47.

[150] Marimoutou, Michèle, *Les engagés du sucre, Editions du Tramail*, La Réunion, 1989, p. 261.

[151] Currently identified number of Indian immigrant ships bound for Reunion Island from 1828 to 1830 (20 from Yanaon and one from Calcutta).

voluntarily and agreed with the terms of recruitment of their own free will and fully aware of the terms of their contract.

The reality was farcical. The Pondicherry Emigration Society was established in 1850 by the business groups of Pondicherry and Karikal. It had absolute monopoly of recruiting the *engages* and delivering them to the ship owners for transportation to Reunion Island. Similarly, an immigration society was created on Reunion Island in 1853 to coordinate the flow of the *engages*.

According to informed sources, for 4,500 workers delivered to Reunion Island in 1850, the profit was ₹90,000 (roughly F225,000).[152] The profits of the traffickers increased by prohibiting the recruitment of children because child labor was lucrative. The brutality was exposed in 1854 by the De Souza affair in 1853 and the *L'Auguste* in Karikal. The former hired goons to kidnap minors who were addicted to hashish (a common Indian intoxicant) and took them on-board. Many atrocities were committed on-board the *L'Auguste*.[153]

Cooperation between the major colonial powers resulted in the Franco-British Agreement of 25 July 1860, resulting in the recruitment of 6,000 *engages*. This agreement was extended on 1 August 1861 to other French sugar producing colonies. Once again, conditions were attached that were never respected. A British Consul based in Calcutta, which was the port of embarkation, was supposed to ensure a fair deal for the *engages*.

The reality was totally different. Even before the emancipation of slaves, engages protested against their harsh treatment. On

---

[152]Weber, Jacques, 'Entre traite et coolie trade: L'affaire de l'Auguste', *La dernière traite: Fragments d'Histoire en hommage à Serge DAGET*, Société Française d'Histoire d'Outre-Mer, Université de Nantes, Université de Lille III, 1994, pp. 150–162.

[153]Weber, Jacques, 'Les conventions franco-britanniques de 1860 et 1861 sur l'émigration indienne', *Cahiers des Anneaux de la Mémoire, n°2, Esclavage et engagisme dans l'océan Indien, La traite atlantique*, Nantes, Édition Les Anneaux de la Mémoire, 2000, pp. 128–68.

17 July 1848, a group of 33 Indians signed a letter which was published in *Le Cri Public*, an underground liberal publication, noting:

> A whole class of unfortunates will not be reduced to the silence of despair. [...] The Indians, of gentle and peaceful habits, who have been introduced into the Colony and who have come here only in the faith of the treaties and of the completely reassuring promises of a nation marching in the forefront of civilization have been inhumanly thrown into the hands of the police. Citizens, such a state of affairs can last no longer. May the cause of our motive for bringing it to the notice of the National Assembly be removed.[154]

Due to unsanitary conditions and the practice of drinking water from the cholera-infested Hooghly River, many died of cholera en route from Calcutta or from Mauritius and were thrown overboard. One horrific example was of the ship *L'Auguste*, which set sail from Pondicherry, overloaded with 339 indentured instead of the mandated 309, and suffered an epidemic of cholera on the journey. An inquest revealed that many of the sick were thrown overboard while still alive. Passengers were ill-treated and deprived of their provisions. Some women were raped and killed.[155] Those who survived, nicknamed 'Calcuttas' and 'Bengalis', were sent on arrival to grim quarantine centres without adequate facilities at Grande Chaloupe Bay. As a result, dwindling numbers of *engages* actually reached the plantations.

There were similar abuses on the return journey. In 1857, on Reunion Island, 550 *engages* were loaded on a small ship of 374 tonnes for repatriation to India. Many died and the accompanying

---

[154]*Le Cri Public*, Ile de la Reunion, 17 July 1848.
[155]Weber, Jacques, 'L'émigration indienne des comptoirs, 1828-1861', *Etudes et Documents n° 11*, Aix-en-Provence, Université de Provence, Institut d'histoire des pays d'outre-mer, 1978, pp. 133–59.

medical doctor noted: 'What may suffice for an inanimate cargo did not suit a live cargo, whose first need is to breathe.'[156]

Living conditions deteriorated in the mid-1860s when disease brought by parasites decimated sugarcane crops. The British Consul was forced to ask for an enquiry commission. The commission was set up in 1877. Commander Miot, who was French, and Major Goldsmith, who was British, jointly exposed the rot that had set in. Many of the *engages* had completed their contract but had been refused repatriation.[157]

Demands made by the British Indian Government, including an agent to protect the rights of the *engages* and the right granted to the British Consul to visit the plantations and inspect the conditions of the workers, were rejected. This forced the British to suspend the Convention of 1861 on 11 November 1882. The last batch on Indian *engages* reached on-board *La Marguerite* in 1885. Girmitya travel to all French colonies came to an end through the Indian Emigration Act of 1883.[158]

The French always referred to the indentured as *engages*. Their travel to Reunion Island from India was named *La Route des Engages*. Were they different from the English indentured? Or was it as the French say in jest: '*Le plus qu'ca change, le plus c'est la meme chose* (The more it changes, the more it remains the same)'?

Sudel Fuma, a historian from Reunion Island, proposed in 2001 that the term 'engagisme' be replaced with 'servilisme'

---

[156] *Health Report of Doctor Guilley on the Voyages of the Condor and La Felicite*, Pondicherry, 30 December 1857, Manuscript no. 799 of Catalogue 121 of the Librarie Bellanger, Nantes.

[157] Commander Miot's confidential report was microfilmed and partially published in *Archives de La Réunion-Recueil de documents et travaux inédits pour servir à l'histoire des îles françaises de l'océan Indien*, Conseil général de La Réunion, 1986, CAOM c. 277.

[158] *Mr Geoghegan's Report on Coolie Emigration from India*, Proquest LLC, 2006; Tupper, C.L., *Note on Colonial Emigration during the Year 1878-1879*, Bengal Secretariat Press, Calcutta, 1879.

or servitude, as being closer to reality. While the proposal was rejected, the suggestion underlined the 'the fraudulent nature of the contracts'.[159]

This 'compulsory labour' or indenture bore an eerie resemblance to slavery. Freedom was illusory. Labour was hard and enforced by supervisors. Contracts were long and could not be terminated midway. Travel was prohibited. There was no right to legal representation. Working conditions had been set out in the decree of 27 March 1852. Their status was not protected by sections of French law relating to the hiring of services. The *engages* came under a different part of French law termed as 'forced' or 'restricted' employment.[160]

Some concessions were made to differentiate the two systems. There was initially no forced conversion to the Christian faith. The new arrivals clung to their religion, customs and rituals. They were allowed to cremate their dead. This was testified to by the health officer in Saint-Paul from 1832 to 1838, Dr Morizot, who wrote: 'Not so long ago they would still burn their dead, in specific places designated by the authorities some distance from the towns.'[161] Interracial marriages were permitted. Some rights of ownership of land were conceded along with the right to pass on their names to their children.

Later, the church embarked on an aggressive proselytizing policy, seeking to evangelize the *engages*. Jesuits like Father Laroche were particularly active from 1855 to 1868. Many influential plantation owners, like the Desbassayns, Villèle and

---

[159]Fuma, Sudel, 'Le servilisme à la place du concept d'engagisme pour définir le statut des travailleurs immigrés ou affranchis après l'abolition de l'esclavage en 1848', *Histoire Reunion*, 2001, https://tinyurl.com/49uuhsyr. Accessed on 16 August 2023.

[160]Boutang-Yann, Moulier, *De l'esclavage au salariat, économie historique du salariat bridé*, Presses Universitaires de France, Paris, 1978, p. 975.

[161]Morizot, Joseph, *Considérations historiques et médicales sur l'état de l'esclavage à l'île Bourbon*, Orphie, 2017, p. 27.

Kervéguen clans, also pushed hard for their conversion. Others were more reticent, fearing social unrest.

Conversion did not make any difference to the treatment meted out to the *engages*. They were deprived of their freedom and liberty. There were instances of youth being drugged and kidnapped from French settlements in India. This was clear from the trial of De Souza in 1853.[162] Those who gained were the unscrupulous recruitment agencies and ship owners in Karikal, Pondicherry and Madras.

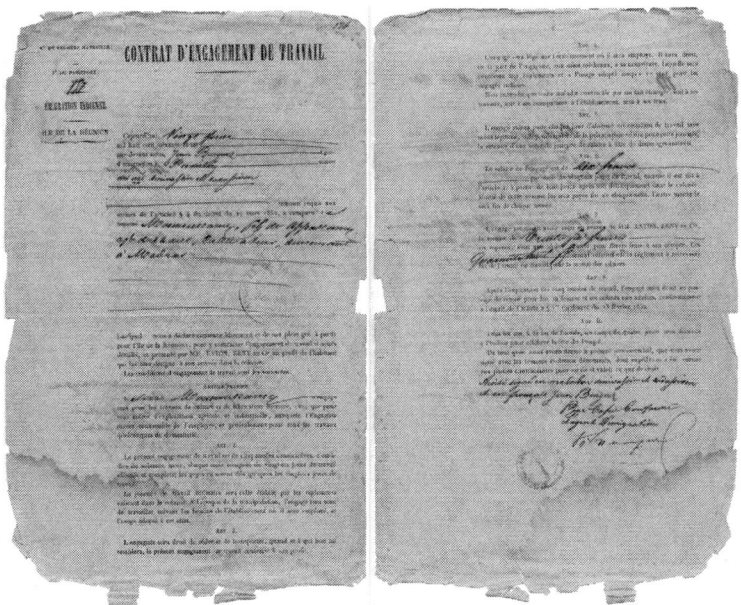

Figure 15: The farcical 'employment contract'

Source: *Société de plantation, histoire et mémoires de l'esclavage à La Réunion*, https://tinyurl.com/2m953u7s. Accessed on 22 August 2023.

---

[162]Weber, Jacques, 'Entre traite et coolie trade: L'affaire de l'Auguste', *La dernière traite: Fragments d'Histoire en hommage à Serge DAGET*, Société Française d'Histoire d'Outre-Mer, Université de Nantes, Université de Lille III, 1994, pp. 150–62.

Conditions promised were attractive but never implemented on the ground. They were intended to entice desperate humans to Reunion Island. The contract was adapted from those used earlier by the French East India Company to entice skilled Indian workers from South India, including masons, carpenters and painters to other French colonies such as Mauritius.

The salary promised was ₹7 (F10) per month along with accommodation and food. An advance of three months' salary was paid upon signing the contract in India. The *engages* were also promised a free trip back to India on completion of their contract. The high and unacceptable mortality rates challenge these seemingly attractive contracts. They were caused by inhuman living and working conditions.

The attitude of the sugar plantation owners was that the *engages* had replaced the slaves and deserved no better than the 62,000 recently 'Freedmen'.[163] The contractual period was extended to seven years. Several *engages* were obliged to share small rooms with primitive facilities. Food was inadequate and wages were deducted for any debts at the plantation shop. Medical facilities were virtually non-existent. Their identity cards resembled those of the former slaves.

In case an *engages* was absent for one day, wages were deducted for two days under a system known as 'double cut'. Anyone outside the plantation was punished for 'vagrancy'. They were hunted down by vagrancy guards, like escaped slaves.

From a psychological and sociological perspective, engages led an abnormal human existence. In an alien land, far from

---

[163] Le Terrier, Xavier, *La main d'oeuvre du sucre: De l'engagisme au colonat: Bourbon-La Réunion, 1848-1914*, Centre de recherches et de documentation Émile Hugot, Musée Stella Matutina, DL 2016, p. 45.

Le Terrier reveals how workshops quickly recovered and even improved their original production levels with the arrival of indentured workers from India (from 1849 in the north and east, and from 1850 in the west and south), thus avoiding a drop in production, as happened in West Indies.

home and family, they were an all-male labour force, in striking contrast to English settlements like Mauritius or Fiji. Initially, there were hardly any women. This phenomenon impacted their behaviour and conduct and later influenced their social and cultural practices. Suicide became a common phenomenon. This forced a change in approach by the colonial administrative authority and gradually some women were inducted as *engages* or as domestic help but under pitiable conditions.

Although the decree of 3 July 1829 established a supervisory committee to ensure that employers would not treat the indentured like slaves, in reality, these laws were never implemented. A trade union was created in 1831. Unfortunately, racist planters, used to treating slaves harshly, complained of the low productivity of *engages* as compared to former slaves and used corporal punishment to increase their output.

Available records show 25 per cent of the Indian indentured workers, including women, died on Reunion Island. The short and miserable lives of the women *engage*s have been documented in a few cases. One example is of Naly Pery, a Dalit woman from Yanaon who was about 35 years of age. She was recruited by Mr Joseph Desbassayns. After seven months of service, she died on 23 November 1830 at Mr Desbassayns' home in Bel Air, Sainte-Suzanne.[164]

Male mortality rates were even higher. A 23-year-old indentured farmer, Abigadou Apaya, who was working for a sugar factory in Sainte-Suzanne died under miserable conditions on 6 October 1829 after a very short stay on the island.[165]

As in France before the revolution, the society of Reunion Island was divided between the extremely rich and *les miserables*,

---

[164]'Indentured Labour in Reunion Island', *Société de plantation, histoire et mémoires de l'esclavage à La Réunion*, https://tinyurl.com/pt5y6b7x. Accessed on 17 August 2023.
[165]Ibid.

(translated as 'the poorest and the most marginalized') comprising the freed slaves and the *engages*, poor, marginalized and desperate and with no social standing. This was acknowledged at the highest official level by Rodolphe Augustin, Baron Darricau, who was Governor of Reunion Island from 1858 to 1863: 'Everywhere I have been struck by sights that have touched me deeply: alongside the lushest of crops and most magnificent produce lies truly saddening shortages; wealth in a few hands, while the majority of the population has less than the bare minimum.'[166]

The emergence of a small settler class of former *engages* was not an easy process. Urban traders and many French Colonial Officers encouraged repatriation on racist grounds. They were opposed to competition from those who they looked down upon as racially inferior. This was defended on the grounds of law and order.

Smaller estate owners supported renewal of contracts because of the increasing restrictions on the recruitment of *engages*. Their methods were illegal and ranged from not repaying their 'debts' to corporal punishment and forcing long working hours between 18 and 20 hours a day.

Despite such obstacles, from the 1860s, small land holdings owned and cultivated jointly by several *engages*, either from their savings or by those who chose to stay on after the completion of their contract, led to some social changes on Reunion Island. They were treated as tenant farmers under a sharecropping system known as *metayage*. It led to the emergence of a small farmer class. According to the law of 1889, their children were given French citizenship rights. Whether they actually enjoyed all those rights is yet to be established.

What conclusion can the reader draw from such a tragic narrative? T.S. Eliot said: 'In my beginning is my end.' A great injustice was done to the *engages*. They were treated in a manner similar to slaves as borne out by Tinker's *A New System of Slavery*.

---

[166] Roussin, Louis-Antoine, *Album de l'Ile la Réunion*, A. Roussin, 1858, p. 43

Reconciliation was never attempted, then or now.

So many living in Reunion believe that *engagisme* was a crime against humanity. Who will reach out and try to make amends? In 2023, the past has neither been accepted nor legally acknowledged.

Reunion Island was officially integrated into France and became a French department (*département d'outre mer*) in 1946. It coincided with the process of decolonization set into motion by the independence of India, Mauritius and several African and Asian colonies. Paradoxically, despite its assimilation with mainland France, economic and social conditions on Reunion Island were abysmal and far removed from conditions prevailing in France.

The French Fourth Republic, in its constitution adopted in October 1946, embraced state sponsored secularism, termed *laïcité*. It ensured the complete separation of the State from all forms of religious activity. Its impact in Reunion Island was catastrophic. Official records deleted all references to the place of origin of the Indian indentured. Indian nomenclature was replaced by French names. As an example, Krishnan became Kitchen and Ganapathy became Canabady. Indian languages gradually became extinct, increasing the feeling of being without roots. Unlike Mauritius, the only language spoken by the *engages* is French. They cannot communicate in English or any Indian language and need French interpreters if they visit India. This too cuts them off from their place of origin, Mother India.

Youth of Indian origin have had to confront a negative narrative regarding India in their high school education. Céline Ramsamy-Giancone recounts how, in class, a geography teacher defined India as 'a huge and poverty-stricken country. Dead people's burnt bodies are thrown in the Ganges while, further down others brush their teeth with that filthy water.'[167]

---

[167] Ramsamy-Giancone, Céline, 'Reunion: My Island, My History', *Girmitiyas: The Making of Their Memory-Keepers from the Indian Indentured Diaspora*, Brij V. Lal (ed.), Primus Books, 2022, pp. 115–35.

Conversion from Hinduism to Catholicism was a sensitive topic and has only recently been discussed on Reunion Island. The French distinguished Hindu practices from Islam by referring to them as popular forms of religion and likening them to paganism and pagan rituals. The Catholic Church actively converted the Indian *engage*s and discouraged them from continuing their religious and cultural practices. Children of the newly converted were given free access to the best education. This was a powerful incentive. Apart from societal pressure and a desire to please the authorities, the disproportionate sex ratio among *engages* increasingly led to mixed marriages and conversions to the Catholic faith. The offspring too would be Catholic.

In an effort to remember their past for the sake of their future generations, *engages* clung desperately to their ancient Hindu rituals and customs. The result was tragic. Although their descendants are Catholic, many continue to practise Hindu rituals, including the worship of photos or small images of their Gods. They have continued practising their cultural and social rituals and cooking the Indian cuisine. Seeds of jackfruit, curry leaves and basic Indian spices and condiments were planted. They flourished in Reunion Island's fertile soil. Laïcité could not prevent Reunion Island from becoming a melting pot of cultures, called *métissage* in French. Hindu practices and worship have continued, justified in the name of 'cultural diversity and differentiation'.

A marked ambivalent approach of the new generations towards their religion, culture and heritage is a direct result of their detachment from their roots, an exercise in assimilation that is yet to take place. It may never happen. This paradoxical situation has never been addressed either within Reunion Island or in France.

Such efforts at déracinement were deliberate and part of the policy to ensure cultural assimilation. A visit to Reunion Island today demonstrates the futility of such politics. Indian cultural associations established by the third or fourth generation of the indentured promote a strong connection with India. Music, dance and yoga are taught with the support of the Indian Government. India too has rediscovered its forgotten children on Reunion Island.

Another and more complex issue was whether France would ever acknowledge the great injustice done to the *engages* of Reunion Island? It took 55 years for the Taubira Law to be adopted on 10 May 2001. It makes a distinction between slavery and the *engages*. While acknowledging that the slave trade in the Atlantic and Indian Oceans and the enslavement of 'African Amerindian, Malagasy and Indian populations' in these regions was a crime against humanity, it makes no mention of the *engages*.

In an effort for reconciliation, Article 4 of the law proclaims that the annual public holiday of 10 May will commemorate the abolition of slavery and 'the end of all indentured contracts signed following said abolition'.[168] Unfortunately, neither the commemoration of 10 May in France and 20 December on Reunion Island has been associated with the end of indenture.

During my two visits to Reunion Island in 2014 and 2016, many of the former *engages* expressed distress and indignation at the refusal to accept the similarity of indenture with slavery or to commemorate its abolition in a manner similar to the end of slavery. They were of the view that indenture or *engagisme* was a crime against humanity.

The *engages* of Reunion Island were pushed into a dark tunnel with no exit and no protection of the law. As early as 1865, British Prime Minister Lord John Russell lamented 'a new system of slavery', later corroborated by Tinker. The anomaly and ambiguity in defining and distinguishing slavery from indenture became part

---

[168] Article 4: The commemoration of the abolition of slavery by the French Republic and that of the end of all Indentured labour contracts signed following said abolition shall be the subject of a public holiday in the departments of Guadeloupe, French Guiana, Martinique and Reunion, as well as in the territorial community of Mayotte.

of a process of political struggle for liberation, embraced by left wing parties. As was said by workers of the Communist Party: 'In the dark nights of slavery, Indian emigration to Reunion took place through three ports [...] these slaves...'[169]

Alessandro Stanziani linked the unequal status of the *engages* of colour to the consequences of the French Revolution of 1789.[170] Abolition of slavery was a difficult process. It was abolished twice and the process was particularly complex on Reunion Island. As Stanziani pondered: 'Was the inferior status of immigrants in the colonies[...] a broader consequence of the way the revolution of 1789 dealt with labour and rights?' This remains a conundrum that should be addressed.

Another profound and complex issue was the legacy of *engages* in relation to Reunion Island. Though slaves but not fully enslaved, were they able to give voice to 'the rhythms, images, and brakes and constraints whose origins were rooted in the slave system, and of which, in spite of themselves, they were the vehicle and the alibi after having been its victims?'[171]

History is witness that the denial of the past can only lead to social unrest and rise of racism and neo-fascism. Professor Frederick Maurice Powicke said: 'The craving for an interpretation

---

[169]*Nous sommes tous de parias* (We are all the same), Saint-Gilles les Hauts, Reunion, 1977, pp. 3–4, 52.

In the same pamphlet, D. Singainy explained to the members of the *cercle de la misère* (Poverty Circle) how he can at the same time be a Malabar priest of a Poverty Chapel and a militant communist: the defence of the poor and the defence of the popular cults come from India and are for him two faces of the same struggle. In popular tradition, fact was more potent than law: coolies, engages, or freed slaves, were considered new slaves for a long time.

[170]Stanziani, A., *Labour and Rights in Eurasia from the Sixteenth to the Early Twentieth Centuries,* Berghahn Books, 2015.

[171]Gerbeau, Hubert, 'Engagees and Coolies on Reunion Island: Slavery's Masks and Freedom's Constraints', *Colonialism and Migration: Indentured Labour Before and After Slavery*, Bernard Delfendahl Emmer (ed.), Martinus Nijhoff Publishers, Dordrecht, Boston/Lancaster, 1986.

of history is so deep-rooted that, unless we have a constructive outlook over the past, we are drawn either to mysticism or to cynicism.'[172]

The *engages* of Reunion Island wait with impatience, frustration and growing anger for that constructive interpretation of their past so that historical injustices can be laid to rest and the weight of history may not be passed on generation to generation, as it is now.

Fiji: A Traumatic Journey into Exile

Generations nurtured from my seeds will clasp their hands and say our ancestors carved those fields which have given us meanings to stand tall. This land is ours too.

—Rooplall Monar, Guyanese poet

Monar's stirring call rings across continents, galvanizing the Girmitya to fulfil an age-long tradition: to claim the land lovingly tilled and cultivated for generations as their own.[173]

Indentured labour came late to Fiji in 1879. The long sea voyage across the Kalapani deterred many from venturing across the Indo-Pacific to an unknown destination. It galvanized the long struggle to end indenture because of the resistance successfully organized in the plantations to sustained malpractices and assault. Women played an important role in the struggle.

There were many myths about the new arrivals. As G.A. Grierson stated in 1882, 'I have been assured by every native from whom I have enquired, and by most Europeans, that only

---

[172]Powicke, F., *Modern Historians and the Study of History*, Odhams Press, 1955, p. 174.

[173]Monar, Rooplall, 'Babu', *They Came in Ships: An Anthology of Indo-Guyanese Prose and Poetry*, Ian McDonald et al. (eds), Peepal Tree Press Ltd., 1998, pp. 203–05.

the lowest castes emigrate, and that nothing will ever induce men of higher class to leave.'[174] The colonial version of this myth that the higher castes refused plantation indenture, fearing social ostracism is only partially correct. The long journey was dreaded by all. Economic circumstances influenced the final decision.

The reality was that the Girmitiyas, who came to Fiji, hailed from varied social backgrounds. Of Fiji's 45,000 Hindu indentured, Brahmins and other upper castes numbered 1,686; the Kshatriyas and mid-level castes numbered 4,565; the Baniya or merchant and money-lending castes numbered 1,592; agricultural labourers and artisans, called Kurmi, Ahir, Jat and Lodha, numbered 15,800; the lowest castes, called Chamar, Pasi and Dusadh, numbered 11,907; and finally, there was also a tiny Muslim minority of around 6,787.[175]

The Fiji authorities tried their best to paint a rosy picture of what awaited the indentured. William Seed, Agent General of Immigration, wrote: 'There is a grand opening in the colony after the indentures are out as [the indentured labourer] can set up as a cow keeper, market gardener, and poulterer, there being no industries of this description amongst the Fijians, nor ever I imagine likely to be.'[176]

Legislation to ensure a fair deal to the new arrivals was never implemented. It existed as a recruitment mechanism to entice the Girmitiyas to undertake the long journey. They were promised rations at fair prices, with children supposedly receiving half rations free. Reasonable and rent-free accommodation and free medical treatment and free medicines were other undertakings that were promised and put aside. The Foundation Indenture Legislation for Fiji (1891) stated: 'Medical inspectors in the

---

[174]Taken from: Emigration Proceedings A Pros., National Archives of India (NAI), New Delhi, 12 August 1882.
[175]Lal, Brij V. (ed.), *Girmitiyas: The Making of Their Memory-Keepers from the Indian Indentured Diaspora*, Primus Books, 2022, pp. 68–90.
[176]Lal, Brij V., *Chalo Jahaji: On a Journey through Indenture in Fiji*, Australian National University Press, 2012, p. 149.

districts were empowered to 'enter upon any plantation and inspect the state of health of the immigrants there on and the conditions of the dwellings and hospital and rations and the general sanitation of such plantations.'[177]

The reality was a grim tale of deception and false promises. There was no process of consultation with the indentured about the choice of their future employers. Once contracted, they had no freedom to change their employer or to voluntarily buy out their contracted period of service. They were confined to their place of work while their employers could arbitrarily shift them from one plantation to another. The writ was not the printed legislation but the careful, calculated exploitative interests of the plantation owners. This was the exploitative pattern across plantations in all colonies. Indenture was 'in essence a model of interlocking incarceration'.[178]

Figure 16: A Girmitiya camp waiting for breakfast
Source: Ministry of External Affairs, Government of India

---

[177] Lal, Brij V., *Chalo Jahaji: On a Journey through Indenture in Fiji*, Australian National University Press, 2012.
[178] Samaroo, Brinsley, and David Dabydeen (eds), *India in the Caribbean*, Hansib Publications Limited, 1987, p. 63.

Similarly, the working conditions, as described in first-hand accounts, were deplorable. There are different sources but the stories are similar. Days were long—the working day started at 5.00 a.m. and ended at sunset at 4.00 p.m. A working day usually entailed nine hours of hard labour. During harvest, the hours would be even longer. A quick breakfast was all that sustained the workforce till the day was done.

The task system was inherited from the earlier slave system. Although William Seed, Fiji's first Agent General of Immigration, tried to justify it stating that the task system suited 'the master and the servant much better',[179] the reality was different. It was a system of over-exploitation of available labour, to get the maximum work done with minimum pay.

Remuneration based on the minimum statutory wage was paltry compared to the hard labour and paid according to tasks accomplished. The indenture agreement entitled men to one shilling per day and women to nine pennies. Employers like the Colonial Sugar Refining Company, the major employer of Indian labour in Fiji, would deny even these wages based on charges of incompetence or inertia. This caused a vicious circle of malnutrition, sickness and absenteeism, leading to a further fall in living standards. Even Henry Anson, the Agent General of Immigration in 1887, had to concede: 'Granted that the Indians are bad, lazy and inferior as a class to those in other colonies, one would even then expect that more than eight per cent would manage during a year to attain over the minimum statutory wage at field work.'[180]

---

[179]For first-hand narratives about this system, see: Gillion, K.L., *Fiji's Indian Migrants*, Oxford University Press, 1976; Soares Ramessar, Marianne, *Survivors of another Crossing: A History of East Indians in Trinidad*, University of the West Indies, School of Continuing Studies, St. Augustine, Trinidad and Tobago, 1994; Carter, Marina, *Voices from Indenture: Experiences of Indian Migrants in the British Empire*, Leicester University Press, Leicester, 1996.
[180]Colonial Secretary's Office (CSO) file 2159/1881, National Archives of Fiji.

It was never the case that the 'meek' Indians did not protest. The process of legitimate dissent was stalled by carefully drafted counter legislation to deter any dissenter. For example, the Indenture Ordinance for Fiji of 1891 prohibited more than five workers employed on the same plantation from collectively bringing complaints against their employers without obtaining formal approval from the employer to leave their place of work.

The evolution of a common demand for fundamental human rights at the workplace was further inhibited by the social and ethnic diversity of the indentured. These differences could have been overcome but for the ingenious provisions contained in the files of the Fijian Colonial Secretary's Office (CSO) (file number 156 dated 1896), which enabled employers to break up promising friendships that had the potential to promote worker solidarity. 'It is desirable to break up a gang of men who have caused or are likely to cause serious disturbance of the peace.'[181]

The human spirit cannot be confined forever. Complaints did get filed. According to Fiji's *Agent General of Immigration Annual Reports* between 1890 and 1897, 251 complaints were filed mainly on charges of physical violence and non-payment of wages. Unfortunately, there were only 86 convictions and the convicted were let off lightly. As a result, only the desperate tried to bring charges. Records indicate that of 402 charges filed against European supervisors, between 1897 and 1912, only 29 per cent were convicted. Counter charges were brought by the employers and their supervisors to instil fear and apprehension in the minds of those who would otherwise have pressed charges.

Nights were long and lonely. Relationships forged during the long and arduous journey, called jahaji bhai or brotherhood of the crossing, gave the indentured much-needed emotional support. Social fragmentation increased the feeling of alienation. These

---

[181]Lal, Brij V., *Chalo Jahaji: On a Journey through Indenture in Fiji*, Australian National University Press, 2012, p. 51.

difficult circumstances were made more challenging by the sharp gender imbalance, which rendered a normal family life for men facing completely alien conditions so far away from home virtually impossible.

The Girmitiyas clung fiercely to their memories of their language, culture and history, their social and ethnic traditions and, above all, their religion. These were transplanted on Fiji's fertile soil. With time and a process of cross fertilization, these cultural practices became part of local lore and as Fijian as the age-old traditional practices of Fiji's original inhabitants. Religious practices, whether Hindu or Muslim, were part of their daily life.

Myths and legends, folklore and religious discourses sustained the indentured in Fiji. These included 'Satyanarayan ki Katha' (a collection of five stories from the 'Reva' chapter of the Skanda Purana), 'Sukh Sagar' (a discourse on the different incarnations of Lord Vishnu) and verses from the Bhagavad Gita. The all-time favourite was the Ramayana, the story of Lord Ram in some 10,000 lines of verse in the Awadhi dialect of Hindustani. The story of Ram, his exile and return, enacted through the Ramlila, was an inspiration to the lonely exiles, hoping one day to return to their Mother land.[182]

By 1916, indenture was formally abolished in Fiji. Those who had completed their contract and had opted to stay on established settlements with schools, temples and mosques. This gave hope to the other remaining indentured that freedom was not far away. Gradually, the feeling of community and solidarity helped develop new links of friendship. Alienation became a nightmare of the past.

Agriculture was the preferred form of sustenance. Indians developed scattered holdings on individually leased parcels of land. To regulate their lives and to maintain social and communal harmony, they used the age-old Panchayat system, which

---

[182]Lal, Brij V., *Chalo Jahaji: On a Journey through Indenture in Fiji*, Australian National University Press, 2012.

represents a village council in India till date. The decisions taken by the Panchayat (called Panchayati system) were respected by all. However, this system declined over time.

As Indians became integrated into the new land and society of their adopted land, another crisis reared its ugly head. The conflict and hostility between the newly freed indentured and the original inhabitants or the freed slaves, who had also opted to remain there, were unfortunate but inevitable. The differences were rooted in deep social and cultural prejudices, bordering on racism. The religious and linguistic divide made a sustained dialogue for reconciliation and harmony impossible to achieve. Brij V. Lal noted: 'Relations between the two groups were characterised by prejudice and the suspicion that one was the nemesis of the other.'[183]

These difficulties existed in all the colonies with sugar plantations but were particularly acute in Fiji, where cultural prejudices were deep-rooted on both sides. The Indians looked down on indigenous Fijians, calling them *junglis*, or 'bushmen'. Native Fijians despised Indians for being 'servile' and exploited by Europeans.

This situation gave rise to dark humour by the colonizer who spoke contemptuously of the conflict between the Creole and the Coolie. This conflict was of great value to the colonizer, since it set two exploited groups of individuals against each other, to the benefit of the exploiter.

> The coolie despises the negro, because he considers him a being not so highly civilized as himself, while the negro, in turn, despises the coolie, because he is so immensely inferior to him in physical strength. There never will be much danger of seditious disturbances among East Indian

---

[183]Lal, Brij V., *Levelling Wind, Remembering Fiji*, Australian National University Press, 2019, p. 44.

immigrants on estates as long as large numbers of negroes continue to be employed with them.[184]

Other important factors contributed to this conflict. Indian indentured were paid lower wages than newly freed Black slaves. The Indians and Black people lived in separate ghettos, as ordained by the Fijian authorities, and social interaction and marriage were strictly prohibited. Ethnic separation was sanctioned by law. Separate schools were established for Fijian, European and Indian children. Later, segregation based on race and ethnic representation in the legislative council was also enforced. This vicious practice, similar to apartheid in South Africa, further divided the two communities.

There was no mechanism to address these irritants. Over time, they evolved into festering sores that threatened communal amity and peace. As Brij V. Lal stated, 'The descendants of the Indian indentured immigrants found themselves suffering and living on the sufferance of others, excluded from the corridors of power, disempowered.' [185]

Ultimately, this conflict tore asunder this beautiful land and sent a large majority of the Indians into exile. The paradise was lost, perhaps forever. Can it ever be reincarnated?

∽

---

[184]42 CSO 3481/1887.
[185]Lal, Brij V., *Levelling Wind, Remembering Fiji*, Australian National University Press, 2019, p. 44.

8

THE JOURNEY OF THE INDENTURED WOMAN: AN UNTOLD STORY

No one who understands the historian's craft would plead seriously that all groups should receive equal time. [...] The problem is that historians have tended to spend too much of their time in the company of the 'movers and shakers' and too little in the universe of the mass of mankind.

—Lawrence L. Levine

Gender imbalance, whether of female migrants or indentured women, was a complex issue that was never fully resolved when the great movements of people occurred in the late eighteenth and nineteenth centuries. The numbers of surplus males, whether migrants or indentured, lay at the root of complex social problems at the final destination.

'A colony that is not attractive to women, is an unattractive colony' was the declaration of Edward Gibbon Wakefield in 1849 after the decision to subsidize passages of female migrants to Australia.[186] Concerns regarding this imbalance were also based on morality, religion and the need to populate the plantation colonies with a continuing labour force. 'Men without women were, it

---

[186] Gibbon Wakefield, Edward, *A View of the Art of Colonization, with Present Reference to the British Empire: In Letters Between a Statesman and a Colonist*, John W. Parker, London, 1849, p. 156.

seemed, an uncivilized force and an uncivilizing presence.'[187]

It was ironic that women migrants or indentured women were simultaneously looked upon with suspicion and as a destabilizing influence upon honest, hardworking, upright male migrants or indentured. One could almost conclude that just as one could not do without them, one had to accept their presence with reluctance and many caveats! Their journey itself was undertaken due to misogynistic, male-dominated beliefs frequently imposed upon them. Male expectations about their future role were also a huge burden. They were expected to work in the plantations and at home, produce children and raise them. How then, one could ask Edward Gibbon Wakefield, could a plantation colony look attractive to indentured women?

Unlike men, the indentured women had greater challenges before them. Their journey, their displacement, often contemptuously dismissed as this 'mass of mankind', remains untold, obscured under layers of social prejudice, misperception and misogyny. Who were these women? Why did they travel to unknown destinations? Were they desperate or were they women of easy virtue, encouraged by wily recruiters to seek a new family life, far away from prying eyes? There are no easy answers. That is why the narration is so complex.

The colonial government was hesitant to include women as plantation labour. Lacking a holistic perspective, they failed to envisage the social unrest that would arise from an all-male indentured labour force, cut off from their roots and families. It was not easy to recruit women either.

There are few known accounts of their lives from the perspective of these women. What was their social origin? Had they embraced indenture to escape the miseries of prostitution or had poverty and famine forced indenture on them? What was their

---

[187] Harper, Marjory and Stephen Constantine, *Migration and Empire*, Oxford History of the British Empire Companion Series, Oxford University Press, 2010, p. 215.

status on arrival at the plantations? Did they enter a new life of liberty or had they exchanged one form of servitude for another? Their narrative is difficult to pen because of its complexity. They were portrayed as either 'powerless victims' or 'immoral' women. The discourse was complicated by the burden of deep-rooted Victorian morality. In 1880, the Protector of Emigrants wrote: '...that the class of women willing to emigrate consists principally of young widows and married or single women who have already gone astray and are therefore not only most anxious to avoid their homes and to conceal their antecedents, but are also at the same time unlikely to be received back into their families.'[188]

Colonial historians ignored the silenced voices of these women in their historiographies and refused to acknowledge their role as the family lynchpin, as carriers of their culture and identity in their new nation. Their position as a civilizing Western influence over their colonial subjects in reality reflected their opposition to personal law, dictated by the religion of their subjects rather than a benevolent or emancipatory approach to these subject-women. Their only point of concurrence was their deep-rooted conviction about the inferior status of women. Considered physically weak and intellectually ignorant, they were only to be tolerated as childbearers and caregivers.

The women, naturally, were neither in the discourse nor ever consulted. On the other hand, the illiteracy of the subject women ensured that their voices would be silenced and their portrayal would remain one sided till the 1940s. The stereotyping of these women has been increasingly challenged by feminist historians. Revisionist scholars like P.C. Emmer, M. Carter and C. Bates have tried to argue that indenture ultimately transformed the lives of these women. They ignored the flaws and gross abuses that led to British abolitionist John Scoble equating indenture with slavery.[189]

---

[188] *Yearly Reports on Emigration of the British Indian Government,* 1880.
[189] Van Den Boogaart, Ernst, and P. C. Emmer (eds), *Colonialism and Migration,*

Figure 17: Indentured women voices silenced forever
Source: Le Morne Cultural Landscape, Le Morne Heritage Trust Fund

H. Tinker, J. Beall, J.D. Kelly and Brij V. Lal also portrayed these women as victims of sexual exploitation.[190] Their narrative

---

Indentured Labour Before and After Slavery, Comparative Studies in Overseas History 7, Martinus Nijhoff, 1986; Carter, Marina, *Voices from Indenture: Experiences of Indian Migrants in the British Empire,* Leicester University Press, Leicester, 1996; Bates, C., 'Coerced and Migrant Labourers in India: The Colonial Experience', *Edinburgh Papers in South Asian Studies 13,* University of Edinburgh, Centre for South Asian Studies, pp. 1–33.

[190]Beall, J., 'Women Under Indenture in Colonial Natal, 1860-1911', *South Asians Overseas: Migration and Ethnicity,* C. Clarke, C. Peach and S. Vertovec (eds), Cambridge University Press, Cambridge, 1990, pp. 57–74; Sanadhya, Totaram, *My Twenty One Years in the Fiji Islands and the Story of the Haunted Line by Totaram Sanadhya,* J.D. Kelly and U.K. Singh (eds and trans), Suva

influenced the leaders of the burgeoning national movement such as Gopal Krishna Gokhale, Mahatma Gandhi, C.F. Andrews, J.W. Burton and Totaram Sanadhya.[191] Stories of their exploitation began to emerge and reach India.

There are complex reasons for women going into indenture. They could range from poverty, marginalization, abandonment by the spouse or family or the determination to make their own destiny. One cannot overemphasize the devastating impact of British imperialism, huge agrarian distress due to refusal by the British to mitigate taxation during periods of devastating famine and the systematic destruction of local industries. The most vulnerable among the poor, the marginalized and the desperate were the women and children. Colonial migration sharply impacted women, either as co-migrants or because they were left behind or abandoned.

Recruiters used devious and cunning ploys, since most married women were reluctant to travel to the unknown. Recruiters went to the extent of kidnapping or misleading women who were illiterate and had no idea of what the future would bring.[192] These unscrupulous agents searched for poor and destitute women in temples, markets, festivals and historical cities like Mathura and Varanasi, which had many abandoned and destitute widows. The premium for recruiting women was higher than men, so the lure was much higher.

Whatever the reasons, these women often regretted their choice but there was no turning back. With courage, they continued and

---

Museum, Canberra, 1991; Kelly, J.D., *A Politics of Virtue: Hinduism, Sexuality and Countercolonial Discourse in Fiji,* University of Chicago Press, Chicago, 1991; Lal, Brij V., 'Kunti's Cry: Indentured Indian Women on Fiji Plantations', *Indian Economic and Social History Review,* Vol. 22, No. 1, pp. 55–71.

[191] Kale, M., *Fragments of Empire: Capital, Slavery and Indian Indentured Labour in the British Caribbean,* University of Pennsylvania Press, Philadelphia, 1998.

[192] McNeill, J. and C. Lal, *Report on the Condition of Indian Immigrants in the Four British Colonies and Surinam or Dutch Guiana,* Government Central Press, Shimla, 1914.

many became the lynchpin of the new family structures they put together in the plantations. Folk poetry has captured their despair at the treatment by their husbands. It is poignant.

> Here, in these lonely fields I, the unfortunate, work alone.
> My lord being in a distant land
> Who will tell me thy lord has come
> The day of their happiness has dawned.[193]

In another such poem, the woman laments the endless strife of family life as follows:

> Alas, I will have to run away with another man
> For my beloved has turned his mind away from me
> But as soon as we lie down to rest, you start quarrelling
> My heart is weary of you.[194]

It was an irony of history and a fitting tribute to the resilience of women that, in the words of Lal, they 'emerged from indenture as productive workers in their own right. They survived the burdens of both racism and sexism.'[195] They played a critical role in facilitating 'the transmission and practice of folk religion and of tradition-based sanctions'.[196] Jeremy Poynting pointed out that in Guyana, for example, women 'were the main preservers of Indian domestic culture', which was 'initially the principal means whereby Indians maintained their identity'.[197] The same was true

---

[193] Lal, Brij V. (ed.), *Girmitiyas: The Making of Their Memory-Keepers from the Indian Indentured Diaspora,* Primus Books, 2022, pp. 113–14.
[194] Ibid.
[195] Lal, Brij V. 'The Odyssey of Indenture: Fragmentation and Reconstitution in the Indian Diaspora', *Diaspora: A Journal of Transnational Studies,* Vol. 5, No. 2, University of Toronto Press, Fall 1996, pp. 167–88.
[196] Carter, Marina, *Lakshmi's Legacy: The Testimonies of Indian Women in 19th Century Mauritius,* Edition l'Ocean Indien, Rose Hill, Mauritius, 1994, p. 142.
[197] Poynting, Jeremy, 'East Indian Women in the Caribbean: Experience and Voice', *South Asian Women Writers: The Immigrant Experience, Journal of South*

for the role played by women in plantations elsewhere. It was the harshness of plantation life that ultimately led to their empowerment. Survival implied organization of resistance and protest against the entrenched male hierarchy of predators and abusers. *Mahila mandals* (women's groups) were formed. Self-defence resulted in women beating those who physically abused and tortured them.[198]

Ultimately, these indentured and former indentured women transformed the society and politics of their new homelands in these plantation colonies. Once considered as a mere footnote of indentured history, indentured women have come back to stake their claim in the history of their new nation states. Their once silent voices today resonate in the international understanding of their story, embodied in UNESCO's Indentured Labour Route.

Indentured Women of Fiji: *Tu Kis Liye Hataash Hai*

Tu khud ki khoj mein nikal
Tu kis liye hataash hai
Tu chal tere wajood ki
Samay ko bhi talaash hai.
(Go out to discover yourself.
What are you waiting for?
Do you not realize that this is your time which has come?
You must search and find your moment in history.)

—'Tu Chal' or 'Women Walk Ahead',[199] Tanveer Ghazi

Asian Literature, Vol. 21, No. 1, Winter–Spring 1986, pp. 133–80.
[198]Mishra, R.M., 'The Emergence of Feminism in Fiji', *Women's History Review*, Vol. 17, No. 1, 2008, pp. 39–55; Naidu, V., *The Violence of Indenture in Fiji*, World University Service, 1980.
[199]This poem was narrated in Hindi by Amitabh Bachchan in the film *Pink*.

Fiji became a British colony in 1874. By 1879, indentured men and women started reaching its shores. Their stories were similar yet starkly different. The story of the Indian indentured women in Fiji is one of struggle, despair and empowerment. Like a phoenix rising from the ashes, they made their destinies and carved a niche for themselves on this beautiful island so far from home.

Despite the efforts of the colonial Indian Government to ensure a semblance of gender parity, there was an acute paucity of women on the plantations. Even more troubling was the discrimination practised against women in every sphere of their personal and working lives. This, in turn, directly impacted their role as wives, mothers, caregivers and workers.

Such gender-based discrimination also impacted the male indentured. It may explain the unusually high suicide rates of male indentured.[200] Why so many suicides? Well-known German philosopher Arthur Schopenhauer argued: 'It will generally be found that as soon as the terrors of life reach the point where they outweigh the terrors of death, a man will put an end to his life.'[201] American historian of medicine and neuroscience Dr Howard I. Kushner argued that suicide is caused by a feeling of total alienation that 'is exacerbated where the ritual and social structures of support, which enable migrants to deal with loss, have been abandoned and are not easily replaced'.[202]

What connects gender imbalance and discrimination, and high suicide rates among the indentured in Fiji? The glaring gap between the number of male and female indentured caused social imbalance as well as violence. According to C.F. Andrews (1871–1940), who made an independent fact-finding tour of Fiji in 1916, a wife 'is a

---

[200] Lal, Brij V., *Chalo Jahaji: On a Journey through Indenture in Fiji*, Australian National University Press, 2012, pp. 215–38
[201] Alvarez, A., *The Savage God. A Study of Suicide*, Harmondsworth, 1971, p. 160.
[202] Kushner, Howard I., 'Immigrant Suicide in the United States: Toward a Psychosocial History', *Journal of Social History*, Fall, 1984, p. 18.

matter for huckstering and bargaining, for fighting and suicides, for jealousy and murder'.[203] C.F. Andrews was told that the housing for the indentured resembled 'a poultry yard of quickly shifting loyalties, indiscriminate, promiscuous sexuality and general moral collapse', and this description, he wrote, was 'painfully accurate of much that we were obliged to see and hear'.[204] It also resulted in a much higher suicide rate for men, according to the Register of Deaths of Indian Immigrants. The suicide rate among adult men was twice that of women: 0.14 per thousand to 0.07 per thousand.[205]

Andrews's conclusions were supported by Fiji's Agent General of Immigration, who was responsible for the administration of indentured labour. He observed, in 1909, that the

> number of cases in which the cause of suicides appears attributable to sexual jealousy is as usual large. It is connected with the disproportion of the sexes at present existing on most plantations and the consequent facility with which women abandon partners to whom they are bound by no legal ties for those who offer better inducements.[206]

Many reasons have been advanced for the dire plight of the male indentured labour in the early days of the system. There can be no doubt that the laissez faire approach of the British Indian Government—who believed that, in accordance with the capitalist and mercantile systems, the laws of supply and demand should govern recruitment and trans-shipment—caused huge distortions in the sex ratio.[207] Given the new and alien conditions in Fiji, this

---

[203] Andrews, C.F., *Indian Indentured Labour in Fiji*, Colortype Press, Perth, 1918.
[204] Ibid. 33.
[205] The ratio only includes the indentured who embarked at Calcutta and went on to commit suicide. Adult males from Calcutta numbered 29,349 and females 12,032.
[206] *Annual Reports on Indian Immigration*, The National Library of Australia, Canberra, MF catalogue no. L42, 1909, p. 19.
[207] Lal, Brij V. (ed.), *Girmitiyas: The Making of Their Memory-Keepers from the*

disturbed the foundations of community and family life, leading many desperate indentured men to end it all. This approach was entirely different to the one adopted earlier by colonial slave masters for the recruitment of slaves.

The high suicide rates provided ample ammunition to the opponents of indenture in the UK as well as to the leaders of the burgeoning national movement within India. It forced the British Indian Government to intervene and adopt the Emigration Act XXII of 1882. It stipulated that, with the exception of Mauritius, which had a balanced sex ratio, the sex ratio should henceforth be 40 to 100, i.e., 40 females should accompany 100 males on each ship leaving India.[208] It was followed by the Act XXI of 1883 (Rule 77), which mandated the proportion of four women to 10 men on every journey to Fiji.

To a degree, these new laws did address the issue but not fully. Between 1882 and 1916, 60,965 Indian men, women and children travelled to Fiji. A strict ratio of 40 women to 100 men was enforced. Of the 45,439 Indian indentured, there were 13,696 women.[209] By 1886, women were arriving in larger numbers based on the demand supply ratio. Recruiters were given a higher commission for women.[210]

Was the higher commission for women due to a more benevolent or egalitarian approach? Not at all! The plantation owners and managers realized that for lower and unequal wages, much more labour could be extracted from these exploited women, who also

---

Indian Indentured Diaspora, Primus Books, 2022.
[208] Ibid. 102–3.
[209] Lal, Brij V., *Chalo Jahaji: On a Journey through Indenture in Fiji*, Australian National University Press, 2012, pp. 99–119.
[210] Reddock, R., 'Freedom Denied: Indian Women and Indentureship in Trinidad and Tobago, 1845 -1917', *Economic and Political Weekly*, Vol. 20, No. 43, 26 October 1985, pp. 79–87; Bahadur, G., *Coolie Woman*, Hachette India, New Delhi, 2013, p. 79; Weller, J.A., *The East Indian indenture in Trinidad, Caribbean Monograph Series, No 4,* Institute of Caribbean Studies, University of Puerto Rico, 1968, p 4.

played the unpaid role of homemakers, cooks and mothers while being a crucial factor of social stability. They were also employed as domestic servants on very low wages, almost akin to slavery. By 1914, the number of women domestic workers exceeded twice the number of women working as agricultural labourers.[211]

It is shameful that because of this deep-rooted gender exploitation, based on unequal and low wages that were legalized by Fiji Ordinance No. XVII of 1887, women faced slander, abuse and sexual harassment right from the moment they entered the recruitment depot.[212] Facing institutionalized violence justified as a norm, women had no option but to seek male protection.

Clearly, mitigation measures did not significantly ameliorate the unequal status of women, especially single women. Those without male protectors were at the mercy of the sirdars and plantation managers and often forced to grant sexual favours to multiple men.[213] Women were not safe on the long sea journey or within their homes. Male members sometimes sold them into prostitution while child marriages became the norm. There are also instances of sexual assaults on children, especially girls.[214]

---

[211] *Annual Report on Emigration from the Port of Calcutta*, 1895, p. 2; *The Report on the Condition of Indian Immigrants in the Four British Colonies*, 1914, pp. 259-60.

[212] Hoefte, R.M.A.L., *Plantation Labor after the Abolition of Slavery: The Case of the Plantation Marienburg (Suriname) 1880-1940*, 1987, Dissertation, University of Florida; Hassankhan, M.S., 'The Indian Indentured Experience in Suriname: Control, Accommodation and Resistance', *Resistance and Indian Indenture Experience: Comparative Perspectives*, M.S. Hassankhan, B. Lal and D. Munro (eds), Manohar Publishers, Delhi, 2014, p. 228; Reddock, Rhoda, 'Freedom Denied: Indian Women and Indentureship in Trinidad and Tobago, 1845-1917', *Economic and Political Weekly*, Vol. 20, No. 43, 26 October 1985, pp. 79–87.

[213] 'Sonarie's Deposition', *Annual Reports of the Protector of Immigrants (ARPE) II 1/162 I3154/1908*, 17 September 1908.

[214] Weller, J.A., *The East Indian Indenture in Trinidad*, Caribbean Monograph Series, No. 4, 1968, Institute of Caribbean Studies, University of Puerto Rico, 1968, p. 3; Morton, S.E., *John Morton of Trinidad*, Westminster Company, Toronto,

The British Empire, in Queen Victoria's reign, witnessed deep-rooted misogyny and racism in the mindsets of colonial administrators. This was evident in their discriminatory approach to marriage between the indentured. Despite requests, there was no legal recognition of Hindu or Muslim marriages. As a result, children born out of such unions had no recognized legal status.

Marriage was considered a mechanism to control the 'morally depraved' native Indian woman, with the Indian man becoming a means of controlling and civilizing her.[215] There also was no definition in the minds of these Victorian prudes 'of what constitutes marriage between Indians'.[216] The absence of legal protection led to men considering their spouses as concubines. They were frequently abandoned or ill-treated. If a woman sought freedom from these shackles, she could be murdered on trumped up charge of infidelity or prostitution.[217]

The increased proportion of Indian women in the indentured population could not change the warped and male chauvinistic approach of the colonial authorities on the island. The tasks allocated to them were discriminatory. There was no equal pay for equal work. Far from it! Men received one shilling a week while women received nine pence. As a result, it was virtually impossible for a single mother with a child to survive.[218] Women

---

1916, p. 185; Andrews, C.F., and W.W. Pearson, 'Indentured Labour in Fiji: An Independent Enquiry, Star Printing Works, Calcutta, 1916, pp. 8–9; Bahadur, G., *Coolie Woman,* Hachette India, New Delhi, 2013, pp. 75–89.

[215]Chief Justice, Letter to Governor of British Guiana, 3 August 1882, Colonial Office Series CO/384/139 PRO.

[216]Legislative Council Debates, Indian Divorce Bill, 1883.

[217]Poynting, Jeremy, 'East Indian Women in the Caribbean: Experience and Voice', *South Asian Women Writers: The Immigrant Experience, Journal of South Asian Literature,* Vol. 21, No. 1, Winter–Spring 1986, pp. 133–80; Samaroo, Brinsley, and David Dabydeen (eds), *India in the Caribbean,* Hansib Publications Limited, 1987, p. 214.

[218]Lal, Brij V., *Chalo Jahaji: On a Journey through Indenture in Fiji,* Australian National University Press, 2012.

were paid only when the task allocated was completed. Children under 15 years of age were left with elderly women who were unfit for work. Since attention spans and concern of these older women for the children were limited, there were many accidents involving children on the plantations.[219]

The total indifference to the legitimate requirements of the female workforce, including respect for maternity leave pre- and post-delivery, as stipulated in the legal contracts or to cater to their maternal healthcare needs, was shocking. 'Women were to have two months of leave before birth and 2–3 months afterwards, this practice was not always observed. [...] During the period of leave, the mother was not provided with milk or rations, which directly led to malnutrition and improper feeding of the infant.'[220]

Even breastfeeding was restricted because it was regarded as detracting or lowering women's productivity.[221] Many women were forced to return to work immediately after childbirth, as testified by Naraini's story.[222] As a direct consequence, there was very high infant mortality in Fiji compared to other plantations.[223] Even when they worked together on the fields, wives or daughters rarely inherited property. Education was not available to the girl child. Child marriage was rampant.

Conditions on the plantations were suitable to the requirements of men only. Things took a turn for the worse after the global fall in sugar prices between 1884 and 1895. The colonial government compounded the problem by failing to send inspectors to the plantations on a regular basis. The human rights situation of women rapidly deteriorated. The Indian public was appalled by Kunti's escape from an attempted rape by the overseer in Fiji. It

---

[219]Ibid. 328–29.
[220]Ibid.
[221]Ibid. 208.
[222]Ibid.
[223]Ibid. 283.

was published in a popular Indian daily *Bharat Mitra* on 8 May 1914. Totaram Sanadhya wrote about this incident in Hindi in his memoirs entitled *Fiji Mein Mere Ikkis Varsh* (My Twenty-One Years in Fiji) in 1914 on his return to India.[224] It was translated into Gujarati, Bengali, Marathi and Urdu. A leading Hindi women's periodical, *Stri Darpan*[225], focussed on the plight of these women in four successive issues.[226]

Maithili Sharan Gupt, a leading Hindi poet of the national movement, who played a definitive role in stirring the national conscience about the plight of the indentured, mourned:

Dekho, dur khet mein hai veh kaun dukhini nari,
padi papiyon ke pale hai veh abla bechari.

(See, who is that suffering woman in the distant fields,
The helpless damsel fallen in the hands of the wicked.)[227]

These publications caused public outrage and forced the British Indian Government to ask for an official enquiry. It was taken up by the leaders of the Indian national movement to demand the end of indenture.

It was only a matter of time before the women, who gradually empowered themselves by accessing education and establishing

---

[224]Sanadhya, Totaram, *Fiji Dwip Mein Mere Ikkis Varsh,* Bharati Bhavan, Varanasi, 1973.

[225]Nijhawan, Shobna, *Women and Girls in the Hindi Public Sphere: Periodical Literature in Colonial North India,* Delhi, 2012, pp. 36–48.

[226]Andrews, C.F., 'Kuli Pratha', *Stri Darpan,* February 1917, pp. 63–4, 100–5; Nehru, Nandrani, 'Striyan aur Bharti', *Stri Darpan,* March 1917, pp. 114–17, 152–60; Nehru, R., 'Striyan aur Bharti', *Stri Darpan,* April 1917, pp. 168–9; Nehru, R., 'The Women's Deputation', *Stri Darpan,* April 1917, p. 170; 'The Response of the Viceroy', *Stri Darpan,* April 1917, p. 171; Nehru, Uma, 'Striyan aur Bharti', *Stri Darpan,* April 1917, p. 200–2; 'Upniveshon Mein Hindustani', *Stri Darpan,* March 1920, pp. 174–5.

[227]Paliwal, Krishnadutt (ed.), *Maithilisaran Gupt Granthavali, Vol. 2,* Vani Prakashan, Delhi, 2008, pp. 94-5.

small business units, started organizing labour protests. By 1886, they were able to establish organized resistance. Initially, their acts of defiance were spontaneous. They would form groups to avenge themselves. 'The most common form of resistance involved physically confronting men who sexually violated indentured women and beating them up. Sometimes the punishment entailed pinning the overseer down and taking turns at urinating on him or walking over him until he excreted.'[228]

Later, they formed committees to press for improvements in their conditions at work, including long working hours, arbitrary wage cuts and inhuman and unsanitary working conditions. The Indian Women's Committee was a formidable group and came to be known as the 'women's gang'. In the 1920s, they organized strikes in Suva, Rewa and Navua. They also participated with men in the great Indian strikes of 1920 and 1921 in Fiji.

Mahatma Gandhi played a crucial role in organizing such resistance. Like in Mauritius, Manilal Doctor was a lawyer sent to Fiji by Gandhi to provide legal support. His spouse Jaikumari Manilal, though not an indentured woman, helped mobilize the women. She was trained in Satyagraha at Gandhi's ashram in South Africa and in Sabarmati, India. Jaikumari was instrumental in leading the successful Indian strike of 1920.[229] She drafted petitions and led a delegation of women to the Governor of Fiji with a letter listing their demands. Subsequently, Manilal Doctor was charged with violence and sabotage and the couple was deported.

In the 1930s, Indian women tried to reassert themselves through the formation of associations. The most famous was the Stri Sewa Sabha (women's empowerment group) in 1934, which exists till today. Other well-known groups were Women's Rights Movement and Women's Crisis Centre. Their agenda included education, advocacy and ending violence against women. In

---

[228] Naidu, V., *The Violence of Indenture in Fiji*, World University Service, 1980.
[229] Kelly, J., 'Jaikumari', *Bittersweet*, Lal, Brij V. (ed.), Pandanus Books, Canberra, 2004.

rural areas, women organized into women's groups called mahila mandals, which tried to nurture social, cultural and religious rituals and norms to be passed down the generations.

It is unfortunate that the role of women in organized resistance was soon forgotten, even by the male indentured. The colonial administration erased their contribution from public record and memory. The post-indentured Indian community remained unaware of their contribution till the late 1970s. Imagined realities, depicting women as weak, backward and docile, influenced the dominant narrative. The voiceless were once again silenced.

Public awareness became possible only when these women's stories were narrated on the radio documentary *Girmit Gatha* (stories of indenture). It was part of the commemoration of Fiji's centenary of Indian indenture. First broadcast in 1979 on Radio Fiji 2, the only Hindi radio station in Fiji at the time, the personalized accounts in the show illuminate the indomitable spirit of these women.[230]

The first narration was by Guldhari Maharaj, who reached Fiji on 23 May 1893 on the ship *Jumna II* with her indentured parents. Guldhari narrated her mother's ordeal from her childlike perspective.

> The women went to the field. Sometimes they returned early; sometimes it would be nightfall. When they had to cut sugarcane, it would be nine o'clock at night when they returned. [...] The long hours and hard tasks, in turn, contributed to the women's exhaustion: Then again, at only three o'clock in the morning, the bell would sound. Then again, the women would get up and run.[231]

---

[230]Gounder, F., *Indentured Identities: Resistance and Accommodation in Plantation-Era Fiji*, John Benjamins Publishing, Netherlands, 2011.
[231]Ibid.

She also spoke of acute food shortages for the working women: 'My mother would keep aside some of the food she had made for dinner the previous evening[…]the women used to take the stale food for their lunch. Sometimes they would eat it; sometimes the food would spoil because of the heat. They would throw it away, and they would go hungry.'[232]

The women were frequently cheated of their wages: 'When Saturday came, payday, some received two shillings, some ten pence, some three shillings. The plantation authorities said, "You didn't complete your full task…." Even the wages they would take away.'[233] There was also coercion, violence and use of force: 'If there was any delay, the Sahib and sirdar would come, carrying the whip. They would growl, "'Get out quickly; you need to work." Then unfurling the whip, they used to hit. In fright of this, the women would begin to run.'[234]

There were many communal songs such as '*Baitha Baitha Hukmam Chalay Rey Bidesia*' and '*Gannay Ki Hari Hari Patiyan*' about the inhuman exploitation of women, which became popular and helped mobilize resistance. Some of these songs are aired on Radio Fiji even today.

Bipat Jhiniki ki suunay ko dayia
Sahiba hai bara pittaya
Hai apna sadar chuggal khore
Vayrun hai Ramdayia

(There is nobody to hear the troubles of Jhinki
The boss is a great beater
Ram dayia is my enemy
And Sardar is a backbiter.)[235]

---

[232]Ibid.
[233]Ibid.
[234]Ibid.
[235]Kanwal, J.S., 'Poem of Indenture Period', *The Fiji Times,* 16 May 2016,

It is tragic that social prejudices and a warped male narrative, fashioned from a deeply conservative, parochial and male-dominated Indian society, regardless of religion, led to society questioning the social origins of the indentured women. It was based on a conviction about the so-called 'immoral' character of the Indian indentured women, mainly Hindus. Chandra Jayawardena noted that it prompted many to regard their marriages in Fiji as a temporary convenience they could disown when they returned to India.[236]

The fact that many women came to the country as family members was conveniently ignored. In the case of Fiji, 70 per cent of women migrated as individuals, but the remaining 30 per cent migrated as members of families. The majority, 70 per cent of the women, were accompanied by their husbands only, 15 per cent by their husbands and children and 12 per cent by their children only.

Why the exclusive focus on Hindu women?[237] Even C.F. Andrews was convinced that the problem lay only with Hindu women whom he defined as follows:

> The Hindu woman in this country is like a rudderless vessel with its masts broken being whirled down the rapids of a great river without any controlling hand. She passes from one man to another, and has lost even the sense of shame in doing so.[238]

No comments were made about indentured Muslim women by either the colonial officials or external commentators. One could

---

https://tinyurl.com/ssc9t6n5. Accessed on 17 August 2023.

[236] Jayawardena, C., 'Social Contours of an Indian Labour Force during the Indenture Period in Fiji', *Rama's Banishment*, V. Mishra (ed.), Heinemann, 1979, p. 50.

[237] Lal, Brij V., 'Kunti's Cry: Indentured Indian Women on Fiji Plantations', *Indian Economic and Social History Review*, Vol. 22, No. 1, pp. 55–71.

[238] Andrews, C.F., *Indian Indentured Labour in Fiji*, Colortype Press, Perth, 1918; Naidu, V., *The Violence of Indenture in Fiji*, World University Service, 1980, pp. 38–9.

legitimately ask if there was an absence of Muslim women among the indentured in Fiji?

Or, alas, was there another reason for the silence? In fact, statistics demonstate the contrary. Indentured women came from every level of society. Their caste composition and religion were varied: 4.1 per cent were Brahmins, 9 per cent were Kshatriyas, 34.1 per cent were mid-level castes, 29.1 per cent were lower castes, 2.8 per cent were from tribal communities and 16.8 per cent were Muslims.[239]

More troubling was the coupling of charges of prostitution only with indentured Hindu women. According to available records, most of the indentured women were unaccompanied. The repeated insinuation that Hindu prostitute women were seeking a safe and new family life in the plantation colonies needs to be re-examined. Such assumptions ignore the economic hardships in colonial India, which forced many women to seek employment elsewhere. Brothels were emptied out in Calcutta by recruiters seeking to satisfy the mandatory 40:100 sex ratio. Prostitution was also rampant because of the imbalanced gender distribution in the plantations.

This bias was common across the plantations, from Mauritius to the Caribbean and Fiji. The Trinidad Emigration Agent noted: 'Of single women, those only will be found to emigrate who have lost their caste, by which all ties of relationships and home are severed, and, having neither religion nor education to restrain them, have fallen into the depths of degradation and vice.'[240]

Denigration of indentured women also distracts from their disproportionate social and economic burden. They worked at

---

[239]Lal, Brij V., *Leaves of the Banyan Tree: Origins and Background of Fiji's North Indian Migrants, 1879 -1916: Vol. 1*, 1981. The Australian National University, PhD thesis, pp. 198–216.

[240]A. Montgomery, Letter to Colonial Secretary, 8 January 1914, Minute Paper M.P. 8779/13, p. 98.

home and on the plantations while bringing up children. At the same time, they were ridiculed and insulted as being immoral. There also was no hard evidence that these women were mainly prostitutes. One cannot accept the assertion of C.F. Andrews that 20 per cent of the women were of 'bad character'.[241]

What is more disturbing is the total absence of an indentured woman's perspective in these narratives. There is a need to shape these women's story from available oral and written evidence. One cannot abandon them to the eternal indignity of being labelled women of dishonour.

Indentured Women in Mauritius

> *You may write me down in history*
> *With your bitter, twisted lies,*
> *You may trod me in the very dirt*
> *But still, like dust, I'll rise.*

—'Still I Rise', Maya Angelou

Women were central to the seamless assimilation of Indian indentured into the rainbow nation called Mauritius. Yet, their journey, their sterling contribution and their sacrifices for a long time lacked a sympathetic narration.

When slavery was abolished, liberated women slaves found remunerative employment as domestic labour at the same rate as Indian indentured men.[242] Indian women, who were not bound by a contract, like men, had to depend on the men folk for survival. For this reason, even Marina Carter described these

---

[241] Andrews, C.F., *Indian Indentured Labour in Fiji,* Colortype Press, Perth, 1918, p. 31.
[242] Carter, Marina, and James Ng Foong Kwong, *Forging the Rainbow: Labour Immigrants in British Mauritius,* Alfran Co., 1997.

Indian women as 'slaves, servants and spouses'.[243]

Patriarchy prevailed and was brilliantly exposed by Carter who penned *Lakshmi's Legacy*, dedicated to these women and their struggle for social and economic equality.[244] Carter's book, with touching testimonies, demonstrates that despite efforts by the plantation owners to impose a new form of slavery, these women assumed roles significantly different from their slave predecessors. Through their letters, petitions and statements, a cogent analysis can be made of their role in developing identity and maintaining cultural linkages with their pasts.

Earlier, Tinker's view of these women resembling a 'sorry sisterhood of single, broken creatures' was widely shared by other scholars.[245] Feminist writers have pointed out that indentured women were portrayed as poor, illiterate and ignorant, closely resembling the 'average Third World woman' of Western feminists writings.[246] This resulted in a negative, male-dominated narrative. Women were held accountable for an alarming rise in cases of polyandry, marital violence, murders, sexual abuse, prostitution and sexually transmitted diseases.

Revisionist and feminist historians have rejected the portrayal of these women as immoral and mercenary, moving seamlessly from one relationship to another. This stereotype was strongly influenced by the misogynistic mindset of European male officials of the time.

---

[243]Carter, Marina, 'Slaves, Servants & Spouses: Indian Women in Mauritian History', *Aapravasi Ghat Trust Fund Magazine*, 2017, pp. 2, 36–37.

[244]Carter, Marina, *Lakshmi's Legacy: The Testimonies of Indian Women in 19th Century Mauritius*, Edition l'Ocean Indien, Rose Hill, Mauritius, 1994, p. 142.

[245]Tinker, Hugh, *A New System of Slavery: The Export of Indian Labour Overseas 1830–1920*, Hansib, London, 1993; Kelly, J.D., *A Politics of Virtue: Hinduism, Sexuality and Countercolonial Discourse in Fiji*, University of Chicago Press, Chicago, 1991.

[246]Talpade, M.C., *Feminism without Borders: Decolonizing Theory, Practicing Solidarity*, Duke University Press, 2003.

It was unfortunate that British Indian officials regarded single indentured women as immoral, and by inference, as prostitutes. As stated by the Protector of Emigrants at Madras: 'As to the so-called single women, many of them are prostitutes, others are kept women, and the remainder after entering the depot in almost every case attach themselves to some man they meet there.'[247] A similar warning was given by the Protector of Emigrants at Calcutta: 'The object of encouraging female emigration is the promotion of colonization; for this purpose the exportation of any but virtuous women is essentially a mistake.'[248]

The acute paucity of women necessitated marriages across social barriers and sometimes across religious boundaries. This impacted deep-rooted conservative patriarchal ties. Families clung to their links with their past, culture, language and religion. Even in remote areas, the fundamental texts of Hinduism, especially the Valmiki Ramayana, was ever present and carried by the indentured wherever they went. The Muslims carried their family Quran. It ensured the preservation of these links with Mother India, along with the celebration of traditional festivals, be it Holi for the Hindus or Muharram for the Muslims. It ensured a near complete preservation of Indian culture.

The sea voyage was a great ordeal, particularly for single women. The easy presumption that single women recruits were usually widows or prostitutes is not supported by statistical evidence. It seems most unlikely that large numbers of women prostitutes had immigrated to Mauritius. Available evidence sourced from immigration registers indicate that the larger proportion of women were not single but travelling in family

---

[247]IPP 434/2 PE, Letter to Chief Secy, Madras, October 1869; BYGP 348/57 Secy. Govt. Bombay, Letter to Medical Board, 11 May 1843; CO 167/339 Higginson, Letter to Pakington, 3 December 1852, mins. Taylor, Elliot; BEP vol. 170 EA, Letter to PE, Madras, 14 October 1869.
[248]BEP 15/83 PE Calcutta to Geoghegan, 28th November 1865.

groups. Moreover, single women were not necessarily prostitutes. Many had come to rejoin male family members in Mauritius.

Of greater concern was the extreme vulnerability of single women travellers to the unwanted sexual attentions of men onboard the ship, including crew members. In the *Woodcock Report*, it was noted that any young single Indian woman on the ship *Drongan* to Mauritius in 1836 'was claimed before we had been at sea three days as the property of three persons'.[249]

In the event of these unfortunate women contracting any disease, usually cholera, they were mercilessly thrown overboard. In case the ship was nearing Mauritius, they could be thrown into the awaiting ocean before death claimed them. In that event, their orphaned children would be looked after by the remaining jahaji bhais and jahaji behens. Many other women died after arrival in quarantine, at the depot or at the hospital. Those who survived were unaware that their real challenge lay ahead—to confront their harsh exploitation at the hands of nineteenth century plantation owners.

Initially, the female indentured were married and came to join their husbands. In the 1840s, married females accounted for around 60–80 per cent of the new arrivals.[250] The remaining women were single. Their compulsions for moving to Mauritius were varied and ranged from extreme poverty to difficult family environment or broken marriages. Some were forced into prostitution and opted for indenture, there being no other option at that time, except suicide. The latter option was exercised out of desperation even in Mauritius.

The single women would wait at the depot for a suitable match in view of the many unmarried Indian male indentured on the island. These were termed 'depot marriages'. Marriage on

---

[249]'PP 1837-8 (180)', *Woodcock Report*, p. 121.
[250]Carter, Marina, and James Ng Foong Kwong, *Forging the Rainbow: Labour Immigrants in British Mauritius*, Alfran Co., 1997.

arrival in Mauritius was defined as 'marriage migration'. Invariably, women hoped for spouses from similar castes and the same region of origin.

Single women were looked upon with suspicion and usually offered domestic work rather than work in the plantations. Unfortunately, many women were victims of trafficking by unscrupulous returnees or agents who would marry them to one or several men simultaneously. Of greater concern was the gradual infiltration of an informal dowry system by Mauritian Indians who would pay the bride's family for a wife. This encouraged the abusive treatment of daughters by their fathers and later, of wives by their husbands, sometimes leading to murder. The wife was invariably regarded as chattel.

In one instance, the accused named Virapatrin noted that he had purchased his wife named Thelamey for a substantial amount, part of which had been borrowed.[251] He accused Thelamey of adultery and believed her to be deserving of death. In such marriages, wives had no rights, including of remarriage after the death of the spouse. She would forever remain the inalienable property of her spouse. In such situations, many women opted for suicide as salvation. These included single destitute women as well as widows with no means of sustenance.

To encourage the recruitment of more women, returnees petitioned the colonial government to allow them to return with their families. To consolidate and increase the Indian indentured, several laws were enacted to allow family reunions. These included provision of free passages for wives and children of male indentured and the payment of a bonus by the colonial authorities to recruiters bringing married couples or spouses of male indentured. The number of female arrivals went up from 49 in 1842 to 4,380 in 1843.[252]

---

[251]Gomm, Letter to Grey, 11 June 1847, Colonial Office Series CO 167/283, (129).
[252]Carter, Marina, Lakshmi's Legacy: *The Testimonies of Indian Women in 19th*

In addition, women migrants were exempted from signing formal indenture agreements. It was argued that 'they were primarily valued for their role in fostering the permanent settlement of the community in Mauritius, as reproducers of labour power force rather than as labourers per se'.[253] The then Governor of Mauritius Sir James Macaulay Higginson even suggested the 'creation of resident labour population' considered 'indispensable to permanent security'.[254]

Despite these measures, women remained a tiny minority of the total Indian indentured population. According to the 1859 *Immigration Report*, between 1834 and 1852, about 1,014 women arrived, 244 returned to India, and 210 died in Mauritius. The report also documented the slow trickle of female arrivals.[255]

A powerful disincentive to increased women's recruitment was the harsh and invasive medical examination they were subjected to against their wishes by European doctors and emigration officials. In 1847, the Protector of Emigrants at Mauritius cautioned against subjecting women 'to so close an examination of their persons for the purpose of requesting their bodily marks [...] it is evident [...] that they are even stripped of their clothes'.[256] Media reports regarding such practices outraged public opinion in India and the practice was discontinued.

Plantation owners remained notoriously reluctant to encourage female indenture or spouses of male indenture to be brought to Mauritius. The returnee recruiters were aware of their instructions

---

Century Mauritius, Edition l'Ocean Indien, Rose Hill, Mauritius, 1994.

[253]Carter, Marina, 'Slaves, Servants & Spouses: Indian Women in Mauritian History', *Aapravasi Ghat Trust Fund Magazine,* 2017, pp. 2, 36–37.

[254]Hazareesingh, K., 'The Religion and Culture of Indian Immigrants in Mauritius and the Effect of Social Change', *Comparative Studies in Society and History,* Vol. 8, No. 2, Cambridge University Press, 1966, pp. 241–57

[255]Pineo, H., *Lured Away: The Life History of Indian Cane Workers in Mauritius,* Mahatma Gandhi Institute Press, 1984.

[256]PL 32 PI, Letter to Col Secy, 16 September 1847, Mauritius Archives PL Series.

as well as the emigration agents at Calcutta and Madras. It has been documented that an Indian planter based in Mauritius, Tiroumoudy, recommended that spouses of the indentured be brought to Mauritius. The Emigration Agent responded in the negative, stating: '[The] returned men all of whom when asked their reason for taking no women invariably replied that their Mauritian masters have forbidden them to bring any, saying their masters require men for their cultivation, not women'.[257]

By 1857, this attitude became known to the Protector of Emigrants at Mauritius and to the Mauritian colonial government. It was decided that further measures would be required to encourage female recruitment. Between 1842 and 1860, the recruiters were paid a lump sum if the proportion of male to female recruits was respected. The proportion was fixed as 40 women to every 100 men immigrants.

This practice was abolished in 1866, since the Protector in Mauritius complained that the sirdars and returnees had manipulated the system to maximize the cash remuneration by bringing back 'two and sometimes three wives'.[258] In some cases, women used to be sold on arrival at Mauritius. This has been documented in the case of a cook named Buskeet who used to work on ships carrying indentured labour as well as women 'whom he sold'.[259]

To encourage female recruitment as well as to establish the conventional family unit, the colonial government had, in the late 1850s, enacted the Indian Marriage Ordinance. Marriages solemnized in India required a marriage certificate issued by the civil registration office in Mauritius. Single women were

---

[257]RA 1129 EA Calcutta, Letter to Col Secy, 31 March 1851, Mauritius Archives RA Series.
[258]PB 6 PI memo, Mauritius Archives PB Series, 7 June 1856; ARI, 1862, 1866.
[259]PA 70 Statements of Jacquin, Buskeet and Boodhoo, Mauritius Archives PA Series, 17 March 1885.

encouraged to marry at the depot post disembarkation. This was followed by the official recognition of religious weddings in Ordinance 3 of 1856.[260]

Feminist historians regard the imposition of legally recognized arranged marriages on newly arrived Indian women as a policy to ensure their continuing subordination in a male-dominated society. If these women had hoped for greater social and economic autonomy in the new society of Mauritius, this was sadly not to be. Through a coalition of conservative male interests, European and Indian, the objective was an 'effective re-institution of patriarchal authority', since 'the state and employers were primarily concerned with securing men's right over the women they formed partnerships with'.[261]

Indentured women in Mauritius were unequally integrated into capitalist production and into the plantation economy in particular. This was in contrast to the central participation of female slaves in plantation agriculture in the pre-Abolition period. As a result, their transition to being a recognized part of the workforce was even more difficult.

Women were harshly treated by plantation owners and managers who tried to restrict their social independence and vilified them for what they characterized as their loose personal relationships. They were regarded as necessary appendages to men, without any notion of equality. Despite these challenges, women were able to keep their families together. They faced great odds but succeeded in the end.

The transition from mere spouses and family helpers to plantation workers was slow. As unpaid householders, women were responsible for carrying water, collecting firewood and

---

[260] Pineo, H., *Lured Away: The Life History of Indian Cane Workers in Mauritius*, Mahatma Gandhi Institute Press, 1984

[261] Carter, Marina, *Lakshmi's Legacy: The Testimonies of Indian Women in 19th Century Mauritius*, Edition l'Ocean Indien, Rose Hill, Mauritius, 1994.

feeding animals by transporting grass from forest land. This was testified in 1846 by the local stipendiary magistrate who noted that women were 'extremely useful in the preparation of food and carrying it to the men when they work at a distance from the camp and many other ways to the comfort of the coolies'.[262]

Figure 18: Waiting for the men folk to return

Source: 'File: Coolie woman.jpg', *Wikipedia*, https://tinyurl.com/2wzvkzrb. Accessed on 2 August 2023.

Initially, in the 1830s, women were recruited as nannies and for domestic labour, including cleaning of toilets. Their employers used to deal with them like slaves. This caused friction and

[262]Ibid.

resentment because the women were not used to this form of labour. Bibee Juhooram, a female indentured, testified: 'I was made to sweep the rooms and do the methranee's (sweeper) work and I complained to the police.'[263]

Later, women joined as regular plantation workers along with their spouses. The monthly remuneration for cutting sugarcane was ₹4. Much later, they became supervisors and overseers and were called 'sardarines'.[264] It took many more years before some select women became returnee recruiters.

Many women acquired assets from their earnings, became owners of property and wisely invested their capital. They demonstrated 'entrepreneurial skills which are a striking testimony to the strength and courage of their gender in the face of much personal and statutory discrimination'.[265] They became fully empowered and participated, along with men, in the evolution of modern Mauritius.

The evolving role of women as householders, breadwinners and carriers of culture, religion and heritage resulted in the development of Indian settlements, called Indian villages, in Mauritius. This was encouraged by the British colonial government. As Secretary of State for War and the Colonies in 1846, Lord Henry Grey requested the then Governor of Mauritius, Sir William Maynard Gomm, to pass enabling legislation in this regard.[266] It was not an easy process, given the negative attitude of plantation managers towards such women. The gradual evolution

---

[263] Pande, Amba (ed.), *Indentured and Post-Indentured Experiences of Women in the Indian Diaspora*, Springer, Singapore, 2020, p. 128.

[264] Pineo, H., *Lured Away: The Life History of Indian Cane Workers in Mauritius*, Mahatma Gandhi Institute Press, 1984.

[265] Carter, Marina, *Lakshmi's Legacy: The Testimonies of Indian Women in 19th Century Mauritius*, Edition l'Ocean Indien, Rose Hill, Mauritius, 1994.

[266] Hazareesingh, K., 'The Religion and Culture of Indian Immigrants in Mauritius and the Effect of Social Change', *Comparative Studies in Society and History*, Vol. 8, No. 2, Cambridge University Press, 1966, pp. 241–57.

of an Indian family-like existence helped foster resistance among the indentured to plantation owners and the determination to safeguard their culture.

Following the Grand Morcellement (the sub-division of large plantations into small plots for sale) in the late 1870s, when sugar prices had crashed globally, Indian indentured gradually became landowners. Accompanied by the setting up of schools for the children of the indentured and the availability of loan facilities to acquire property, villages of Indian settlers became a familiar feature. They subsequently became citizens of Mauritius. The wheel had turned full circle.

The positive role of women in this absorption into the rainbow culture of Mauritius cannot be overestimated. As correctly noted, it was 'easier for the immigrants to save money when accompanied by their wives and to retain their customs, language and religion'.[267] As a result and encouraged by their spouses, the new Mauritian citizens generously donated money and land to build temples. Available records document the efforts of Doya Kishto, along with spouse Songor, to build a Tamil temple while Gokoola, Dabeedin Reetoo, Dookhee Gungah and Ramtohul donated money for building temples, cremation grounds and establishing publishing houses for Hindi publications.[268]

As village life prospered with the support of womenfolk, the emergence of village councils resembling the Indian Panchayati system, for governance at grassroot level, facilitated locally administered law enforcement. Women ensured the building of community centres that helped preserve and disseminate religion and culture for future generations. This included teachings from the Ramayana and Hindi language lessons for children. Women

---

[267] Pineo, H., *Lured Away: The Life History of Indian Cane Workers in Mauritius*, Mahatma Gandhi Institute Press, 1984.
[268] Sooriamoorthy, R., *Les Tamouls a L'Ile Maurice*, Port Louis, Henry and Cie., Mauritius, 1977.

have rightly been identified 'as the transmitters of cultural traditions, customs, songs, cuisine and [...] mother tongue.' As their roles evolved, women became the 'carriers of culture and preservers of identity'.[269]

It is remarkable that traditional Bhojpuri folk culture such as *saadi ke geet* (wedding songs), *lalna* or *sohar* (birth songs), *harparawri* (invoking the God of rain), *janeo* (wearing of the sacred thread), *Gopal gaari* (teasing song) and *jantasar* (songs of the grinding stone), all sung exclusively by women, are preserved in their entirety in modern Mauritius.[270] Unfortunately, the few male Bhojpuri traditions like *birha*, *sabadh* and *gamat* or *l'accroche* (encounter) are less well preserved and have virtually disappeared.

In 2016, the UNESCO Committee on Intangible Cultural Heritage of Humanity inscribed the *Geet-gawai* or Bhojpuri pre-marriage folk songs on the Representative List of Intangible Cultural Heritage of Humanity. This achievement testifies to the untiring efforts of Mauritian women to preserve Bhojpuri culture.

Carter underlined that these women contributed not just to the forging but also to the colouring of the rainbow nation of Mauritius. She noted that these Indian women 'made the journey across the kalapani to Mauritius, and became the forerunners of the present Indo-Mauritian population'.[271] This serves as a timely

---

[269]Mukherjee, Bhaswati, 'Journey of the Women of Indian Diaspora: Carriers of Culture, Preservers of Identity', *Ministry of External Affairs, Government of India*, 2015, https://tinyurl.com/4mn9x25j. Accessed on 17 August 2023.

[270]Boodhoo, S., *Kanya Dan: The Why's of Hindu Marriage Rituals?*, Mauritius Bhojpuri Institute, 1993; Mishra, K., *Morisasa ke Bhojpuri Lok Geeton Ka Vivechanatmak Adhyayana*, Second edition, Sanjay Book Centre, Varanasi, 1999; Ramdin, S., *Sanskar Manjari, Mauritius ke Bhojpuri Sanskar Geet*, Mahatma Gandhi Institute Press, 1989; and *Cultural and Linguistic Aspects of Bhojpuri in Mauritius with Special Reference to Jantsar Work Songs*, 2004, University of Mauritius, Doctoral thesis.

[271]Carter, Marina, *Lakshmi's Legacy: The Testimonies of Indian Women in 19th Century Mauritius*, Edition l'Ocean Indien, Rose Hill, Mauritius, 1994.

reminder of 'their rich and important contribution to the island's development'.²⁷²

The testimonies of women like Lakshmi and Bibee Juhooram demonstrate that Indian women 'never accepted the status of slaves and their litigiousness became proverbial'.²⁷³ Their struggle demonstrated their ability to trigger change and reject injustice. It is important to recognize and pay tribute to Indian women who pioneered change in Mauritius rather than stereotyping them as immoral prostitutes or loose women.

Modern Mauritius now pays tribute to their resilience, their determination to surmount all odds and to overcome. Recognition and liberation from the negative parochial narrative has finally come. Their souls are invincible:

> Out of the night that covers me,
> Black as the pit from pole to pole.
> I thank whatever gods may be,
> For my unconquerable soul.²⁷⁴

Finally, their human spirit prevailed and won. The rainbow nation was created not just by the jahaji bhais but also by these jahaji behens.

---

[272] Ibid.
[273] Ibid., 236.
[274] Henley, William Ernest, 'Invictus', *Poetry Foundation*, https://tinyurl.com/2p8w8r6e. Accessed on 17 August 2023.

9

INDIA RISES AGAINST INDENTURE: MAHATMA GANDHI AND A NEW DAWN

*The world outside existed in a kind of darkness;
And we enquired about nothing.*

—V.S. Naipaul

Many including those from within India have questioned why a system that so closely resembled slavery was not fiercely resisted by Indians immediately after the process of transportation of the so-called coolies commenced sometime in the mid-nineteenth century. It is to the credit of the abolitionists that their resistance to indenture initially helped mobilize public opinion within India.

Among the earliest Indians who clearly articulated India's increasing impoverishment at the hands of her colonizers, leading to desperate Indians seeking to leave the shores of India, was Dadabhai Naoroji (1825–1917). Affectionately called 'Grand Old Man of Indian Nationalism', Naoroji painstakingly calculated India's enormous burden in the form of continuing drain of gold and resources and the destruction of her nascent industries. He understood that indenture, a successor to slavery, was the natural corollary of imperialism. Nationalist leaders following him, including Madan Mohan Malaviya and Gandhi, were continuously engaged with the critical conditions of the indentured, resulting in a powerful stimulus, through the Indian national movement, for the eventual abolition of indenture.

Among Western critics who perceived that, in many respects, indenture resembled a form of slavery were the activists who founded the Anti-Slavery Society in the UK[275]. Joseph Sturge was instrumental in its foundation while John Harfield Tredgold became the first secretary of the organization. George William Alexander acted as the first treasurer along with the Anglican Thomas Fowell Buxton, the Quaker William Allen and the Congregationalist Josiah Conder who were prominent members of the society. They termed indenture as 'a new system of slavery'.[276]

Due to sustained pressure from the government of the day in Whitehall, their opposition started declining around 1870. By that time, indenture had become entrenched as part of British colonial policies. Nevertheless, critics of indenture remained. Located in influential positions within the Empire, they played an important role in swinging domestic opinion within Britain.[277]

So effective was the colonial propaganda of the time of hailing indenture as the panacea to poverty and unemployment that the burgeoning national movement and its leaders like Mahadev Govind Ranade and Surendranath Banerjee were taken in and initially welcomed it. Many of these leaders were bhadralok (so-

---

[275] The Anti-Slavery Society was an abolitionist society founded in London in 1823. It functioned till 1838 before being succeeded by the British and Foreign Anti-Slavery Society in 1839.
[276] Barrett, William Garland, *Immigration to the British West Indies: Is it the Slave-Trade Revived or Not?*, Gray and Warren, London, 1859; Beaumont, Joseph, *The New Slavery: An Account of the Indian and Chinese Emigrants in British Guiana*, W. Ridgway, London, 1871; Jenkin, Edward, *The Coolie: His Rights and Wrongs*, George Routledge and Sons, New York, 1871; Scoble, John, *British Guiana: Facts! Facts! Facts!, 28th February*, Johnson & Barrett Printers, London, 1840.
[277] *The Modern Review* regularly featured articles and editorials critiquing the system between 1913 and 1917.

called gentry) who sought to project British rule as benign. In an article written on 6 February 1892 in *The Bengali*, Banerjee opined that indentured emigration represented a form of migration with great potential for future economic development.[278] The bhadraloks were late converts to Indian nationalism!

Figure 19: The commemoration of India's lost children who left Calcutta Ghat for unknown shores forever

Source: 'File:Baba and Mai, Suriname Ghat,Kolkata.jpeg', *Wikimedia Commons*, https://tinyurl.com/mrym9neh. Accessed on 21 August 2023.

These naïve and early views rapidly changed with the rise of the social and religious reform movements that profoundly impacted the fate of British colonialism. The rise of the Arya Samaj[279], based in Uttar Pradesh and Bihar, was very effective in developing a

---

[278] Ray, Karen A., *The Abolition of Indentured Emigration and the Politics of Indian Nationalism, 1894-1917*, 1981, McGill University, unpublished PhD thesis.
[279] Arya Samaj, a Hindu reformist organization, was of the view that the indenture system was an evil and was diminishing the cultural and moral values of Hinduism. Their leaders were sent to the different colonies to establish branches and schools to disseminate the essentials of Hinduism.

propaganda campaign including through popular folklore, poetry and songs against indenture. This was timely, since it was in the United Provinces of Agra and Oudh and the east that the poor and marginalized were being targeted by unscrupulous agents. In Bihar, the Arya Samaj distributed pamphlets and campaigned against indentured emigration in the districts of Patna, Muzaffarpur and Darbhanga.[280] The movement was led by the fiery Swami Satyadev who was very effective in propagating the anti-indenture campaign in Muzaffarpur and Darbhanga.

The Arya Samaj found, among others, an effective leader in Purushottam Das in Muzaffarpur. His pamphlets conveyed a clear warning against the recruiters, which had a huge public impact. One of his pamphlets has been translated below:

> Escape from deceivers.
> Escape from the depot people
> Beware! beware! beware!
> Don't fall in to their snare. They will ruin you.[281]

As a counter to early bhadralok approval of indenture, the influential and prosperous Marwari community of Calcutta also started an anti-indenture campaign. The Marwaris required the cheap labour that was being shipped to other colonies.[282]

---

[280]Government of India (GoI) C&I, Emigration, A Progs Nos. 43, December 1915, National Archives of India, New Delhi; E.L.L. Hammod, Secretary Government of Bengal (GoB) and Orissa, Municipal Department, Letter to Secretary GoI, C&I, Emigration, 7 June 1915, Ranchi.

[281]Kumar, Ashutosh, 'Anti-Indenture Bhojpuri Folk Songs and Poems from North India', *Man in India* Vol. 93, No. 4, 2013, pp. 509-19.

[282]Marwari is a Vaishya or trader caste originally belonging to the Marwar region of Rajasthan. In Calcutta, after 1897, they emerged as the wealthiest and most successful business and industrial communities widely known by a homogenous category Marwari. They ran the mills of Calcutta. They were seeking cheap and plentiful labour. Indenture created problems in obtaining cheap and reliable labour force for their, ills. See: Banārasīdāsa, *Ardhakathanak*, Rohini Chowdhury (trans), Penguin Books, 2009.

In Calcutta and its adjoining areas, the Marwaris established the Marwari Sahayak Samiti. Their association was named the Indentured Cooly Protection Society or Anti-Indentured Emigration League and had its office at 160, Harrison Road (Sutta Patti), Calcutta.[283]

Bhojpuri poet Babu Raghubir Narayan contributed to popular folklore and poetry. He composed a *purbi*, a Bhojpuri song that metaphorically portrayed the loneliness of indentured Indians who longed to return home. His song titled 'Batohiya' was heart wrenching. As translated by Ashutosh Kumar in 'Anti-Indenture Bhojpuri Folk Songs and Poems from North India', it reads:

> Beautiful good land brother India its country is,
> Want to go O traveller to see Hindustan,
> [...]
> Scented air breeze slowly from the sky,
> My Hindustan is essence of world O traveller.[284]

These efforts were supplemented well before the First World War by institutionalized resistance organized through anti-indenture associations in the major cities like Calcutta, Madras and Allahabad. Through pamphlets, songs and theatre as well as societies, like Arya Samaj, and public meetings, the message was disseminated that indenture was an evil and akin to slavery.

In 1914, one Hindi pamphlet available in the English records and signed by a campaigner by the pseudonym Satyadeva of Allahabad ominously warned: 'Save yourself from the Depot Wallas.

---

[283]James Donald, Secretary to the Government of Bengal (GoB) Financial Department, Letter to the Secretary to Government of India (GoI), C&I, Emigration, 14 October 1915, Letter No. 322, Darjeeling.

[284]Sahay, Raghubir Narayan, 'Raghuvir Patra-Pushpa', in Sri Durga Prasad Singh, *Bhojpuri Ke Kavi aur Kabya*, Bihar Rashtra Bhasha Parishad, Patna, 2001, pp. 216–17; see also 'Gramophone Recordings from the Linguistic Survey of India', South Asia Digital Library, https://tinyurl.com/mttehsxm. Accessed on 24 August 2023.

Be careful!!! Be careful!!! Be careful!!! It is not a service but pure deception. Don't get enmeshed in their meshes, you will repent. They take you overseas!!! [...] They are not Colonies but Jails.'[285]

By this time, resistance was being mobilized by leaders of the Indian national movement representing different political ideologies. They included moderates like Gopal Krishna Gokhale, Pandit Madan Mohan Malaviya, and Indian Member of the British Parliament Sir Mancherjee Bhownugree. A special mention must be made of Gandhi's English associate, the Anglican priest C.F. Andrews, a lecturer in St. Stephen's College, Delhi, who denounced the immoral and unethical aspects of indenture as totally unbefitting the British Empire.[286]

On 9 January 1915, Gandhi returned to India after an absence of 25 years. Shortly thereafter, on 19 February 1915, Gokhale died, leaving a vacuum in the Indian national movement. The First World War was raging and British ships were being targeted by German submarines on the high seas. The outward flow of indenture declined rapidly.

---

[285]BNA Colonial Office Series CO 323/646 (1914), 100–107, here in 107. This pamphlet appears only in the English translation in the records. See also the discussion of the resonance between indenture and convict transportation for Indian villagers: Anderson, Clare, 'Convicts and Coolies: Rethinking Indentured Labour in the Nineteenth Century', *Slavery & Abolition*, Vol. 30, No. 9, 2009, https://tinyurl.com/3mnw8ruu. Accessed on 17 August 2023.

[286]Tinker, Hugh, *A New System of Slavery: The Export of Indian Labour Overseas 1830–1920*, Hansib, London, 1993, pp. 288–366.

Gokhale moved a resolution calling for the abolition of the system in the Indian Legislative Council on 4 March, 1912. See: Gokhale, Gopal Krishna, *Speeches of Gopal Krishna Gokhale*, G.A. Natesan and Co., Madras, 1916, pp. 616–43.

Malaviya moved a similar resolution in the Imperial Legislative Council on 20 March, 1916. See: Malaviya, Madan Mohan, *Speeches and Writings of Pandit Madan Mohan Malaviya*, G.A. Natesan and Co., Madras, pp. 323–47.

Gandhi, in addition to regular journalistic writings on the subject, also discussed it at length in *Satyagraha in South Africa*. See: M. K. Gandhi, M.K., *Satyagraha in South Africa*, Jitendra T. Desai Navajivan Publishing House, 1968.

Several organizations established to fight indenture including Indian Coolie Protection Society (Anti-Indentured Immigration League) of Bengal had become very active. C.F. Andrews had become a vociferous crusader to abolish indenture. In his interactions and writings, C.F. Andrews gave vivid descriptions of the exploitation of the Indian indentured, their fear and desperation, the disproportionate and harsh punishments, the confinement within the estate and the alarming and rising suicide rates. He was convinced that single indentured women were being forced into prostitution. C.F. Andrews concluded that indenture was a system akin to slavery and that the indentured were treated no better than cattle. The words of C.F. Andrews carried weight. Being English, the Viceroy and Whitehall were forced to listen to him.

The toxicity of the debate ultimately forced a response from the British Indian Government. It is to the credit of Lord Hardinge (Viceroy, 1910-1916) that after consultations and reflection, he soberly noted that indenture was an evil that needed to be abolished. In an extensive memorandum titled 'Memorandum by H.E. the Viceroy upon questions likely to arise in India at the end of the war', Lord Hardinge gave a detailed review of indenture. He concluded:

> I venture to urge very strongly upon His Majesty's Government the total abolition of the system of indentured labour in the four remaining British colonies and Surinam ... and thus to remove as racial stigma that India deeply resents and which reflects upon His Majesty's Government and the Government of India in the sanction granted by them to a system of forced labour differing but little from a form of slavery.[287]

---

[287] Tinker, Hugh, *A New System of Slavery: The Export of Indian Labour Overseas 1830-1920*, Hansib, London, 1993, p. 339.

The moot issue here was the belated recognition by the British of the evils of indenture had so aroused public opinion in India, especially the conviction that single Indian women were being forced into prostitution, that it was galvanizing the national movement and could hasten the departure of the British from India. The dispatch—signed by Hardinge and sent to London on 15 October 1915— after describing in detail the evils of indenture, concluded by stating that while a substitute for indenture may be difficult, 'it is not the duty of the Government of India to provide coolies for the colonies'.[288]

As expected, Hardinge's dispatch was not welcomed by Whitehall. It was decided to inform the Viceroy that indenture could not be abolished until an acceptable substitute had been found by the colonial government. In effect, the intention was to delay the abolition indefinitely.

Delaying tactics could hardly succeed in the charged political atmosphere in India. Hardinge's dispatch was followed by the launch of Gandhi's campaign against indenture, commencing with a speech in Bombay on 28 October 1915. Gandhi insisted that indenture should be abolished within a year and repeated the demand in his articles and speeches as well as at the annual session of the INC at the end of December 1915. In a well-articulated editorial in *The Leader*, an Allahabad-based newspaper on 25 February 1916, Gandhi questioned why the British had allowed indenture to continue for so long when it was based on racism and the notion of racial supremacy.

More damaging were reports coming from Fiji, published by C.F. Andrews and W.W. Pearson in *Indian Labour in Fiji:*

---

[288]The dispatch and the subsequent Whitehall responses (1915–1918) can be found in *Indentured Emigration from India-Discontinuance,* a file of the Judicial and Public Department of the India Office (J and P 4522: 1915). See: Tinker, Hugh, *A New System of Slavery: The Export of Indian Labour Overseas 1830–1920,* Hansib, London, 1993, p. 341.

An Independent Enquiry, dated 19 February 1916. This report underlined the appalling housing provided to the indentured in Fiji, the absence of medical facilities and the courage and patience of the indentured in the face of such challenges.

While there were different nuances in the messaging by different leaders, their concerns were similar. Gokhale and Gandhi highlighted the coercive and fraudulent aspects of the system and its racist and demeaning undertones in treating Indians as coolies. Malaviya also expressed concern at the lack of support in the system to safeguard and preserve the religion of the indentured.[289]

Figure 20: Pandit Madan Mohan Malaviya, seen here with Gandhi. The former contributed immensely to the abolition of indenture.
Source: Dinodia Photos/Contributor.

---

[289]Malaviya, Madan Mohan, *Speeches and Writings of Pandit Madan Mohan Malaviya*, G.A. Natesan and Co., Madras, pp. 330–31; Sturman, Rachel, 'Indian Indentured Labor and the History of International Rights Regimes', *The American Historical Review*, Vol. 119, No. 5, 2014, p. 1463.

Gokhale regretted the existing situation and said: 'Wherever the system exists, Indians are known as coolies, no matter what their position may be'. He added: 'India is currently the only country supplying indentured labour—why should India be marked out for this degradation?'[290] Gandhi said it reduced the status of Indians across the empire as the empire's 'hewers of wood and drawers of water'.[291]

The nature of the contract was also strongly criticized. A trained barrister, Gandhi noted that the penal sanctions in the contract for indentured Indians' refusal to work had been eliminated in the contracts for White labour. This was another instance of stark and overt racism. Gokhale, too, highlighted this point:

> First, what is the treatment of us, Indians, in this Empire? Secondly, what is the extent of the responsibility which lies with the Imperial Government to ensure to us just and humane and gradually even equal treatment in this Empire? And, thirdly, how far are the self-governing member s of this Empire such as South Africa] bound by its cardinal principles?[292]

Later leaders of the national movement were strongly influenced by persistent reports of abuse of indentured women and their reported rape and repeated violations of their dignity by colonial and Indian overseers. Deep concerns were expressed about the treatment of Indian women. Some of the comments reflected the deeply patriarchal nature of Indian society of the time.[293]

---

[290]Gokhale, Gopal Krishna, 'Indentured Labour, 4 March 1912', *Speeches of Gopal Krishna Gokhale,* G.A. Natesan and Co., Madras, 1916, pp. 628–34.
[291]'Mahatma Gandhi, His Life, Writings and Speeches/Indian Colonial Emigration', *WikiSource,* https://tinyurl.com/mr4dsput. Accessed on 25 August 2023.
[292]Gokhale, Gopal Krishna, 'Indentured Labour for Natal, 25 February 1910', *Speeches of Gopal Krishna Gokhale,* G.A. Natesan and Co., Madras, 1916, pp. 615.
[293]Niranjana, Tejaswini, 'Left to the Imagination: Indian Nationalisms and Female

On Gandhi's return in 1915, the Champaran Satyagraha in Champaran, Bihar[294,] initially helped swing public opinion against indenture. Gandhi brought new hope and a new dawn to the descendants of the indentured.

Figure 21: Champaran satyagraha: Gandhi's first strike against indenture
Source: 'File: Gandhiji and Sub-Inspector Qurban Ali in Champaran (1917).jpg', *Wikimedia Commons*, https://tinyurl.com/4r3jx82e. Accessed on 21 August 2023.

The report by Andrews–Pearson on Indian indenture in Fiji proved to be the last nail in the coffin of indenture.[295] A motion was moved by Malaviya on 20 March 1916 in the Imperial Legislative Council

---

Sexuality in Trinidad', *Public Culture*, Vol. 11, No. 1, 1999, pp. 223–43; Kelly, J.D., *A Politics of Virtue: Hinduism, Sexuality and Countercolonial Discourse in Fiji,* University of Chicago Press, Chicago, 1991.

[294]Champaran was the first mass protest after Gandhi's return to India in 1915. Organized in 1917, it was a farmer's uprising in Champaran district of Bihar, India. Satyagraha became a mass movement against British rule.

[295]Andrews, C.F. and W.W. Pearson, *Report on Indentured Labour in Fiji: An Independent Enquiry,* Star Printing Works, Calcutta, 1916.

in Delhi stating: 'That this Council recommends to the Governor-General in Council that early steps be taken for the abolition of the system of Indian indentured labour.' He concluded: 'My Lord, no reform will prove sufficient; tinkering will not do; the system must be abolished root and branch.'[296]

The motion was accepted by Viceroy Lord Hardinge who, unfortunately, was forced to add a reservation that would, in effect, maintain indenture until an acceptable substitute had been established. Hardinge also outlined several reforms that had also been initiated, including the abolition of imprisonment for indentured offenders in Fiji.

Demonstrating his true feelings, Hardinge concluded passionately:

> Why should the labourer have to journey thousands of miles over the 'black water' to settle in a strange country [...] when he can do as well in the jute mills of Bengal? The coolie himself does not stand to gain very much by emigration.[297]

In effect, this was Hardinge's last public statement as Viceroy. A few days later, on 4 April 1916, he departed from India. He reportedly treasured his efforts to abolish indenture as an important part of his legacy.

The engine that drove indenture may have slowed down but had not stopped running. The new Viceroy Lord Chelmsford (1916–1921), a cold and calculating man, neither shared the natural affinity with Indian leaders as his predecessor, nor was he willing to dialogue with C.F. Andrews who, from his perspective, was just an ordinary teacher in St. Stephen's College, Delhi.

---

[296]The motion to abolish indentured labour, called coolitude, was proposed by Madan Mohan Malaviya on 20 March 1916. It was defeated with assurances given by the British Indian Government that indenture would end once a suitable, alternative system was in place. It was finally halted in March 1917.

[297]Tinker, Hugh, *A New System of Slavery: The Export of Indian Labour Overseas 1830–1920*, Hansib, London, 1993.

Fortunately for India, the system was slowing down due to other challenges. There was little enthusiasm for recruitment. The British military, facing a humiliating defeat in Mesopotamia, had stepped up recruitment for the British Indian Army. On 24 December 1915, the Colonial Office instructed that army recruitment had the highest priority.

By January–February 1917, Gandhi had stepped up his resistance to indenture, accusing the government of betraying the agreement arrived through the Malaviya resolution of 20 March 1916. Gandhi highlighted the racist ideology behind indenture as well as the economic exploitation. Separately, C.F. Andrews denounced the moral evils of indenture, reminding his Indian and British audience that the system was a blot on British rule in India.

The year 1917 coincided with heightened German attacks on the British Navy in the high seas through submarines. On 15 February 1917, the Colonial Office suspended recruitment because of the threat to civilian transportation. In the meantime, on 12 July 1917, the British Parliament debated the debacle in Mesopotamia and censured the British Indian Government for its failures that had let down the British Indian Army. The Secretary of State, Austin Chamberlain, stepped down immediately on 13 July 1917. His successor, Edwin Montagu, who had piloted the censure resolution on Mesopotamia, became the new Secretary of State.

In one of his earliest dispatches to India, Secretary of State Montagu informed the British Indian Government that indentured emigration could not be resumed. There was an important caveat. It referred to a proposal to permanently settle the indentured with a land settlement scheme after three years of employment. The dispatch noted that since Dominions were closed to Indians, they could settle in the Crown Colonies. The report was officially released by the British Indian Government from Shimla, India, on

21 September 1917. It sought a response from the Indian side.[298]

Gandhi's response was available soon thereafter in the *Indian Review* on 1 October 1917. While he welcomed the end of indenture, he unreservedly rejected the offer of any process to permanently settle the indentured in the plantation colonies. In Gandhi's view, the proposal was a continuance of the system of indentured immigration rather than a full abolition. He concluded by noting: 'The system of indenture was one of temporary slavery; it was incapable of being amended and it is to be hoped that India will never consent to its revival in any shape or form.' Others were of the same view as Gandhi with Jinnah remarking: 'I should stifle it.'[299]

The plan was fiercely debated in London. While acceptable to the Anti-Slavery Society, it was rejected by the Indian Overseas Association, the successor body to the South Africa British Indians Committee. On their behalf, Henry Polak wrote a long rebuttal asserting that India 'was no longer content to be regarded as a Coolie country'. Polak was of the view that this form of emigration was involuntary, not free.[300]

In the last months of the First World War, at a meeting of the representatives of the Dominions and India in London in July 1918 at the Imperial War Conference, it was agreed:

> It is an inherent function of the Governments of the several communities of the British Commonwealth, including India, that each should enjoy complete control of the composition of its own population by means of restrictions on immigration from any of the other communities.[301]

---

[298] Ibid. 354–55.
[299] Ibid. 355–56.
[300] Ibid. 356.
[301] Ibid. 359.

India Rises Against Indenture: Mahatma Gandhi and a New Dawn 159

During the debate in the legislature on 11 September 1918, Malaviya once again moved the motion that all existing indenture be cancelled immediately. He was particularly concerned about Fiji. Indenture had almost come to an end. It was Malaviya's opposition that facilitated its total abolition. The system was finally brought to an end on 1 January 1920.

However, the story does not end there! The British Indian Government tried to put in place an emigration policy. On 20 January 1921, a year after the definitive abolition of indenture, a proposed bill was sent by the Viceroy to Secretary of State Montague for approval. The approval was conveyed on 11 March 1921.

No time was lost! The Indian Emigration Bill was introduced to the Legislative Assembly by Sir George Barnes on 22 March 1921. It prohibited the emigration of unskilled workers. The bill became law after the Viceroy's approval in March 1922 as Act VII.

An emigration committee was established in May 1922. Efforts were made for stringent regulation of such emigration through rules which was ratified by the Indian legislature.[302] Emigration, however, had virtually ended for Fiji and existed in very small numbers to Mauritius and the Caribbean. As noted by Tinker: 'The Sugar Islands left immigration behind them as an uneasy memory.'[303]

The end of indenture in all its forms enabled the formerly indentured to develop into self-sufficient communities. They became like tenant farmers, growing sugarcane for sale and export. Their enslavement and bondage had given way to a pioneering spirit that their descendants would carry on. This was documented by C.F. Andrews on a journey to Fiji in the 1930s. He attributed these positive developments to the efforts of the Arya Samaj and Sanatan Dharma Sabha.[304]

---

[302] Ibid. 369. The rules were published in the Gazette of India (5 August 1922 and 10 March 1923).
[303] Ibid. 372.
[304] Andrews, C.F., *India and the Pacific*, G. Allen & Unwin, London, 1937.

Following their liberation, the indentured described the inhuman conditions of indentured life as *narak* (hell).³⁰⁵ Indenture was an imperialist structure whose dynamics were along imperialist lines to exploit plantation economies to benefit Britain. To this end, the transportation of the indentured was intended to strengthen imperialism at every level. As Radica Mahase correctly stated:

> A labour force can be more easily subjugated and controlled when it is seen as inferior. The colonial attitude during the nineteenth and twentieth century's was one of superiority and indifference to a less-civilized labour force. In all the territories, the difference between immigrants and planters extended beyond ethnicity. The disparity was noted in the levels of development in the societies from where both groups had come and ideologies of dominance and power of one group over the other.³⁰⁶

The bitter truth was that colonized Indians were at the mercy of the British, second-class citizens with no human rights or benefits of citizenship. They were to be as mercilessly exploited as the slaves who preceded them.

It was correctly concluded by Tinker in the last sentence of his iconic masterpiece *A New System of Slavery*: 'With the formal termination of indenture and of other forms of servitude, there can be no end to the unequal situation of the Indians. They arrived as coolies [...] for slavery is both a system and an attitude of mind. Both the system and the attitude are with us still.'³⁰⁷

---

[305] Gillion, Kenneth L., *Fiji's Indian Migrants: A History to the End of Indenture in 1920*, Oxford University Press, 1962; Tinker, Hugh, *A New System of Slavery: The Export of Indian Labour Overseas 1830-1920*, Hansib, London, 1993; Ali, Ahmed (ed.), *Girmit: Indian Indenture Experience in Fiji*, Fiji Museum, Suva, 1979.
[306] Mahase, Radica, *Why Should We Be Called 'Coolies'?: The End of Indian Indentured Labour*, Routledge, 2020, p. 79.
[307] Tinker, Hugh, *A New System of Slavery: The Export of Indian Labour Overseas*

No wonder then, a century later, the terminology 'route of the coolies' is detested as an enduring symbol of the racist terminology of the day.

∼

1830–1920, Hansib, London, 1993, p. 383.

10

RISE OF INDIA'S DIASPORA: CULTURE AS SAVIOUR AND REDEEMER

When thy mind leaves behind its dark
forest of delusion, thou shall go beyond the
scriptures of times past and still to come.
When thy mind, that shall be wavering
in the contradictions of many scriptures,
shall rest unshaken in divine contemplation,
then the goal of Yoga is thine.

—Bhagavad Gita 2. 52–3.

As this story winds to a conclusion, the discussion centres on the Indians outside India, the people of Indian origin overseas, the great Indian Diaspora. But what do they represent? Since India's culture and civilization are complex and layered, perceptions about the role of her Diaspora have undergone many changes as India has come of age.

A common and widely acknowledged belief is that they represent the concept of '*Udarcharitana tu Vasudhaiva Kutumbakam*' or 'It is only for the generous hearted that the world is one family', flowing from India's Maha Upanishads, part of her great civilizational heritage. They are India's greatest assets outside India. They constitute India's soft power.

The movement of one-and-a-half million Indians across continents from the mid-nineteenth century was dictated by the demands of imperialism and finance capitalism. The ideology behind it has been honestly and brutally acknowledged by Joseph Conrad in *Heart of Darkness*: 'The conquest of the earth, which mostly means the taking it away from those who have a different complexion or slightly flatter noses than ourselves, is not a pretty thing when you look into it too much. What redeems it is the idea only.'[308]

In this relentless quest for resources, territory and subordinate peoples, the narratives were decided by those who conquered. This was essential in plantation economies to ensure a culture based on servility and subjugation. As stated by Edward W. Said: 'The power to narrate, or to block other narratives from forming and emerging, is very important to culture and imperialism, and constitutes one of the main connections between them.'[309]

The question has been legitimately raised how such few Europeans, spread out across the Empire and so far from home, could exercise control over and subjugate so many millions? In the 1930s, Gandhi said: 'A mere 4,000 British civil servants assisted by 60,000 soldiers and 90,000 civilians had billeted themselves upon a country of 300 million persons.'[310]

In the imposition of this imperial culture, the mental enfeeblement of the colonized subject was essential. This was accomplished by his tacit acceptance of the superior culture of the colonizer. The conservative historian of empire D.K. Fieldhouse reasons: 'The basis of imperial authority was the mental attitude of the colonist. His acceptance of subordination-whether through a positive sense of common interest with the parent state, or through inability to conceive of any alternative-made empire durable.'[311]

---

[308]Conrad, Joseph, *Heart of Darkness,* Coyote Canyon Press, 2007.
[309]Said, Edward W., *Culture and Imperialism,* Chatto & Windus, London, 1993, p. xiii.
[310]Smith, Tony, *The Pattern of Imperialism: the United States, Great Britain, and the Late Industrializing World since 1815,* Cambridge University Press, Cambridge, 1981, p. 52.
    Smith quotes Gandhi on this point.
[311]Fieldhouse, D.K., *The Colonial Empire: A Comparative Survey from the*

These efforts to suppress a so-called subordinate culture, a culture transported across the oceans by the Indian indentured, was doomed to failure. India's culture was their identity, the raison d'être for survival. Their victory and the flowering into the second-largest global Diaspora after China became interlinked with India's own struggle for freedom.

India's first Prime Minister Jawaharlal Nehru presciently said in 1937: 'Our countrymen abroad must realize that the key to their problems lies in India. They rise or they fall with the rise and fall of India… Surely, the only way is to put an end to their subjection, to gain independence and the power to protect our people wherever they might be.'[312] Indeed, after Independence, India strongly supported liberation movements in Africa and Asia. In doing so India also helped liberate her own people.

The evolution of India's Diaspora and soft power into the phenomenon they are today was not an easy process. It was rendered more complex by India's Partition. Efforts by the colonialists to divide the Diaspora on the basis of religion and caste were rejected by the children of India's indentured. It did not take into account the invisible bonds made during the crossing by the jahaji bhais and jahaj behens or the unity forged in fighting subordination.

Gandhi's leading role in advising the Diaspora in the plantation colonies, along with others, including the Englishman C.F. Andrews, cannot be overstated. Tagore and Vivekananda before him were able to sensitize international audiences about the strength and tenacity of India's culture and heritage, represented by millions of Indians spread across continents.

The descendants of the indentured built new rainbow nations in the erstwhile plantation colonies as free and independent states. They became the protagonists of a hybrid culture, similar to India

---
Eighteenth Century, Macmillian, 1991, p. 103.
[312]Gregory, R.G., *India and East Africa: A History of Race Relations within the British Empire, 1890-1939,* Oxford University Press, 1971, p. 414.

but also different. It included the evolution of a creolized culture. Spread across former colonies, it disrupted the erstwhile imperial culture of the Empire. In doing so, they also embraced their new nations as their own. Memories of India slowly faded in the absorption and assimilation of counter cultures. This made them more resilient and accommodative, more inclined to accept an evolved culture. Hugo of Saint-Victor, a twelfth-century monk from Saxony aptly summarized the stirrings of a new nationalism as:

> The person who finds his homeland sweet is still a tender beginner; he to whom every soil is as his native one is already strong; but he is perfect to whom the entire world is as a foreign place. The tender soul has fixed his love on one spot in the world; the strong person has extended his love to all places; the perfect man has extinguished his.[313]

Nationalism had awoken in the minds and souls of Indians. It was stirring but it lacked a proper articulation. The echoing silence reflected the absence of voices to write a new narrative until their final liberation. Unfortunately, the narrative was controlled and manipulated by the instruments of imperialism. As articulated by Toni Morrison in *Playing in the Dark*: 'Silence from and about the subject was the order of the day. Some of the silences were broken, and some were maintained by authors who lived with and within the policing strategies. What I am interested in are the strategies for breaking it.'[314]

The diktat of imperialism in the plantation colonies, indeed the dialectic between slavery and indenture, resulted in an ambivalence bordering on hostility between the emancipated slave and his indentured Indian successor. Like with the communal

---

[313] Hugo of Saint-Victor, *Didascalicon*, Jerome Taylor (trans), Colombia University Press, New York, 1961, p. 101.

[314] Morrison, Toni, *Playing in the Dark: Whiteness and the Literary Imagination*, Harvard University Press, 1992.

narrative, this was systematically and cleverly encouraged by the former slave masters and plantation owners.

Over time, these poisoned grapes resulted in hostility bordering on hatred between the Creole and the freed Black slave on the one hand and the Indians on the other. The results were particularly dramatic in Fiji but they regrettably continue to fester in the Caribbean, East Africa and South Africa, Reunion Island and even Mauritius.

As with India's Partition, these internal contradictions between different Diaspora and formerly subordinate peoples continue to cast a long shadow over political, economic and cultural issues in the former plantation colonies, now independent states and members of the United Nations.

E.H. Carr said, 'In a sense, a fact is and cannot be more sacrosanct than a perception.'[315] Such perceptions influence collective consciousness about past traumatic experiences. They shape the memories of survivors and their descendants who have been victims of extreme violence and human indignity perpetrated on slaves and indentured. These memories influence thinking and behaviour of communities and shape their writing of history.

As with slavery, the indentured too need a healing touch. Experts from UNESCO, in a special study on subjugation and slavery, speak of the need for 'a healing map to better understand how to heal the persons and communities impacted inter-generationally and the structures of social and economic inequalities founded on historic wrongdoing.' The same study concluded that:

> Violence against enslaved people [...] involved slave owners, non-slaveholders and public authorities. Such violence has a function: it creates a climate of chronic fear and demands submission of enslaved bodies [...] The violence of slavery

---
[315]Carr, E.H., *What Is History?*, Penguin Books Limited, 2018.

did not end with abolition. Its contemporary consequences are still active in the form of the terrible poison of racism that continues to contaminate societies. Even today, racism kills, discriminates and humiliates.[316]

For the indentured, the balm or healing lay in India's culture, tangible and intangible, forever present in their minds. Here, too, they were confronted by the notion of inferior or subordinate cultures. Such racist notions had fuelled the imperial acquisition of territory during this period. The culture of imperialism entailed venerating one's own culture to the exclusion of other cultures, a notion antithetical to the Indian approach. This imperial approach is best symbolized in Lord Macaulay's minute of 1835:

> I have never found one among them who could deny that a single shelf of a good European library was worth the whole native literature of India and Arabia. It is I believe no exaggeration to say that all the historical information that has been collected from all the books which have been written in the Sanskrit language is less valuable than what may be found in the most paltry abridgement used at preparatory schools in England.[317]

As the descendants of the indentured came into political and economic power, they traced their roots to India and asserted their cultural identity. It was their unique contribution to their new countries. In diverse ways, their culture interacted with the local culture of the former slaves and colonial masters. Often, a hybrid culture emerged. At other times, it remained intact as with the oral traditions, such as the Bhojpuri language and songs that are still sung in Mauritius, Guyana and Suriname and all over

---

[316] *Healing the Wounds of Slave Trade and Slavery: Approaches and Practices: A Desk Review*, UNESCO Slave Route Project/GHFP Research Institute, June 2020, https://tinyurl.com/58hj8n5y. Accessed on 17 August 2023.
[317] English Education Act of 1835

the Caribbean. In this way, the cultural traditions brought to the island over 150 years ago were strengthened and energized.

In Mauritius, Hindus comprise 52 percent of the total population and a majority speak Bhojpuri and understand Hindi, which is recognized as the ancestral language of Hindus in Mauritius and a symbol 0f Hindu identity. Establishment of linkages to Indian sacred sites and their replication in Mauritius has resulted in a pilgrimage sites, perhaps more impressive than India!

A remarkable representation of this interconnect is the annual pilgrimage to Grand Bassin, a mountain lake in the southwest of Mauritius known to Hindus as Ganga Talao (Ganges pond) on the occasion of Shivratri, which is a Hindu festival. Shivratri is an official national holiday in Mauritius. About 300,000 pilgrims make the pilgrimage annually, mainly on foot. They collect the sacred water from the lake, which is offered to the Shivling, a phallic representation of God Shiva.

Figure 22: Ganga Talao (Grand Bassin), Mauritius

Source: 'Grand Bassin', *Wikimedia Commons*, https://tinyurl.com/2ett8ket. Accessed on 3 August 2023.

The Grand Bassin was built to recreate the ghats or bathing places on the banks of the Ganges in Varanasi and other cities on the river. This facilitates prayers on the banks of the lake and collection of the sacred water. The ghats are overlooked by four temples resembling traditional Indian temple architecture.

During the commemoration of the 100th anniversary of the pilgrimage in February 1998, a container of Ganges water flown in from Haridwar with the assistance of the Indian Government was emptied into the lake, which was named Ganga Talao.

Charming popular legends abound regarding this Mauritian pilgrimage spot. It was suggested that this distant lake earlier known as Pari Talao (fairies' pond) was connected to the Ganges by a subterranean passage beneath the ocean.

Another legend is that it originated from the tear shed by Goddess Ganga, saddened by the long journey of her children— the Indian indentured—to this distant island. Her tear was carried by the God of the winds, Vayu, to the uplands of southwest Mauritius, now known as Ganga Talao. German professor, historian and anthropologist Patrick Eisenlohr noted:

> Grand Bassin/Ganga Talao as a site of pilgrimage stands in an iconic relation to a sacred religious geography in India, while the Shivratri pilgrimage to the site can be seen as if it is on the river Ganges. This iconicity is manifest in multiple kinds of likeness between the sacred Hindu geography of India and its replication in Mauritius.[318]

Such developments resulted, over time, in the evolution of an Indian Diaspora in Mauritius, whose soft power outreach, connectivity with India and emotional bonding with the past,

---

[318]Eisenlohr, Patrick, 'Temporalities of Community: Ancestral Language, Pilgrimage, and Diasporic Belonging in Mauritius', *Journal of Linguistic Anthropology*, Vol. 14, No. 1, 2004, pp. 81–98, https://tinyurl.com/y5c7676w. Accessed on 17 August 2023.

provided a unique example of cross fertilization of cultures. It is not surprising that Mauritius, supported by India, took the lead in October 2014 to present the Indentured Labour Route to UNESCO's Executive Board.

The Indo-Fijian experience is in total contrast to Mauritius. It was marked by an unfortunate clash of cultures. In Fiji, neither a hybrid culture nor a dominant culture developed. A cultural, social and ethnic conflict fuelled by the colonizers kept the two communities apart. Indeed, inter-ethnic conflict was the bane of Fiji's development for decades.

The efforts of C.F. Andrews to publicize the horrific conditions of Indian indentured in Fiji, including forced prostitution of the women, had a deep impact on Indian public opinion. Dr P. Harper, district medical officer of Navua, wrote in a Fiji government medical report: 'One indentured Indian woman has to serve three indentured men, as well as various outsiders.'[319] On being further questioned by the Fijian colonial authorities, Dr Harper stated: 'The average coolie woman is forced to allow sexual intercourse to the majority of the coolies in the lines in which she lives, as well as to various outsiders, such as Europeans, free Indians, half-castes, and in many cases, Fijians. She is in fact demoralized.'[320]

It resulted in the major focus of the INC on the urgent need to abolish indenture in Fiji. By the end of 1920, four ships brought back 4,700 Fijian Indians to India. Unfortunately, the majority had been born in Fiji and found the process of adjustment in India exacting. They also did not obtain suitable employment. Many went back to Calcutta in the hope of finding ships to take them back to Fiji or to any other plantation colony. It was indeed ironic, as concluded Hugh Tinker: 'India, which had called so loudly for the removal of their disabilities, had no place for them

---

[319] Tinker, Hugh, *A New System of Slavery: The Export of Indian Labour Overseas 1830–1920,* Hansib, London, 1993.
[320] Ibid. 361.

when they finally came home. The sugar plantations, where they had been used so badly, offered their only hope. It was a strange end to a strange story.'³²¹

Fiji's ethnic and racial composition is unique. Ethnic Fijians constitute 54 per cent and Indo-Fijians 38 per cent of the total population. The remaining is a motley mix of Chinese, Europeans and Pacific Islanders. There was a steady flow of Indians to Fiji from 1879 to 1916. During this period, about 60,965 Indians settled in Fiji. The great majority (about 80 per cent) came from Uttar Pradesh. Another 13 per cent came from Bihar and Bengal. The rest were from South India.

In contrast to other Fijians, they spoke different Indian languages, including Bhojpuri-based Hindi along with Urdu, Tamil, Telugu, Gujarati and Punjabi. Hindi/Bhojpuri is the main written and spoken language among Fiji Indians. The vast majority (about 85.3 per cent) were Hindu and about 14.6 per cent were Muslim. The rest were Sikhs and Christians. As Indian Diaspora, they remained strongly connected to India. They clung to the Indian family life, their culture, traditions and belief systems. They were emotionally connected through shared history and ethnicity to other former indentured globally.

Due to persistent racism, the compatriots of the Fiji Indians, the former indentured, spread over the former plantation colonies did strongly support the Indians in Fiji. The ethnic Fijians had no such external support. This exacerbated the 'troubled and often hostile relationship' between the two groups.³²² There were other reasons including a 'mismatch between formal political institutions and the underlying culture of a society may also have resulted in political instability.'³²³

---

³²¹Ibid. 366.
³²²Cohen, R., *Global Diasporas: An Introduction,* University of Washington Press, Seattle, 1997, pp. 60–65, 79–80.
³²³Kamrava, M., *Understanding Comparative Politics: A Framework for Analysis,*

By 1945, the Fijian Indians constituted the majority population. By 1947, when India became independent, many Fijian Indians advocated a new Fiji, attached as a form of a dominion, with the status of a dominion, to India. India.[324] On the other hand, the leaders of Indo-Fijians were committed to being citizens of the new nation State of Fiji formed in 1970. They 'called for a new emphasis on being fully Fijian'.[325] In retrospect, it seems politically naïve that they failed to understand the need to effectively counter or address the problems caused by the ethnic nationalism of indigenous Fijians.

About 98 per cent of Indo-Fijians utilized their option to become citizens of the new state. The economic choices they made would influence their future. They were never permitted to be fully integrated. They faced different kinds of discrimination. They were prohibited from owning land. They focussed on education and opportunities available in other professions, especially business. Hard working and close knit, they became economically prosperous. These included the later Indians, Gujaratis and Sikhs, who retained even closer ties with their communities in India. This made them a sub-diaspora within the overall Indian Diaspora.

Over time, the Indians who owned land and dominated Fiji's money-making sectors, including the sugar industries, branched out into classic white-collar professions. Indo-Fijians controlled the civil service, the judiciary and provided most of Fiji's doctors, teachers and chartered accountants. The native Fijian was much less prosperous, working on copra production and the fishing industry. They also were recruited at a low level into the local police and armed forces. This later gave them a clear advantage over the Indo-Fijians when the coups took place later. In the process, after the coup, Indians were driven out of their lands.

Routledge, London, 1996, pp. 43–48, 71, 175–80.
[324]Scarr, D., *Fiji: A Short History,* George Allen & Unwin, Sydney, 1984, p. 149.
[325]Kelly, J.D., 'Bhakti and Postcolonial Politics: Hindu Missions to Fiji', *Nation and Migration: The Politics of Space in the South Asian Diaspora,* P. van der Veer (ed.), University of Pennsylvania Press, Philadelphia, 1995, pp. 43–72.

Thakur Ranjit Singh is an Auckland-based journalist and a media commentator, who runs his blog *Fiji Pundit*. He also opted to retain his Fijian citizenship. The Indo-Fijians did try to reach out to the indigenous Fijians. Prime Minister Frank Bainimarama was popular with the Indo-Fijian community because of his impartial approach to Fijian Indians. Unfortunately, he was not been able to stop the rot or the daily assaults on the culture, language and customs of Indo-Fijians.

As Thakur Ranjit Singh stated on his blog:

> Fiji Prime Minister Frank Bainimarama was seen as a ray of hope, and savoir for Fiji Indians in the doom and gloom of past ethno-nationalist leaders and Fijian Governments. He was seen by some as a reincarnation, as promised by Lord Krishna in Gita that he would come back when people are in strife. Therefore, this act of assault on Fiji Indian culture is seen as something foreign from his government.[326]

Unfortunately, no such ray of hope is provided by the present incumbent, Sitiveni Rabuka, a retired general with deep prejudices against ethnic Indians. He has been Prime Minister since 24 December 2022. His presence has ensured the further exodus of ethnic Indians from Fiji.

Fiji so far remains an ugly exception to the otherwise harmonious integration of India's children into the culture and societies of their final destinations. Two racist coups in 1987 and 2000, seeking to disempower Fijian citizens of Indian origin, resulted in their mass exodus of more than 100,000 Indians, mainly to Australia. Very few, surprisingly, opted to return to India.

Since most of the departing Indians were professionals, including the majority of Fiji's lawyers, doctors, teachers,

---

[326] 'An Open Letter To Fiji PM: The Great Fiji Hindi Debate - An Assault On Fiji Indian Culture Through Stealth', *Fiji Pundit,* 26 January 2020, https://tinyurl.com/5ev9yfxx. Accessed on 3 August 2023.

accountants and civil servants, Fiji's economic and social development was adversely affected. Fiji was also expelled from the Commonwealth and was shunned by her immediate neighbours in the Southern Pacific as well as by Australia and New Zealand along with India.

The experience of indenture and its aftermath in Fiji holds a mirror to a system of tacit apartheid used by the colonial rulers to separate the native Fijian from the Indo-Fijian. Given their totally different racial, linguistic, religious and cultural background, their efforts fell on fertile soil. The division of labour ensured development of ethnically and racially separate enclaves with no interaction or intermarriage in what was after all a small island.

Many have remarked that unlike Mauritius, Trinidad, Guyana and other parts of the Caribbean, Fiji has no Creole or Creolized culture that is an amalgam of native and Indian cultures. What is unfortunate is the conscious segregation of communities since birth, with native Fijian and Indo-Fijian children attending separate schools even if there was some interlapping or intermingling of communities. Inter-community marriages were frowned upon on both sides and were virtually non-existent. Neither side wished to adopt any cultural or linguistic practices from each other. As a result: 'Even after more than a century of living together, few know more than a few words of each other's language.'[327]

Similar to apartheid, it resulted in the formation of ethnic alliances based on race. In 1980, C. Jayawardena noted that within both communities, 'social elites dominate class interests in the operation of the power structure in Fiji.'[328]

---

[327]Harrison, D., 'The World Comes to Fiji: Who Communicates What, and to Whom', *Tourism, Culture & Communication,* Vol. 1, No. 2, 1998, p. 130.
[328]Jayawardena, C., 'Culture and Ethnicity in Guyana and Fiji', *Man,* Vol. 15, No. 3, 1980, p. 446.

Even the terminology used by either side to describe each other was pejorative and racist. The native Fijians referred to Indo-Fijian as *kaisi* (coolies) and *vulagi* (outsiders), guests, rather than co-owners of Fiji. The Indo-Fijian, not to be outdone, referred to the native Fijian as *jungali* (people of little culture). As noted by many, the two groups viewed each other 'through a prism of prejudice, reinforced by contrasting life-styles, cultural attitudes and historical experiences'[329], which resulted in mutual distrust and suspicion.

It is difficult to avoid being judgemental about present-day Fiji when one witnesses the pitiable conditions of those Indo-Fijians who stayed behind since they regard Fiji as their only home but live an unequal life compared to native Fijians. The questions that arise are '[Do] collective indigenous rights trump individual human rights? How ought self-determination for the entire nation to be squared with the special claims of a native people?'[330]

Whatever be the response, Fiji's economy and social development have been impacted as a result. Its social and ethnic tensions have affected tourism and prevented foreign investments from its prosperous neighbours, notably Australia and New Zealand. Fiji has a complex and difficult relationship with India. Indo-Fijians continue to leave Fiji in large numbers. According to *World Population Review* and *Find Easy*[331], in 2021, the percentage of Indo-Fijians, at around 314,000 constituted

---

[329]Lal, Brij V., *Broken Waves: A History of the Fiji Islands in the Twentieth Century*, University of Hawaii Press, Honolulu, 1992, p. 304.

[330]Srebrnik, Henry, 'Indo-Fijians: Marooned without Land and Power in a South Pacific Archipelago? Indian Diasporics', *Tracing an Indian Diaspora: Contexts, Memories, Representations,* Parvati Raghuram et al., (eds), SAGE Publications India, 2008.

[331]'Fiji Population 2023 (Live)', *World Population Review,* https://tinyurl.com/535x6bsk. Accessed on 17 August 2023; 'Indians in Fiji', *Find Easy*, https://tinyurl.com/38n5cyaz. Accessed on 17 August 2023.

about 38 per cent of the total population of Fiji. This was a steep drop since Indo-Fijians, since even in 1966, they constituted 51 per cent of the population. Those who remain are embittered and live in ethnically secure settlements.

During my own visit to Fiji in 1998 on an official mission from India to ascertain the possibility of reopening the Indian Mission in Fiji, I met with many sections of the Indo-Fijian Diaspora. The majority had never visited India and clung to fashions and customs that are no longer in vogue in India. In fact, though they do not accept it, they do represent an Indo-Fijian version of a creolized culture. Perhaps, some form of social reconciliation is still possible.

Fiji remains a striking exception to the manner in which India's inclusive culture permeated across the other plantation colonies. In general, it is a process that recalls India's own way of assimilating the culture of her invaders. As William Dalrymple acknowledged, 'India has always had a strange way with her conquerors. In defeat, she beckons them in, then slowly seduces, assimilates and transforms them.'[332]

Today, that culture has transformed India's Diaspora, the second largest globally, into a mutually supportive and beneficial relationship that is the envy of the global community. Mother India, having let her children go, calls them back on 9 January every alternate year on Pravasi Bharatiya Divas, which commemorates the contribution of India's overseas community. The date was selected to coincide with 9 January 1915, when Mahatma Gandhi, the greatest *pravasi* (overseas Indian) of all, returned to India via Mauritius from South Africa, to lead India to freedom.

The children of the indentured now contribute to the greatness of India. Who can predict what destiny has in store?

---

[332]Dalrymple, William, *White Mughals: Love and Betrayal in Eighteenth-Century India*, Penguin Books India, 2004.

As Bhishma said in the Mahabharata:

'*Dharamasya gahana Vati.*
(Deep and subtle are the ways of Dharma.
Let us not predict or pre-empt it).'

~

11

OLD SINS CAST LONG SHADOWS

*I am the tree,
creaking in the wind,
outside in the night,
twisted and stubborn:
I am the voice
Crying in the night
that cries endlessly
and will not be consoled.*

—Dennis Brutus, 'In Shrill Sad Protest'[333]

It was in the fitness of things that the UN and its primary specialized agency, UNESCO, should have first sought and obtained international recognition for the Slave Route before seeking similar recognition for the Indentured Labour Route. One flows from the other. Both slavery and indenture result in human bondage. Both are based on the principle of racial superiority versus inferiority. Both slaves and indentured were treated like children of a lesser God. Both their stories need to be known, narrated, recognized and inscribed on UNESCO's flagship projects.

UNESCO's Slave Route Project was pioneered by the African Group to seek international recognition and acknowledgement of one of humanity's greatest human rights violations and to commence a process of reconciliation. Unfortunately, this

---
[333] Written during South Africa under apartheid

process can only be completed if the principle of reparations is accepted by the international community. That seems most unlikely. So, will it linger on forever in the memories of their descendants?

Nouréini Tidjani-Serpos (of Benin, West Africa), former Deputy Director-General of UNESCO, who conceptualized the project pointed out: 'Memory is first of all a land and its routes.'[334] The successful process enabling its inscription was due to another great son of Benin, the late Ambassador Olabiyi Yaï, the charismatic former chairman of UNESCO's Executive Board.

The process was complex. The Executive Board of UNESCO was politically divided. Efforts were repeatedly made to divert discussions on technical grounds. With the strong support of the Asian and Arab groups as well as the Caribbean, truth and justice finally prevailed. The Slave Route is now inscribed on what UNESCO describes as Memory of the World Register. Slave trade and slavery are on the international agenda. There is global recognition that it represents a gross crime against humanity.

The beginning can be traced to its launch on 23 August 1994 in Benin, under the title UNESCO Routes of Enslaved Peoples: Resistance, Liberty and Heritage Project. Like Senegal and Ghana, Benin was the focal point of slave drivers and recruiters when slavery first cast its sinister net on the African continent. Intended to imprint on the global memory the injustices and horrors of the Slave Route, it is now solemnly commemorated annually by UNESCO on 23 August at its headquarters in Paris.

Global recognition of the devastation wrought upon peoples and societies affected by centuries of slave trade should remain a sombre reminder of a horrific epoch in human history. In the process, it was hoped that new patterns of recognition, reconciliation and new perspectives for the future would be built.

---

[334]'Ouidah the Slave Route', The Ministry of Culture and Communication of the Republic of Benin.

Its main aim was to eventually 'de-racialize' people's vision and 'decolonize' their perception of history through:

- deconstructing discourses based on the concept of race that justified these systems of exploitation;
- promoting the contributions of people of African descent to the general progress of humanity; and
- questioning the social, cultural and economic inequalities inherited from this tragedy.[335]

It is unfortunate that despite the passage of time, neither racism nor racialism have faded into the distant past. Instead, new forms of racism, racial hatred, White supremacy, human bondage and slavery have emerged.

Tidjani-Serpos, in his introduction to UNESCO'S Slave Route, rightly points out: 'The womb that produced the Beast is still fertile. If we remain silent now in the face of acts of racism, intolerance, exclusion and marginalization, more modern forms of either slavery or indenture will arise. It is time that the indentured and their route be declared a crime against humanity.'[336]

This is a timely reminder. As memories of slavery followed by the Holocaust fade, it becomes easier for neo-fascists, neo-Nazis, White supremacists and racists to once again raise their ugly heads. In the decade after the Second World War, memories of mass extermination of the human population in concentration camps spread across Europe were a powerful reminder of the dangers of the rise of such toxic ideologies challenging notions of racial equality among peoples, notions denied by slavery, indenture, apartheid and the Holocaust.

---

[335]'Routes of Enslaved Peoples', *UNESCO*, https://tinyurl.com/4spxc7zd. Accessed on 24 August 2023; 'Outreach Programme on the Transatlantic Slave Trade and Slavery', *UNESCO*, https://tinyurl.com/548bpnjr. Accessed on 24 August 2023.
[336]'Ouidah the Slave Route', The Ministry of Culture and Communication of the Republic of Benin.

Figure 23: Holocaust—a successor of slavery and the indenture: Gas chambers and crematorium of Natzweiler-Struthof concentration camp, Alsace, France

Source: Mrindholt, 'Crematorium at Natzweiler-Struthof Concentration Camp', *Wikimedia Commons*, 8 July 2016, https://tinyurl.com/2p9ebdbs. Accessed on 3 August 2023.

Posted in France shortly after joining the Indian Foreign Service, I decided in March 1980 to understand better the horrors of the Holocaust by visiting a perfectly preserved concentration camp in Alsace-Lorraine, simply named the Natzweiler-Struthof camp. It is the only concentration camp built by the Nazis on French soil after the Third Reich overran France in the Second World War.

As I paused at the entrance, the plaque at the gate starkly stated in English and French:

Humanity, pause and reflect.
Never again must the human race experience this again.

Nothing that I had ever seen or studied in India had prepared me for the ordeal that was to come. According to the guide, the prisoners were forced to enter the gas chambers completely disrobed, knowing their fate. The heat generated from mass extermination and cremation of humans was used to warm the bathwater of the wife of the German commander who enjoyed her ablutions twice a day. The ashes of the incinerated were used as manure for her beautifully manicured rose garden that was tended to by the unfortunates until they, too, met their predetermined destiny.

It was also a site for unethical and inhuman medical experiments on unwilling prisoners. The Holocaust museum inside the camp has preserved to this day the small items of day-to-day life left behind by the victims.

That the Holocaust succeeded slavery and the indenture system gives us cause to reflect that these inhuman practices may have been outlawed, but they linger on in the dark thoughts of those who practice racial inequality and who believe in the notion of the superior races. As Professor Achille Mbembe reminds us:

> The imperative to 'deracialise' is [...] valid for Europe, for the United States, for Brazil and for other parts of the world. The emergence of new varieties of racism in Europe and elsewhere, the reassertion of global white supremacy, of populism and retro-nationalism, the weaponization of difference and identity are not only symptoms of a deep distrust of the world. They are also fostered by transnational forces capable of making that same world inhospitable, uninhabitable and unbreathable for many of us.[337]

Flowing from the above is the complex issue of compensating the descendants in return for forgiveness and reconciliation. The Truth and Reconciliation Commission set up in post-apartheid South Africa in 1995 remains a fine example of creating a mechanism to proactively address past sins in order to move forward. In the South African context, it helped to partially heal the wounds of a nation and begin a process of reconciliation. The

---

[337] Bangstad, S. and T. Tumyr, 'Thoughts on the Planetary: An Interview with Achille Mbembe', *New Frame,* 5 September 2019.

wounds remained, since it was unable to provide reparations and skirted the issue of compensation.

It is unfortunate that despite the proclamation of the International Decade of People of African Descent (2015–2024)[338], not much has changed for former slaves or the descendants of the indentured. With the return of racial prejudice and discrimination on one hand and the refusal to pay reparations on the other, the descendants of liberated slaves are not yet ready to forget and turn this page of history into a mere memory. What is required is a UN Truth Commission that puts to rest the agonized memories of the survivors and helps them move from the tragedy of the past to the complexities of the present and to a future based on the principles of racial equality, human dignity and justice for all.

The same is true for the victims of indenture. It was once again Africa led by Mauritius and supported by India that took the lead. The Indentured Labour Route Project of UNESCO was launched with India's full support and co-sponsorship. After all, if Africa's children were forced into slavery, it was India's teeming millions—colonized, poor, inadequately educated and vulnerable or marginalized—who were driven into indenture. These tragic histories bind Africa and India together in a common determination to ensure that the past is not forgotten.

Memory constitutes history that should never be forgotten. Basil Davidson said: 'History unfolds in the mind and the imagination, and it takes body in the multifarious responses of a people's culture, itself the infinitely subtle mediation of material realities, of underpinning economic fact, of gritty objectives'.[339]

It took the Africans to remind the UN that the comfortable assertion that slavery was a thing of the past, an unfortunate aberration to be buried in history books, was a completely false

---

[338]'International Decade for People of African Descent (2015–2024)', *UNESCO*, https://tinyurl.com/yp8xpj4m. Accessed on 24 August 2023.
[339]Davidson, Basil, *Africa in Modern History*, Touchstone Books, 1995.

narrative. The status quo may have shifted but many complex questions remain unanswered. The reality was that slavery and slave-like practices persisted for decades, long after their formal and legal abolition. They were often presented in benign forms that disguised the reality, which was the continuation of human bondage inflicted upon the poor and the marginalized.[340]

Interwoven into this debate was the complex issue of compensation. As stated starkly by Eric Foner: 'Former slaves received "Nothing but Freedom."'[341] The reason for this complex assertion was also economic. Abolition was not accompanied by transfer of economic power, wealth and resources from the exploiter to the exploited.

Freedom from eternal bondage is joyful. It must be accompanied by material compensation. When freed slaves and former indentured returned to their land of origin or remained in the plantation colony as settlers, they lacked the material means to fully enjoy freedom and emancipation. As Frederick Cooper explained:

> Never, as far is as known, has a slave community regretted its freedom; never, even in the face of the most-dire poverty, has it wished to return to the security and oppression of slavery. But emancipation—in the southern United States, in the Caribbean, in Brazil, and in parts of Africa as well—has been a time of disillusionment as well as joy. The individual plantation owner may have ceased to be lord and master over his slaves, but the planter class did not lose its power [...] in case after case, a particular class [...] kept land from the eager hands of ex-slaves and vigorously applied the instruments

---

[340] Quirk, Joel and Wilberforce Institute for the study of Slavery and Emancipation, University of Hull, *Unfinished Business: A Comparative Survey of Historical and Contemporary Slavery,* UNESCO, Paris, 2009.

[341] Foner, E., *Nothing but Freedom: Emancipation and Its Legacy,* Louisiana State University Press, Baton Rouge, 1983.

of state and the law to block ex-slaves' access to resources and markets, to restrict their ability to move about, bargain or refuse wage labour, and to undermine their attempts to become independent producers.[342]

It took courage for an Englishman, John Oldfield, to observe:

> Britons—and Britain's colonial subjects—were taught to view transatlantic slavery though the moral triumph of abolition [...] Whether seen through the lens of abolitionists relics or celebrations and commemorations, what is so often striking about this specific 'history' is its silencing of African perspectives, and, in particular, the suffering of the millions who were sold into slavery.[343]

UNESCO has created the Memory of the World to ensure that history is not forgotten, since otherwise it can repeat itself. Otherwise, as Hegel said, 'The only thing we learn from history is that we learn nothing from history.'[344]

Why did UNESCO play the lead role? The Second World War and the Holocaust greatly influenced US President Franklin D. Roosevelt to build bridges to destroy racial hatred leading to great wars and, in particular, the Second World War.

This is beautifully articulated in the Preamble of UNESCO's Constitution, adopted in London on 16 September, 1945. The Preamble states:

> Since wars begin in the minds of men, it is in the minds of men that the defences of peace must be constructed [...] That the wide diffusion of culture and the education of humanity for

---

[342]Cooper, F., *From Slaves to Squatters: Plantation Labor in Agriculture in Zanzibar and Coastal Kenya, 1890–1925*, Yale University Press, New Haven, 1980, p. 1.
[343]Oldfield, J., *'Chords of Freedom': Commemoration, Ritual and British Transatlantic Slavery*, Manchester University Press, Manchester, 2007, p. 2.
[344]'Georg Wilhelm Friedrich Hegel > Quotes > Quotable Quote', *Goodreads*, https://tinyurl.com/3szuaffc. Accessed on 18 August 2023.

justice and liberty and peace are indispensable to the dignity of man and constitute a sacred duty which all the Nations must fulfil in a spirit of mutual assistance and concern.[345]

It is no coincidence that UNESCO, the only UN specialized agency for diffusion of soft power through education, culture, science and information, pioneered the Slave Route and Indentured Labour Route Projects. It continues to be a bridge between differing ideologies, cultures and civilizations. It has promoted a dialogue between culture and civilization and between religions. It is a testimony to the power of multilateralism in confronting dangerous ideologies of hatred and supremacy.

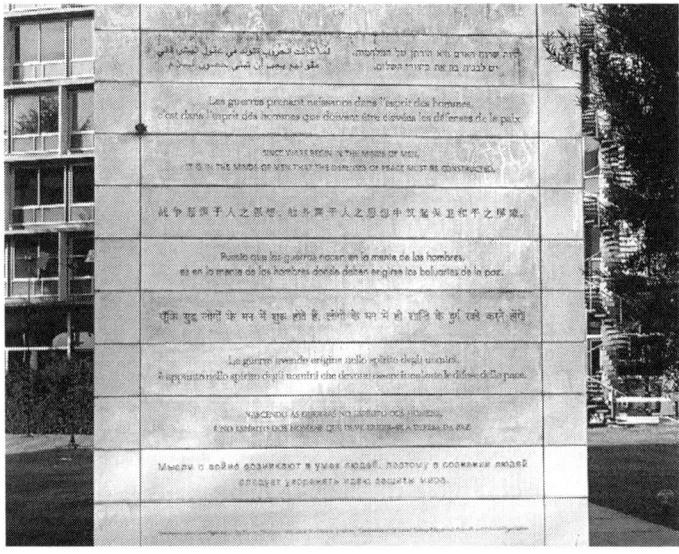

Figure 24: Building defences in the minds of men: Preamble to UNESCO's constitution

Source: UNESCO

[345]'Constitution of the United Nations Educational, Scientific and Cultural Organization', *UNESCO,* https://tinyurl.com/mryuve2y. Accessed on 25 August 2023.

The process of international recognition and acceptance was not an easy one. Mauritius decided to inscribe Aapravasi Ghat, the symbol of indenture and servitude on the World Heritage List of UNESCO at the 30th meeting of the World Heritage Committee in Vilnius, Lithuania, in 2006. The process was complex and mired in former colonial politics. The advisory body concerned, International Council on Monuments and Sites led by a British expert tried to portray indenture as a pre-modern form of immigration so that Indians could leave behind their lives of poverty and destitution for a golden future. At one point, it seemed the British expert was swaying the opinion of developed countries, members of the World Heritage Committee.

At that point, the Minister of Culture of Mauritius turned to the author, the Indian Ambassador to UNESCO, requesting India explain the evils of indenture to the committee. The moment was dramatic, since India was not supposed to introduce the item brought by Mauritius on behalf of the African group. In an extempore 15-minute presentation, the Indian Ambassador explained the tragedy of indenture, of innocent people dying on the route and oblivious of their final destination and of what awaited them on arrival. Nor did they have, unlike modern immigrants, the freedom to return to their homeland. As they crossed the steps of Aapravasi Ghat, they were not to know that they would, for the rest of their lives, cultivate sugarcane of which they knew nothing or would be sent in another ship to Reunion Island or to the Caribbean.

For the first time in the history of the World Heritage Committee, after this explanation, brief but emotional supportive statements were expressed by leaders of delegations of the US, the Netherlands and New Zealand. Thereafter, Aapravasi Ghat was inscribed on the World Heritage List of UNESCO without debate and by acclamation.

This was the moment when Mauritius and India jointly

conceived of eventually bringing the Indentured Labour Route Project as an UNESCO project to the UNESCO Executive Board for approval.[346] The International Labour Route Project, to be centred at Aapravasi Ghat in Mauritius, would represent the oldest surviving entry and transit point associated with indenture.

With 26 UNESCO Member States as members of the Route, the International Indentured Route, after its adoption, complemented the Slave Route. Both mark the mass and forced movements of peoples around the world during the worst periods of imperialism and colonialism. As a result of indenture more than 2.2 million indentured were moved from India to more than 26 countries in various parts of the world, making it one of the greatest mass movements of India's future Diaspora worldwide.

The date of adoption was deliberately chosen to coincide with Gandhi's birthday (2 October). It was adopted on 2 October 2014, at the 195th Session of the Executive Board of UNESCO as 195 EX/30. In doing so, the Executive Board noted that its adoption would:

- contribute to a better understanding of the dynamics of the movement of millions of peoples and cultures in that age;
- highlight the global transformations and cultural interactions that has resulted from this history; and
- contribute to a culture of peace by promoting reflection on culture pluralism, intercultural dialogue, sustainable development and peace.[347]

Subsequently, an international secretariat was established in Aapravasi Ghat, Mauritius, with a corpus of experts and professionals who are establishing an international database on

---

[346]30th Session of the UNESCO World Heritage Committee, Vilnius, Lithuania, 9–16 July, 2006.
[347]UNESCO Executive Board resolution at its 195th Session: 195 EX/30.

indentured labour. The AGTF in Mauritius, under the aegis of the Ministry of Arts and Culture, is leading the project.

It is seeking to facilitate a better understanding of the importance of this event in global history and facilitate the need for reconciliation and rehabilitation.

UNESCO's seminal contribution to healing the ugly wounds of slavery and indenture has resulted in a process of reconciliation without forgetting history or historical events. Rigorous research has also helped such a dialogue. We are reminded: 'Communities carry the history of catastrophic events and their consequences, not only as the content of their DNA, but also as part of their representation of life in general and the way they remember history. It also opens the possibility of a deep questioning into the consequences of collective traumas and the "naturalisation" of pathological functioning expressed in pathological frameworks structured by the disaster itself.'[348]

The UNESCO Slave Route Project tells us: 'The challenge is extending this approach to acknowledge the impacts of postcolonial cognitive dissonance, and to develop a "healing map" to better understand how to heal the persons and communities impacted inter-generationally and the structures of social and economic inequalities founded on historic wrongdoing.'[349]

The healing process has commenced but is far from complete. Today, even the process of abolition is being challenged by the rise of fascism and fascist ideologies and parties across Europe and North America. These ideologies are mutating and developing into new and more dangerous forms of racism and racial discrimination. Unless challenged and checked, the world could be confronted by dark and evil forces inexorably leading to

---

[348] *Healing the Wounds of Slave Trade and Slavery. Approaches and Practices: A Desk Review*, UNESCO Slave Route Project / GHFP Research Institute, June 2020, https://tinyurl.com/58hj8n5y. Accessed on 17 August 2023.
[349] Ibid.

another Great War. Dark clouds of war are gathering on European skies and could rapidly spread eastwards.

EPILOGUE

That justice is a blind goddess
Is a thing to which we blacks are wise:
Her bandage hides two festering sores
That once perhaps were eyes.

—'Justice', Langston Hughes[350]

As this narrative comes to an end, we need to reflect on why identity is important and how the descendants of indentured made their new identity. Identity is a raison d'être for human existence. In the relentless quest for their identity, the indentured had to combat many and different racist and pejorative definitions of their origin and work. The ideological underpinnings of the debate were centred on the so-called Coolie Route.

Khal Torabully, the Indo-Mauritian poet and sociologist, brilliantly coined the term 'coolitude'. What is coolitude? Is it similar to 'Negritude', a definition put forward by Aimé Césaire and other African and Caribbean intellectuals in the 1950s and 1960s? The answer is a resounding 'yes'. Both demolish the inherent racism towards slaves and indentured. Both definitions facilitate the process of building a separate identity.

Negritude was the Black consciousness movement that championed pride in African history and culture in response to years of repression and denigration under colonialism. Césaire wrote:

---

[350] A Black poet and writer who shaped and led the Harlem Renaissance from the 1920s to the 1960s

My negritude is not a stone, its deafness heaved against the clamour of day my negritude is not a film of dead water on the dead eye of earth my negritude is neither a tower nor a cathedral.[351]

Césaire, who was a poet and politician, was one of the three founders of the Negritude movement, along with Léopold Sédar Senghor, who later became the first President of Senegal as well as Léon-Gontran Damas, a poet and politician from French Guiana. Their first journal, published in 1934 in France, focussed on negritude and was appropriately titled *L'Étudiant noir* or *The Black Student*.

Césaire was born in Martinique and acquired French citizenship. His leadership of the movement did much to enable the descendants of slaves to be treated as equals in the West. Césaire died on 17 April 2008, aged 95, and was buried in Martinique. On 6 April 2011, his name was inscribed on the Pantheon in Paris, the first Black citizen of France to be so honoured. Negritude had travelled a long way.

As cogently argued by Hugh Tinker in *A New System of Slavery*, the indentured, termed coolies, conveniently replaced slaves, especially on the plantations. They were two faces of one coin, the Black slave on one side and the Brown indentured on the other. Their suffering due to their inhuman bondage represented one of the greatest tragedies of human history.

Khal Torabully and historian Marina Carter have edited a collection of meaningful essays on coolitude. Torabully underlined that all indentured, called coolies, were in exile from India, their Mother land. 'Coolitude emphasizes their shared history.' As explained in the book: 'Coolitude encapsulates both an interpretation and an artistic immersion in the world of the

---

[351]'Poem of the Week', *Duke University Press*, https://tinyurl.com/3pfhcbfd. Accessed on 24 August 2023.

"coolie". It seeks to understand migration and indenture across the globe as a trans-cultural process in non-essentialist ways through poetry, art and prose, both conventional and experimental.' He noted that indenture and coolitude should 'remain within the realm of reasoned discourse and debate that will do justice to a complex human experience. The Girmitiyas deserve that at the very least.'[352]

Torabully's powerful medium of poetry is able to do full justice to both negritude and coolitude, unlike what any prose could symbolize.

> Like spume, each body
> wakes up on a wave.
>
> We are molasses, we are bagasse
> my African brother descended from slaves
> our skin is the trace
> like yours, of the same dark race.
>
> a seedless man
> destitute die-rolling race
> hanged from pandanus trees,
> in the name of the stunning sea.[353]

Kalapani is another perception, laden with different interpretations, that needs to be rationally addressed if the children of indentured are to finally find justice. We have read in the earlier chapters that crossing the ocean was not confined to the lowest castes in Indian society. It was economic deprivation and famine, due to a vicious system of colonialism and finance imperialism, that compelled the exodus. How much did caste impact the future status of those who had survived the ocean crossing?

---

[352]Carter, Marina and Khal Torabully, *Coolitude: An Anthology of the Indian Labour Diaspora,* Anthem Southeast Asian Studies, Anthem Press, 2002.
[353]Torabully, Khal, 'Three Poems', *World Literature Today,* https://tinyurl.com/ysetuxf3. Accessed on 18 August 2023.

The most socially conservative Hindus clung to the notion that crossing the oceans meant a separation from the Ganges, thus breaking the cycle of reincarnation that impacted one's caste. Many maharajas (royalty) like those of the Jaipur royal family transported thousands of litres of Ganges water on the sea journeys.[354]

While deciding on undertaking such journeys, religion and caste ultimately did not play the dominant role. A study of the earliest Indian texts is instructive. The fifth century BC sutra of Baudhayana only expresses reservations about Brahmins undertaking sea voyages.[355] Historians have theorized that the social taboos applied only to Brahmins and Rajputs and were never explicitly forbidden for any caste.[356] Taking this further, Michael Pearson commented that the sastra prohibitions 'are to be seen as precepts rather than strict rules. This is demonstrated by the way Hindus have crossed the ocean since time immemorial, even if the sea does not play a major role in Hindu thought.'[357] Dr Tapan Raychaudhuri adds a new dimension when he suggests that the critical approach to Kalapani could be due to historical reasons 'involving "the destruction of Indian merchant fleets by Arab pirates"'.[358]

Of particular interest were the first-hand reports of two recruiters, George Grierson and Major Pitcher, who were deputed

---

[354] 'The most famous instance of this social custom revolves around Maharaja Madho Singh II of Jaipur who commissioned a pair of silver vessels to transport Ganges water to London and back for the coronation ceremony of Edward VII. The vessels, known today as Gangajalis are on permanent display in the Diwan-i Khas of the Jaipur City Palace.

[355] Bates, Crispin and Marina Carter, 'Kala Pani Revisited: Indian Labour Migrants and the Sea Crossing', *Journal of Indentureship and Its Legacies,* Vol. 1, No. 1, 2021, pp. 36–62, https://tinyurl.com/2p8pzx97. Accessed 14 August 2023.

[356] Bindra, S.C., 'Notes on Religious Ban on Sea Travel in Ancient India', *Indian Historical Review,* Vol. 29, Nos. 1–2, 2002, pp. 34–7.

[357] Pearson, Michael, *The Indian Ocean,* Routledge, London, 2007, p. 47.

[358] Raychaudhuri, Tapan, *Europe Reconsidered: Perceptions of the West in Nineteenth Century Bengal,* Oxford University Press, Oxford, 1988, p. 37.

to investigate the system of recruitment. Grierson recorded, during his visit to a recruitment depot in Bankipur, that the potential indentured were informed of their final destination being a *tapu* (island). The term 'Kalapani' was totally avoided.[359] This account is corroborated by Tinker, who noted that the plantation colonies were called tapu, stating: 'Anyone who disappeared from the village (absconded, lost, or murdered) was said to have gone to Tapu.'[360]

How much did this really matter? Were the socially adverse consequences of crossing the ocean really linked to the Indian caste system or did the colonizers cleverly manipulate existing prejudices to bring in transportation as the preferred mode of punishment? After all, transportation of White criminals from England to the Americas started in 1717 and to the so-called 'penal colonies' of Australia in 1787, about three decades after the Battle of Plassey in 1757, just as colonialism was tightening its grip on India.[361]

Over time, as the national movement acquired strength, this term became synonymous with transportation.

> 'kalapani' was acquiring an increasingly political meaning within India, one entirely different from its original significance as a religious injunction occasionally encountered among upper-caste Hindus. Between 1905 and 1908, just as in 1857, transportation overseas became once again the preferred punishment for political offenders during

---

[359]Grierson, George A., 'Report on Colonial Emigration from the Bengal Presidency', Diary, IOLR V/27/820/35, 1883, pp. 4–5.
[360]Hugh Tinker, A New System of Slavery, p. 120.
[361]The Piracy Act, also known as the 'Transportation Act' was passed by the British Parliament in 1717 to institutionalize the shipment of convicted criminals to British colonies across the Atlantic in the Americas. Once those destinations became saturated, Australia was chosen as the new site for 'penal colonies' from 1787.

the 'Swadeshi' movement in Bengal and in suppressing the strikes organised by Arya Samajists in the canal colonies in the Punjab. Ghadrites and other so-called terrorists were next to be shipped to the cellular jail in the Andaman Islands in their hundreds during World War I, according to the terms of the Defence of India Act of 1915.[362]

Transportation served the dual purpose of permanent exile and supporting the labour requirements of plantation colonies. Today, we are familiar with the transportation and imprisonment so far from home of Vinayak Damodar (Veer) Savarkar. He was imprisoned in the Cellular Jail in Andaman in 1911 for abetment in the murder of the collector of Nashik and conspiracy against the imperial government arising from his involvement with a revolutionary organisation called Abhinav Bharat (Young India).

Sarvarkar wrote about his life changing experience in 1927 in his Marathi memoir titled *Majhi Janmathep* (My Life-Term). It was translated into Hindi with the simple title *Kala Pani*. He was sentenced for 50 years and remained imprisoned for 15 years. He was released in 1924. It is generally agreed today that the conditions of imprisonment resembled that a concentration camp.

In Savarkar's words:

'काला पानी की भयंकरता का अनुमान इसी एक बात से लगाया जा सकता है कि इसका नाम सुनते ही आदमी सिहर उठता है। काला पानी की विभीषिका, यातना एवं त्रासदी किसी नरक से कम नहीं थी।'[363] As translated by the author, Sarvarkar said: 'An idea of Kalapani's terrible conditions can be ascertained by the fact that taking its very name chills you to the bone. Kalapani's horror, the tragedies and the sufferings it entailed were no less than that of hell itself.'

Such accounts by political prisoners resulted in a body of literature creating the imagery of Kalapani and the horrors

---

[362] Crispin Bates and Marina Carter, "Kala pani revisited", pp. 36-62.
[363] Savarkar, Vinayak Damodar, Kala Pani, Prabhat Prakashan, 2020.

suffered by those transported. For the burgeoning national movement, Kalapani became synonymous with the humiliation inflicted upon India and Indians by the colonizer. The Lucknow poet Shikohabadi (1819–1981) symbolized India's pain when he wrote: 'The prisoners' evil fate made the water black (Kalapani). [...] In the darkness of the evening of exile, they were granted the kohl of Solomon.'[364]

Prejudices regarding the crossing resulted in social ostracism, particularly in Bengal. Such individuals included Swami Vivekananda, who, after returning from the World's Parliament of Religions in Chicago in 1893, was barred access to a temple. It was Nobel Laureate Rabindranath Tagore who offered a rational explanation and a way forward to address the Kalapani phenomenon.

According to Tagore's letters, analysed by Shamsad Mortuza, Tagore was of the view that both 'imported imperialism and home-grown nationalism were [...] the metaphorical black waters—kalapani, that needed to be crossed to [...] engages with the West in equal terms'. Mortuza was of the view that Tagore was advocating that Indians needed to overcome, 'the metaphorical Kalapani, required for cultural engagement'.[365]

Coolitude offers an alternative and more rational narrative but it also challenges the nationalist moorings of the Kalapani concept. As explained by Torabully, the Kalapani crossing provides 'a metaphorical framework for an understanding of migrancy'.[366] It also enables the sharing of experiences and memories between

---

[364]Anderson, C., 'A Global History of Exile in Asia c 1700–1900', *Exile in Colonial Asia: Kings, Convicts, Commemoration*, in R. Ricci (ed.), University of Hawaii Press, Honolulu, 2016.

[365]Mortuza, S., 'Beyond "Kalapani" and Tagore's Search for a Shared Regional Identity', *Journal of the Indian Ocean Region*, Vol. 13, No. 3, 2017, p. 284.

[366]Bragard, V., 'Transoceanic Echoes: Coolitude and the Work of the Mauritian Poet Khal Torabully', *International Journal of Francophone Studies*, Vol. 8, No. 2, 2005, p. 229.

slaves and indentured who survived the crossing.[367] This is reinforced by the jahaji behen and jahaji bhai concepts, which enable further bonding. The effort by Torabully is to transform the Kalapani narrative 'into a space of enlightenment whilst Kalapani remains a potent metaphorical memorialisation. It is evoked as a symbol of remembered pain and servitude.'[368]

It is the search for identity of the indentured that offers a possible response to the dialectics of coolitude versus nationalism. It does not involve the rewriting of history but its reinterpretation. As Hilary Mantel said, the job of history is not to issue 'report cards' to the past.[369] History must make us think and to interpret the past as we see and understand it. That thinking should ideally lead to a better understanding of past injustices and human rights violations. One day, it could result in reconciliation as the indentured find a new identity in their rainbow nations.

The Bhagavad Gita provides the final response to the traveller in the long journey to discover the lost identity after the long exile from Mother India: 'I am what is and I am what is not.'[370] Identity comes from both and this is what the indentured need to discover. Only then will their relentless quest in search of their identity find fruition.

∽

---

[367] Bannerjee, R., 'The Kala Pani Connection: Francophone Migration Narratives in the Caribbean Writing of Raphaël Confiant and the Mauritian Writing of Ananda Devi', *Anthurium: A Caribbean Studies Journal*, Vol. 7, No. 1, 2010, pp. 1–11.
[368] Amharai, V., 'Récits postcoloniaux, retour colonial et diaspora indienne à Maurice', *Loxias-Colloques*, Vol. 3, 2013.
[369] 'British Museums and Galleries Are Dealing with the Past, Clumsily', *The Economist*, 11 January 2023.
[370] Verse 19, 'Chapter 9', *Bhagavad Gita*, Penguin, 1962.

ACKNOWLEDGEMENTS

This is my fourth book and truly a labour of love. I have been closely involved in the recognition of the indentured and their route as one of the greatest movements in human history, with 1.5 million Indians leaving the shores of their Mother land and ultimately creating the rainbow nations where reside our great Diaspora.

Like the one on Bengal's partition, its writing facilitated my rediscovery of India's painful colonial past. Indenture was conceived by the British as a substitute for slavery. It is a forgotten part of our history.

The journey of India's children across the Kalapani, their suffering and humiliation at the hands of the colonizers and their relentless quest for identity cannot remain an untold narrative.

In retrospect, their salvation lay in their refusal to abandon their culture and civilization and their ties to their Mother land. They walked a lonely and troubled path but never gave up. A special mention must be about indentured women and their unique path to liberation.

As Tagore said:

> If they answer not to thy call, walk alone,
> If they do not hold up the light when the night is troubled with storm,
> O thou unlucky one,
> With the thunder flame of pain, ignite thy own heart
> And let it burn alone.

Ultimately, their indomitable spirit and courage resulted in the creation of new rainbow nations with the great Indian Diaspora.

The inspiration came from that memorable moment in Lithuania in 2006 when, as India's Ambassador to UNESCO and India's Representative to the World Heritage Committee, my extempore intervention at the request of the African group enabled, for the first time ever, Aapravasi Ghat's inscription, by acclamation on the World Heritage List. Aapravasi Ghat, the 'Door of No Return', was finally acknowledged as one of humanity's great tragedies.

In weaving this narrative, let me pay tribute to the role played by UNESCO and my African friends, fellow Ambassadors, who reminded the international community that the world must not forget the horrors of the Slave Route, which was followed by the Indentured Route. I owe a debt of gratitude to the late Ambassador Olabiyi Yaï of Benin, Chairman of UNESCO's Executive Board, who pioneered the Slave Route Project along with his countryman, late Nouréini Tidjani-Serpos, former Deputy Director General of UNESCO.

Subsequently, India and Mauritius developed the Indentured Route Project. I owe a huge debt to my friends in Mauritius for their support, particularly former Minister and Chairperson of Aapravasi Ghat, late Mahen Utchanah, and the former Minister of Culture of Mauritius, Mookhesswur Choonee, who is now the President of GOPIO International (Global Organization of People of Indian Origin).

My dear friend, indeed my adopted elder brother, Dr Shahid Amin, former Head of Delhi University's History Department, historian and prolific author, provided great support. He introduced me to Hugh Tinker's masterpiece *A New System of Slavery* and to Brij V. Lal. The latter sadly passed away during the pandemic.

As always, I greatly benefitted from the support of my close friend, diplomat and foreign policy expert as well as bestselling author, Ambassador Rajiv Dogra, who carefully went through the manuscript. His suggestions and inputs were invaluable and enriched the narrative.

Akash Chattopadhyaya, a trained historian and independent researcher, was my right hand throughout the process. He gave me outstanding support and painstakingly helped with the background research as well as the endnotes and references. I would like to thank and acknowledge Akash's important contribution.

This book would not have been possible but for the invisible support, including through innumerable cups of coffee, of my devoted housekeeper and friend of 45 years, Dulari Minj. Coming as she does from East India—Jharkhand—she too enjoyed revisiting the past, recreating the Indentured Route and empathizing with the Girmitiyas in their relentless quest for identity!

I would like to thank the entire Rupa team for their unstinting support and encouragement.

Finally, the views expressed in the book are entirely mine as is the responsibility of any errors that may remain.

BIBLIOGRAPHY

'20th December 1848: The Abolition of Slavery in Reunion Island', *Société de plantation, histoire et mémoires de l'esclavage* à La Réunion, https://tinyurl.com/2m953u7s. Accessed on 11 August 2023.

'Breaking the Silence, the Transatlantic Slave Trade Education Project', Associated Schools Project Network Division for the Promotion of Quality Education UNESCO, 2004.

Bandyopadhyay, Shekhar, *From Plassey to Partition and After*, Orient Blackswan Private Limited, 2014.

Bates, Crispin and Marina Carter, 'Kala Pani Revisited: Indian Labour Migrants and the Sea Crossing, *Journal of Indentureship and Its Legacies*, Vol. 1, No. 1, September 2021, pp. 36–62.

Bissessur-Doolooa, Varsharanee, 'Women and Culture in the Hard Days of Indenture: The Case of Mauritius', *International Journal of Research and Innovation in Social Science*, Vol. IV, No. VII, July 2020, pp. 634–41.

Carter, Marina, 'Strategies of Labour Mobilisation in Colonial India: The Recruitment of Indentured Workers for Mauritius', *The Journal of Peasant Studies*, Vol. 19, No. 3–4, pp. 229–45.

Carter, Marina, 'The Transition from Slave to Indentured Labour in Mauritius', *A Journal of Slave and Post-Slave Studies*, Vol. 14, No. 1, 2008, pp. 114–30.

'Cholera on the Emigrant Ship "Sheila"', *Untold Lives Blog*, 19 March 2013, https://tinyurl.com/2n5uv97k. Accessed on 11 August 2023.

Eisenlohr, Patrick, 'Temporalities of Community: Ancestral Language, Pilgrimage, and Diasporic Belonging in Mauritius', *Journal of Linguistic Anthropology*, Vol. 14, No. 1, June 2004, pp. 81–98.

Emmer, Pieter C. (ed.), *Colonialism and Migration; Indentured Labour: Before and After Slavery, Comparative Studies in Overseas History*, Martinus Nijhoff Publishers, 1986.

Fuma, Sudel, 'La traite des esclaves dans le basin du Sud-Ouest de l'Océan Indien et la France après 1848', *La route des esclaves: Système servile et traite dans l'est malgache,* Rakoto Ignace (ed.), Paris, L'Harmattan, 2000, pp. 247–61.

Green, William A., 'Emancipation to Indenture: A Question of Imperial Morality', *Journal of British Studies,* Vol. 22, No. 2, Spring 1983, pp. 98–121.

Gupta, Charu, 'Saving "Wronged" Bodies: Caste, Indentured Women And Hindi Print–Public Sphere In Colonial India', *Proceedings of the Indian History Congress,* Vol. 75, Platinum Jubilee 2014, pp. 716–22.

Healing the Wounds of Slave Trade and Slavery: Approaches and Practices: A Desk Review, UNESCO Slave Route Project / GHFP Research Institute, June 2020, https://tinyurl.com/58hj8n5y. Accessed on 17 August 2023.

'Indentured Labour from India in 19th Century Reunion Island', *Société de plantation, histoire et mémoires de l'esclavage* à La Réunion, https://tinyurl.com/2m953u7s. Accessed on 11 August 2023.

'Indentured Labour in Reunion Island', *Société de plantation, histoire et mémoires de l'esclavage* à La Réunion, https://tinyurl.com/2m953u7s. Accessed on 11 August 2023.

Jha, Aditya Prasad, 'Tenants' Rights in Bengal and Bihar after Permanent Settlement (1793–1819)', *Proceedings of the Indian History Congress,* Vol. 23, No. II, 1960, pp. 78–90.

Kothari, Uma, 'Geographies and Histories of Unfreedom: Indentured Labourers and Contract Workers in Mauritius', *The Journal of Development Studies,* Vol. 49, No. 8, April 2013, pp. 1042–57.

Kumar, Ashutosh, 'Anti-Indenture Bhojpuri Folk Songs and Poems from North India', *Man in India,* Vol. 93, No. 4, 2013, pp. 509–19.

Kumar, Ashutosh, 'Feeding the Girmitiya: Food and Drink on Indentured Ships to the Sugar Colonies', *Gastronomica,* Vol. 16, No. 1, Spring 2016, pp. 41–52.

Lal, Brij V., 'Indian Indenture: History and Historiography in a Nutshell', *Journal of Indentureship and Its Legacies,* Vol. 1, No. 1, September 2021, pp. 1–15.

Lal, Brij V., *Chalo Jahaji: On a Journey through Indenture in Fiji*, Australian National University Press, 2012.

Lal, Brij V., *Levelling Wind, Remembering Fiji*, ANU Press, 2019.

Mishra, Amit Kumar, 'Indian Indentured Labourers in Mauritius: Reassessing the "New System of Slavery" vs Free Labour Debate', *Studies in History*, Vol. 25, No. 2, 2009, pp. 229–51.

Panda, Amba (ed.), *Indentured and Post-Indentured Experiences of Women in the Indian Diaspora*, Springer, 2020.

Quirk, Joel and Wilberforce Institute for the study of Slavery and Emancipation, University of Hull, *Unfinished Business: A Comparative Survey of Historical and Contemporary Slavery*, UNESCO, Paris, 2009.

Sen, Sunanda, 'Indentured Labour from India in the Age of Empire', *Social Scientist*, Vol. 44, No. 1/2, January–February 2016, pp. 35–74.

Sturman, Rachel, 'Indian Indentured Labor and the History of International Rights Regimes', *The American Historical Review*, Vol. 119, No. 5, December 2014, pp. 1439–65.

'Summary Records', UNESCO Executive Board, 197th Session, Paris, 7 to 21 October 2015.

'The Abolition of Slavery and the Case of Reunion Island', *Société de plantation, histoire et mémoires de l'esclavage à La Réunion*, https://tinyurl.com/2m953u7s. Accessed on 11 August 2023.

'The Economic Consequences of the Abolition of Slavery on Bourbon Island', *Société de plantation, histoire et mémoires de l'esclavage* à La *Réunion*, https://tinyurl.com/2m953u7s. Accessed on 11 August 2023.

'The First Abolition of Slavery in France and Its Delayed Application in Reunion Island', *Société de plantation, histoire et mémoires de l'esclavage* à La *Réunion*, https://tinyurl.com/2m953u7s. Accessed on 11 August 2023.

'The International Indentured Labour Route Project', UNESCO Executive Board, 195th Session, Paris, 2 October 2014.

'The International Slave Route Monument Within Le Morne Cultural Landscape', World Heritage Convention, UNESCO.

INDEX

Aapravasi Ghat, iii, xvii, 5, 6, 63, 73, 74, 75, 76, 78, 79, 88, 89, 133, 137, 187, 188, 189, 200
Aapravasi Ghat Trust Fund (AGTF), 133, 189
Abhinav Bharat (Young India), 196
Abolitionists, 83, 145, 185
Abwab, 17
Act XXI, 52, 122
Agent General of Immigration, 106, 108, 121
Agent General of Immigration Annual Reports, 109
Agra, 16, 35, 148
Alexander, George William, 146
Allahabad/Treaty of Allahabad/ Prayag, 13, 16, 35, 37, 149, 152
Allen, William, 146
Alsace-Lorraine, 181
Anderson, Warwick, 56
Andrews, C.F., 117, 120, 121, 126, 130, 132, 150, 151, 152, 155, 156, 157, 159, 164, 170
A New System of Slavery, 3, 6, 7, 24, 26, 29, 78, 83, 100, 133, 150, 151, 152, 156, 160, 170, 192, 195, 200
Angelou, Maya, 132
Annas, 35, 40
Anson, Henry, 108
Anti-Slavery Society, 146, 158
Apartheid, 8, 41, 112, 174, 178, 180, 182
Apaya, Abigadou, 99
Apprentices, 80
Arabia, 167
Arkatias, 37, 38, 39, 50
Arya Samaj, 147, 148, 149, 159
Awadhi, 110

Bachchan, Amitabh, 119
Bainimarama, Frank, 173
Bakewell, Dr., 58
Baldewsingh, Rabin S., xiv, 48
Banerjee, Surendranath, 146
Baniya, 106
Bankipur, 195
Barnes, George, Sir, 159
Bates, Crispin, 194, 196
Batohiya, 149
Battle of Plassey, 5, 12, 13, 195
Baudhayana, 43, 194
Beall, 116
Bel Air, 99
Belle Vue Harel Sugar Estate, 88
Bengal, 5, 12, 13, 14, 15, 16, 18, 19, 20, 33, 34, 37, 38, 39, 54, 78, 81, 95, 148, 149, 151, 156, 171, 194, 195, 196, 197, 199
Bengal Famine, 12, 15
Bengali(s), 35, 94
Benin, 179, 180, 200
Bentinck, William, 14
Bhadralok(s), 62, 146, 148
Bhagavad Gita, 32, 110, 162, 198
Bharat Mitra, 126
Bhishma, 177

Bhojpuri, 43, 49, 53, 89, 143, 148, 149, 167, 168, 171, 193
Bhownugree, Mancherjee, Sir, 150
Bidesia, 49, 129
Bigha, 17
Bihar, xvii, 5, 13, 16, 18, 19, 20, 33, 34, 35, 39, 49, 59, 147, 148, 149, 155, 171
Bihar Gazette, 39
Birha, 143
Black Death, 15, 63
Board of Enquiry, 51
Board of Revenue, 19
Bourbon dynasty, 90
Bourbon Island, 90
Brabant Mountain, 76
Brahmin(s), 57, 82, 106, 131, 194
British Empire, xv, 6, 7, 21, 24, 27, 28, 31, 32, 42, 71, 78, 80, 108, 113, 114, 116, 124, 150, 164
British Guiana, 9, 26, 27, 32, 35
British Indian Army, 157
British Indian Government, 26, 33, 39, 40, 41, 51, 95, 115, 121, 122, 126, 151, 156, 157, 159
British Navy, 157
British Parliament, 3, 150, 157, 195
Brown, Laurence, 54
Brutus, Dennis, 178
Bures, 67
Burton, J.W., 117
Bushmen, 111
Buskeet, 138
Buxton, Thomas Fowell, 146

Calcutta, 9, 17, 23, 35, 36, 37, 38, 39, 44, 45, 46, 47, 48, 54, 57, 60, 69, 70, 71, 74, 81, 83, 84, 85, 92, 93, 94, 95, 121, 123, 124, 131, 134, 138, 147, 148, 149, 155, 170

Calcutta Port, 123
Campbell, A.C., 53
Canal colonies, 196
Caribbean, xi, xvi, 6, 23, 25, 26, 27, 32, 35, 45, 51, 74, 79, 89, 107, 117, 118, 122, 123, 124, 131, 159, 166, 168, 174, 179, 184, 187, 191, 198
Carr, E.H., 166
Carter, Marina, 44, 85, 108, 116, 118, 132, 133, 135, 136, 137, 139, 141, 192, 194, 196
Catholic, 102
Catholicism, 102
Cellular Jail, 196
Césaire, Aimé, 191
Chakraborty, Rakhi, 15
Chamberlain, Austin, 157
Chamberlain, Joseph, 30
Champaran Satyagraha, 155
Chaudhuri, B.B., 15
Chelmsford, Viceroy Lord, 156
Chief Cakobau, 67, 68
Cholera, 45, 48, 60, 63, 64, 65, 66, 67, 68, 69, 70, 71, 72, 74, 94, 135
Chota Nagpur, 81
Chura, 53, 54, 58
Colebrooke, E., Sir, 19, 20
Colonial Office, 23, 30, 66, 78, 124, 136, 150, 157
Colonial Sugar Refining Company, 108
Commonwealth, 158, 174
Communist Party, 104
Compulsory labour, 91, 96
Conder, Josiah, 146
Congress of Vienna, 90
Conrad, Joseph, 163
Commander Miot, 95
Coolie, 7, 9, 36, 52, 53, 55, 58, 56, 92, 97, 111, 122, 124, 140, 146,

151, 156, 158, 170, 193
Coolie Route, 7, 191
Coolie ships, 60
Coolitude, 78, 156, 191, 192, 193, 198
Coopen, Anjalay, 88
Cooper, Frederick, 184
Corn Laws, 27
Coromandel Coast, 92
Court of Directors, 18
Courts of Justice, 19
Creole, 111, 166
Crown Colonies, 8, 38, 157

Dalrymple, William, 16, 31, 176
Damas, Léon-Gontran, 192
Darbhanga, 148
Darricau, Reunion Governor, 100
Das, Purushottam, 148
Davidson, Basil, 183
Deen, Dhibby, 84
Defence of India Act, 196
Delhi, 16, 34, 36, 57, 58, 106, 122, 123, 124, 126, 148, 150, 156, 157, 200
Demarara, 60
Departement d'outre Mer, 101
Depot marriages, 135
Déracinement, xiii, xiv, 90, 102
Desbassayns, Eugène Panon, 91
Desbassayns, Joseph, 99
De Souza, 93, 97
Des Voeux, George William, 66, 68
Dhangars, 35, 81
Dharma, 159, 177
Diwani, 13
Doctor, Manilal, Barrister, 86
Dominions, 157, 158
Donne, John, 63
Door of No Return, 74, 200

Double cut, 98
Dow Alexander, 15
Drongan, 135
Duffadars, 83

East Africa, 25, 70, 164, 166
Eisenlohr, Patrick, 169
Emancipation, 23, 25, 27, 29, 30, 184
Emancipation Act, 23
Emigration Act XXII, 122
Emigration Agent, 84, 85, 131, 138
Emigration commission, 92
Emigration committee, 159
Emmer, P.C., 4, 46, 115
Engages, xvii, 90, 91, 92, 93, 94, 95, 96, 97, 98, 99, 100, 101, 102, 103, 104, 105, 197
Engagisme, 93, 95, 96, 98, 101, 103
English East India Company, 15
Enquiry commission, 95

Fieldhouse, D.K., 163
Fiji, xi, xvi, 4, 6, 25, 27, 35, 36, 41, 59, 63, 64, 65, 66, 68, 81, 99, 105, 106, 107, 108, 109, 110, 111, 112, 116, 117, 119, 120, 121, 122, 123, 124, 125, 126, 127, 128, 129, 130, 131, 132, 133, 152, 153, 155, 156, 159, 160, 166, 170, 171, 172, 173, 174, 175, 176
Fijian Colonial Secretary's Office, 109
Fijians, 67, 68, 106, 111, 170, 171, 172, 173, 175, 176
Fiji Mein Mere Ikkis Varsh, 126
Fiji Ordinance No. XVII, 123
First World War, 10, 32, 42, 149, 150, 158
Fiske, John, 15

Foner, Eric, 184
Foundation Indenture Legislation for Fiji, 106
Fourth Republic, 101
France, 1, 73, 74, 90, 91, 96, 99, 101, 102, 103, 181, 192
Francis, Philip, 15
Franco-British Agreement, 93
Freedmen, 98
French, xi, xiii, 72, 73, 74, 90, 91, 92, 93, 95, 96, 97, 98, 100, 101, 102, 103, 104, 181, 192
French East India Company, 73, 90, 98
French Revolution, 90, 104
Fuma, Sudel, 95

Gamat, 143
Gandhi, Mahatma, 29, 34, 117, 127, 137, 139, 141, 142, 143, 145, 154, 176
Ganga, 43, 168, 169
Ganga Talao, 168, 169
Gangetic plains, 34
Garriga, Sarda, 91
Geet-gawai, 143
Ghadar Party/Ghadrites, 196
Ghana, 179
Ghats, 169
Ghazi, Tanveer, 119
Girmit, xi, 6, 32, 128, 160
Girmit Gatha, 128
Gladstone, William, 22
Gokhale, Gopal Krishna, 29, 86, 87, 117, 150, 153, 154
Gokoola, 142
Gomm, William Maynard, Sir, 141
Gopal gaari, 143
Gorakhpur, 35, 84
Gordon, Arthur, Sir, 59

Government of Bengal, 39, 81, 148, 149
Governor General, 12, 14, 17, 21, 156
Grand Bassin, 168, 169
Grande Chaloupe Bay, 94
Grand Morcellement, 142
Great Experiment, xi, xiv, 4, 73, 75
Green, William A., 29, 30
Grierson, George A., 50, 105, 194, 195
Gungah, Dookhee, 142
Gupt, Maithili Sharan, 50, 126
Guyana, xvi, 35, 60, 74, 80, 81, 89, 118, 167, 174

Habib, Irfan, 34
Haftam, 18, 19
Halal, 56
Hardinge, Viceroy Lord, 156
Haridwar, 169
Harlem Renaissance, 191
Harmand, Jules, 72
Harparawri, 143
Harper, P., 170
Hastings, Warren, 14
Hazareesingh, 87, 137, 141
Hegel, xvii, xviii, 185
Henry Anson, 108
Hicks, Michael, Sir, 66
Higginson, James Macaulay, Sir, 137
Hinduism, 35, 102, 117, 133, 134, 147, 155
Hindu(s), 56, 58, 130, 134, 168, 194, 195
Hindustani, 110, 126
Hittoo, 84
Holocaust, xiii, 180, 181, 182, 185
Hooghly, 54, 64, 94
Hotentote, Jean Michel, 77

Index

Hughes, Langston, 191
Hugo of Saint-Victor, 165
International Council on Monuments and Sites, 187
Ile de France, 73, 74
Imperial Conference, 30
Imperial War Conference, 158
Indenture, xiii, 1, 5, 6, 22, 25, 29, 30, 36, 41, 65, 68, 83, 85, 91, 106, 107, 108, 109, 110, 116, 118, 119, 120, 122, 123, 124, 127, 129, 130, 145, 148, 149, 159, 160, 199
Indentured Cooly Protection Society or Anti-Indentured Emigration League, 149
Indentured Labour Route (Project)/ La Route des Engages, xvi, xvii, 95, 119, 170, 178, 183, 186, 188
Indenture Ordinance for Fiji, 109
Indenturing, 9
India Emigration Act V, 51, 52
India Emigration Act VII, 159
Indian Civil Service, 50
Indian Diaspora, xii, xviii, 4, 5, 61, 118, 141, 143, 162, 169, 171, 172, 175, 199
Indian Emigration Act, 95
Indian Emigration Bill, 159
Indian Marriage Ordinance, 138
Indian Mission, 176
Indian National Congress (INC), 87, 152, 170
Indian Overseas Association, 158
Indian Women's Committee, 127
International Decade of People of African Descent, 183
International Slave Route Monument, 77

Jagannath, 50
Jahaji behens, 135, 144
Jahaji bhais, xvi, 63, 65, 135, 144, 164
Jaipur, 194
Jallianwala Bagh, 42
Jamaica, 26, 27, 81
Janeo, 143
Jantasar, 143
Jayawardena, Chandra, 130
Jinnah, Muhammad Ali, 158
Johannesburg, 86
Juhooram, Bibee, 141, 144
Jungali, 175
Justice Field, 19

Kalapani, xi, 43, 44, 45, 48, 60, 61, 62, 74, 105, 143,193, 194, 195, 196, 197, 198, 199
Kanungos, 13, 19, 20
Karikal, 92, 93, 97
Kelly, 17, 116, 117, 127, 133, 155, 172
Kervéguen, 97
Khan, Munshi Rahman, 35, 36, 57, 58
Kisan, 50
Kishto, Doya, 142
Kolkata Port, 123
Krishna, 173
Kshatriyas, 35, 106, 131
Kumar, Ashutosh, 54, 149
Kunti, 117, 125, 130
Kushner, Howard I., 120

L'accroche, 143
La Grande Chaloupe, 69
laissez faire, 121
Lakshmi, 118, 133, 136, 139, 141, 143, 144

Lal Brij V., 4, 5, 35, 36, 41, 57, 65, 67, 68, 81, 101, 106, 107, 109, 110, 111, 112, 116, 117, 118, 120, 121, 122, 124, 127, 130, 131, 175, 200
Lalla Rookh, 48, 74
Lancashire, 14
Laroche, Jesuit Father, 96
La Route des Engages, 95
La Topaze, 69
La Turquoise, 92
L'Auguste, 93, 97
Law, Thomas, 15
Lazaret, 68, 69
Leader, 29, 148, 152
Le Cri Public, 94
Legislative Assembly, 159
Legislative Council, 87, 124, 150, 155
Le Mastere, 91
Le Morne, 5, 76, 77, 116
Le Morne Cultural Landscape, 5, 76, 77, 116
Leonidas, 63, 64, 65, 66, 67, 68
Les miserables, 99
Levine, Lawrence L., 113
Levuka, 64, 65, 67
London, 3, 6, 7, 9, 10, 16, 20, 24, 25, 26, 27, 29, 30, 34, 38, 51, 63, 66, 68, 78, 79, 80, 86, 113, 133, 146, 150, 151, 152, 156, 158, 159, 160, 161, 163, 170, 172, 185, 194
Lord Cornwallis, 14, 17
Lord Glenelg, 80
Lord Grey, 141
Lord Minto, 21
Lord Rama, 84
Lord Stanley, 26
Lord Vishnu, 110
Lucknow, 61, 197

Lutchmun, 84

Macaulay's minute, 167
MacGregor, William, 59, 65, 66, 68
Madras, 9, 23, 84, 85, 97, 134, 138, 149, 150, 153, 154
Mahabharata, 177
Maharajas, 194
Maharaj, Guldhari, 128
Mahase, Radica, 54, 160
Mahila mandals, 119, 128
Maistries, 119
Majhi Janmathep, 196
Major Goldsmith, 95
Malaviya, Madan Mohan, Pandit, 61, 145, 150, 153, 155, 156, 157, 159
Manilal, Jaikumari, 127
Mantel, Hilary, 198
Marquess of Salisbury, 7
Marriage migration, 136
Marwari, 148, 149
Marwari Sahayak Samiti, 149
Mascareignes, 70
Mathura, 117
Mauritius, xi, xiii, xvi, xvii, 5, 25, 26, 27, 32, 45, 60, 63, 69, 70, 73, 74, 75, 76, 78, 79, 80, 81, 82, 83, 84, 85, 86, 87, 89, 90, 91, 94, 98, 99, 101, 118, 122, 127, 131, 132, 133, 134, 135, 136, 137, 138, 139, 141, 142, 143, 144, 159, 166, 167, 168, 169, 170, 174, 176, 183, 187, 188, 189, 200
Mbembe, Achille, 182
Memory of the World Register, xvii, 179
Mersey, 61
Mesopotamia, 157
Metayage, 100

Index 211

Methranee, 141
Métissage, 102
Mirich Dwip, 73, 74, 80, 81
Monar, Rooplall, 105
Montagu, Edwin, 157
Morizot, Health Officer, 96
Morrison, Toni, 165
Mortuza, Shamsad, 197
Mouat, Dr., 54, 55, 56
Mughals, 13, 82, 176
Muslims, 35, 56, 58, 82, 131, 134
Muzaffarpur, 148

Naipaul, V.S., 145
Nandi Durg, 87
Naoroji, Dadabhai, 33, 34, 145
Napoleon, 90
Naraini, 125
Narak, 160
Narayan, Babu Raghubir, 149
Nassau, Stadholder Maurits van, 73
Natzweiler-Struthof camp, 181
Navua, 127, 170
Nazis, 180, 181
Negritude, 191, 192
Nehru, Jawaharlal, 164
Neo-Nazis, 180
Nourse, James, 64

Orissa, 13, 34, 148
Oldfield, John, 185
Ovalau, 65

Pagan, 29, 102
Panchayat, 110, 111
Panchayati, 111, 142
Paris, 3, 90, 96, 179, 181, 192
Pari Talao, 169
Partabia, 37
Partition, 12, 13, 15, 164, 166

Patna, 49, 148, 149
Patta, 16
Patwaris, 13, 20, 21
Pearse, Dr., 58
Pearson, Michael, 194
Pearson, W.W., 124, 152, 155
Penal colonies, 195
Permanent Settlement, 3, 4, 12, 14, 18, 19, 20, 34, 44
Persad, Sital, 62
Pery, Naly, 99
Petit, the chief Navy Physician, Dr., 70
Pink, 119
Pitcher, Major D.G., 38
Pivert, 69
Plantation colonies, xi, 9, 10, 21, 23, 25, 27, 32, 67, 68, 72, 113, 119, 131, 158, 164, 165, 166, 171, 176, 195, 196
Plantation studies, xvi
Polak, Henry, 158
Pondicherry, 91, 92, 93, 94, 95, 97
Pondicherry Emigration Society, 93
Poor Law Amendment Act, 23
Port Louis, 26, 74, 78, 79, 88, 142
Powicke, F., 104, 105
Poynting, Jeremy, 118, 124
Pravasi, 176
Pravasi Bharatiya Divas, 176
Protector of Emigrants, 39, 45, 84, 115, 134, 137, 138
Pudai, 37
Purbi, 149

Queen Victoria, 124
Quran, xiv, 134

Rabemananjara, J., 78
Rabuka, Sitiveni, 173

Radio Fiji, 128, 129
Rajputs, 35, 82, 194
Ramayana, xiv, 110, 134, 142
Ramlila, 110
Ramsamy-Giancone, Celine, 101
Ramtohul, 142
Ranade, Mahadev Govind, 146
Raychaudhuri, Tapan, 194
Reetoo, Dabeedin, 142
Register of Deaths of Indian Immigrants, 121
Reign of Terror, 90
Representative List of Intangible Cultural Heritage of Humanity, 143
Returnee recruitment, 87
Returnees, 84, 85, 136, 138
Reunion Island, xiii, xvi, 5, 30, 63, 68, 69, 70, 74, 90, 91, 92, 93, 94, 95, 98, 99, 100, 101, 102, 103, 104, 105, 166, 187
Rewa, 127
Riviere du Rempart district, 88
Rocke, R., 20
Roosevelt, Franklin D., 185
Russell, Lord John, 103
Ryots, 13, 17, 18, 19, 21

Saadi ke geet, 143
Sabadh, 143
Sahib, 129
Sahiba, 129
Said, Edward W., 163
Saint-Denis, 68
Sainte-Suzanne, 99
Saint-Paul, 96
Salisbury, Lord, 40
Sanadhya, Totaram, 116, 117, 126
Sanatan Dharma Sabha, 159
Sanskrit, 167

Sardar, 129
Sastra, 194
Sattu, 53
Satyadeva, 149
Satyadev, Swami, 148
Satyagraha, 127, 150, 155
Satyanarayan ki Katha, 110
Savarkar, Vinayak Damodar, Veer, 196
Saxony, 165
Schelkly, medical officer Dr., 70
Schoelcher, Victor, 90
Schopenhauer, Arthur, 120
Scoble, John, 115
Second World War, 180, 181, 185
Secretary of State, 7, 30, 40, 141, 157, 159
Secretary of State for the Colonies, 30
Seed, William, 106, 108
Senegal, 74, 179, 192
Senghor, 192
Servilisme, 95, 96
Shah Allam, 60
Sheila, 70
Shikohabadi, 61, 197
Shimla, 117, 157
Shiva, 168
Shivling, 168
Shivratri, 168, 169
Singh, Thakur Ranjit, 173
Skanda Purana, 110
Slave Route, xii, xiii, xvi, xvii, 77, 167, 178, 179, 180, 186, 188, 189, 200
Slavery, 1, 3, 4, 6, 7, 22, 24, 26, 29, 46, 51, 62, 73, 78, 83, 90, 101, 104, 116, 117, 123, 133, 146, 150, 151, 152, 156, 158, 160, 167, 170, 180, 184, 185, 189, 192, 195, 200

Index 213

Songor, 142
South Africa, xii, 4, 25, 27, 31, 86, 112, 127, 150, 154, 158, 166, 176, 178, 182
South Africa British Indians Committee, 158
Spanish Flu, 42
Stadholder, 73
Stanziani, Alessandro, 104
Stipendiary magistrate, 140
Stri Darpan, 126
Stri Sewa Sabha, 127
St. Stephen's College, Delhi, 150, 156
Sturge, Joseph, 146
Suddar, 19
Sugar Islands, 159
Sukh Sagar, 110
Supervisory committee, 99
Surinam(e)/Surinamese, xi, xii, xiv, xvi, xvii, 4, 35, 36, 38, 46, 47, 48, 57, 62, 70, 71, 74, 89, 123, 147, 167
Suva, 6, 116, 127, 160
Swadeshi, 196
Swami Vivekananda, x, 164, 197
Syria, 59

Tagore Dwarkanath, 43
Tagore, Rabindranath, 44, 197
Task system, 108
Taubira Law, 103
Telinga, 92
Telucksing, Mr., 31
Terms of Engagement of Intending Emigrants, 39
Thakur, Bhikhari, 49
The Bengali, 147
Thelamey, 136
Third Reich, 181

Thomas Hamlin, 60
Thurston, J.B., 66
Tidjani-Serpos, Noureini, 1, 179, 180, 200
Tinker, Hugh, 2, 170, 192, 195, 200
Tiroumoudy, 138
Tolstoy Farm, 86
Torabully Khal, 6, 78, 191, 192, 193, 197
Trade union, 99
Transvaal, 86
Treaty of Allahabad, 13, 16
Tredgold, John Harfield, 146
Triangular Trade, 4, 10
Tribal groups, 81
Trinidad, 26, 27, 35, 37, 39, 58, 74, 108, 122, 123, 131, 155, 174
Trinidad Emigration Agent, 131
Truth and Reconciliation Commission, 182

United Nations Educational, Scientific and Cultural Organization (UNESCO), xii, xiii, xvii, 1, 5, 75, 76, 77, 119, 143, 166, 167, 170, 178, 179, 180, 183, 184, 185, 186, 187, 188, 189, 200
UNESCO Committee on Intangible Cultural Heritage of Humanity, 143
UNESCO Routes of Enslaved Peoples: Resistance, Liberty and Heritage Project, 179
United Kingdom (UK), 1, 3, 28, 31, 41, 42, 122, 146
United Provinces, xvii, 5, 33, 35, 36, 148
United States of America (US), 1, 185, 187
Utchanah, Mahen, 88, 200

Vagrancy, 98
Vaillant, Alfred, 70
Valley of Bones, 77
Varanasi, 117, 126, 143, 169
Vasudhaiva Kutumbakam, 162
Vayu, 169
Viceroy, 126, 151, 152, 156, 159
Victorian Age, 24
Victorian England, 23, 28
Victorian morality, 115
Villèle, 96
Vilnius, 187, 188
Virapatrin, 136
Vulagi, 175

Wakefield, Edward Gibbon, 113, 114
Wardha, 88
Washington, George, 22
Weisel, Elie, xiii

West Indies, 6, 25, 26, 27, 71, 108, 146
Whitehall, 30, 146, 151, 152
White Man's Burden, 8, 28
Wilk, Richard, 56
Women's Crisis Centre, 127
Women's gang, 127
Women's Rights Movement, 127
Woodcock Report, 135
World Heritage Committee, 187, 188, 200
World Heritage List, 5, 75, 187, 200
World's Parliament of Religions, 197
Wragg Commission, 31

Yanaon, 92, 99
Yanuca Lailai, 67

Zamindar(s), 16, 17, 18, 19